READER'S DIGEST

Container Gardening
for all Seasons

Container

READER'S DIGEST

Gardening
for all Seasons

PUBLISHED BY
THE READER'S DIGEST ASSOCIATION LIMITED
LONDON • NEW YORK • SYDNEY • MONTREAL

editor
Brenda Houghton

art editor
Joanna Walker

senior assistant editor
Alison Candlin

assistant editor
Helen Spence

senior designers
Kate Harris
Jane McKenna

editorial assistant
Rachel Weaver

picture researcher
Rosie Taylor

proofreader
Barry Gage

reader's digest general books

editorial director
Cortina Butler

art director
Nick Clark

executive editor
Julian Browne

development editor
Ruth Binney

**publishing projects
manager**
Alastair Holmes

picture resource manager
Martin Smith

style editor
Ron Pankhurst

contributors

writers
Richard Day
Daphne Ledward
Gilly Love
Barbara Segall
Sarah Wilson

plant stylists
Richard Day
Clare Louise Hunt
Gilly Love
Sarah Wilson

principal photographer
Debbie Patterson

additional photography
Linda Burgess
Nick Clark
Alex MacDonald
Jason Smalley
Joanna Walker
Francesca Yorke

illustrator
Charlotte Wess

studio
Ian Atkinson

botanist
Sarah Wilson

indexer
Hilary Bird

visit our web site at
www.readersdigest.co.uk

contents

taking a closer look

Be inspired by the changing seasons and thrill your senses with an inviting container garden of your very own design

▲ **Stark cacti line up** along a whitewashed wall

▲ **Bright summer flowers** shine against Mediterranean stucco

▲ **The romance of a roof garden** is enhanced by glowing lanterns

Do you yearn for the hot baked colours of Provence or the brilliant whitewashed walls and scarlet geraniums that typified that village you loved on a Mediterranean holiday? Do you long for sweetly scented cottage-garden blooms, or the stillness and simplicity of oriental gardens? Whatever your preference, and no matter how small your space or budget, you can create exactly the mood you want with a container garden. Your particular style may come from a single inspiration such as a powerful childhood memory – the sight of a field of scarlet poppies, say, or the distinctive spicy scent of wallflowers. Perhaps you can still visualise that painted narrowboat with its colour-washed barrels brimming with flowers. With a little careful planning you can create a container garden that not only fulfils your vision, but also thrives ▶

11

▼ **A river barge** becomes a floating garden

OXFORD CARRIAGES

IPSWICH

in your particular garden environment and local climate. In this book, we show you how to achieve just the effect you want, whether you have a sunny terrace or a windswept balcony, an exposed flat roof or a tiny, shady basement yard.

an ancient passion

Container gardening may seem a modern trend, but people have been growing plants in containers ever since the tending of gardens began. Some of the earliest gardens were small contained spaces within buildings such as the inner courtyard of a Roman villa, or the cloisters of a medieval monastery where medicinal herbs were cultivated for the infirmary and flowers were grown for religious festivals. Herbs are still popular subjects for growing in containers and you will find fresh ways of presenting them here.

In the 8th century the Moors invaded Europe and brought with them an idea of the garden as a 'paradise on Earth'. Roses were particularly valued and often grown in pots placed on the banks of canals where their beauty was reflected on the water and their prized perfume dispersed by scores of fine spray jets. Today, beautiful water features can be created in containers, offering both soothing sound and the opportunity to grow a range of marginal plants in pots.

The grand French and Italian gardens of the 18th century featured stately classical urns, usually in pairs on elegant plinths. This classical symmetry survives today in the imaginative plantings found in paired pots beside many front doors. Then in the early 20th century Gertrude Jekyll, the pioneering garden designer, ▶

People have been growing plants in containers ever since the tending of gardens began

◀ **Pots of scented lilies** frame a cottage doorway

▲ **Huge matching urns** emphasise perspective in a grand garden

Round-bellied seaside pots look free and easy in this wild setting ▶

▼ **A shiny blue glaze** enhances pale lilac blooms

The garden is a restful retreat offering peace and privacy in natural surroundings

▼ **Urns add drama** to a country border

planned rows of seasonal pots to adorn the elegant terraces of Edwin Lutyens' country houses. Following her lead, we show you how to group pots, whether you want a formal or an informal look.

setting the scene

Many gardens are restful retreats, offering a place to escape for a little peace and privacy in natural surroundings – and you can use containers to create just the environment that suits you best. So if you feel happiest surrounded by flowers that evoke the old-fashioned English countryside – thatched cottages, roses round the door, tabby cats and home baking – then fill weathered terracotta pots with a profusion of daisies, foxgloves, hollyhocks, lupins and roses.

Containers also allow you to plant flowers with herbs and vegetables in ways that look decorative as well as being practical, a juxtaposition that reflects back to traditional cottage gardens. Edible flowers such as nasturtiums and violas thrive happily in wall-hung pots and hanging baskets. Even a window box can produce cherry tomatoes. This style of container garden will need regular watering and feeding if it is to look its best throughout the growing seasons, but the rewards will make it more than worth while – fresh cut flowers and home-grown salads and vegetables all summer long.

high style, low maintenance

In complete contrast, and perfect if you want a low-maintenance garden, consider an oriental style typified by a subtle and harmonious blend of evergreen plants and shrubs. If you have a water feature inspired by the seaside rather than the Orient, choose timber decking stained soft grey or pale blue, pots decorated with seashells and fishing nets to filter the wind and support climbers.

Whatever your chosen style, it is essential to select container plants for their shape as well as their colour. In a shaded area, for example, you could combine the broad leaves of hosta with the arching fronds of feathery ferns and the tall rustling leaves of bamboo and other ornamental grasses.

And if you are choosing a large specimen plant such as a tree, you can achieve magical effects by deciding whether you want a tall spire shape, a soft weeping effect or a branching outline. ▶

Create your own **miniature world.** Just fill the pot with the **right mixture** and you can grow whatever **you like**

For pure indulgence you might opt for a romantic garden where scented flowers and shrubs fill the air with aromatic perfume. In such a scheme the colours should be soft and restful on the eye. Choose delicate pinks and blues, pale mauve, apricot and white – which is the colour of the most highly scented flowers.

Scented flowers tend to give off their strongest perfume towards the end of the day so place your scented containers near your seats, fix up some soft lighting and enjoy the scene and the scents as the sun goes down.

a manageable garden

Container gardening lets you fashion your own miniature world. You may want to grow acid-loving shrubs such as camellias or rhododendrons in an area with an alkaline soil, or create a boggy environment in a sandy area. Just fill the pot with the right mixture and you can grow whatever you like. And if you want a different sort of garden next year, simply choose a new range of plants: container gardening allows you to change your mind as often as you like.

You also have complete control over the level of maintenance in a container garden. No heavy digging or weeding is involved, just the manageable tasks of watering, feeding and perhaps occasional pruning and deadheading. Pot-grown plants generally need far more watering than those in open ground but there are many ways of reducing this chore. And in any case, watering a container garden by hand can be wonderfully soothing at the end of a stressful day. You change down a gear mentally as you sprinkle your charges, examine your plants at close hand, take pleasure in their development, move those at their best into prime positions, nip off spent flowerheads and check for signs of any pests or diseases.

Most modern gardens need some sort of screen to provide areas of privacy and a container allows you to do this by positioning the right plant just where it is needed. You may need a tall bushy shrub to create a windbreak or a scented climber to make a bower. To enable you to roll large plants around safely and easily, we show you how to make a sturdy timber platform mounted on castors.

The portability of containers also means that if you ever decide to move house you can take all your pots and plants with you, and immediately your new garden will feel like home.

Any small enclosed space can become an opportunity for creative planting: raised beds, the narrow strip between walls and paving, a tiny crevice in a flight of steps or planting pocket in a area of gravel all offer wonderful potential for growing.

Whether you are trying to build a garden with only a balcony or yard at your disposal, struggling to cover up a bare wall or to cheer up a dull patch in the border, you'll find the right plants in the right container can fulfil your purpose without breaking the bank. With the help of *Container Gardening For All Seasons*, you will discover a year-round, life-long passion for pots – and plants. ■

▼ **Snowdrops brave** wintry weather

▲ **Ice buckets** make great pots for spring bulbs

▲ **The tiniest space** can become a flower garden

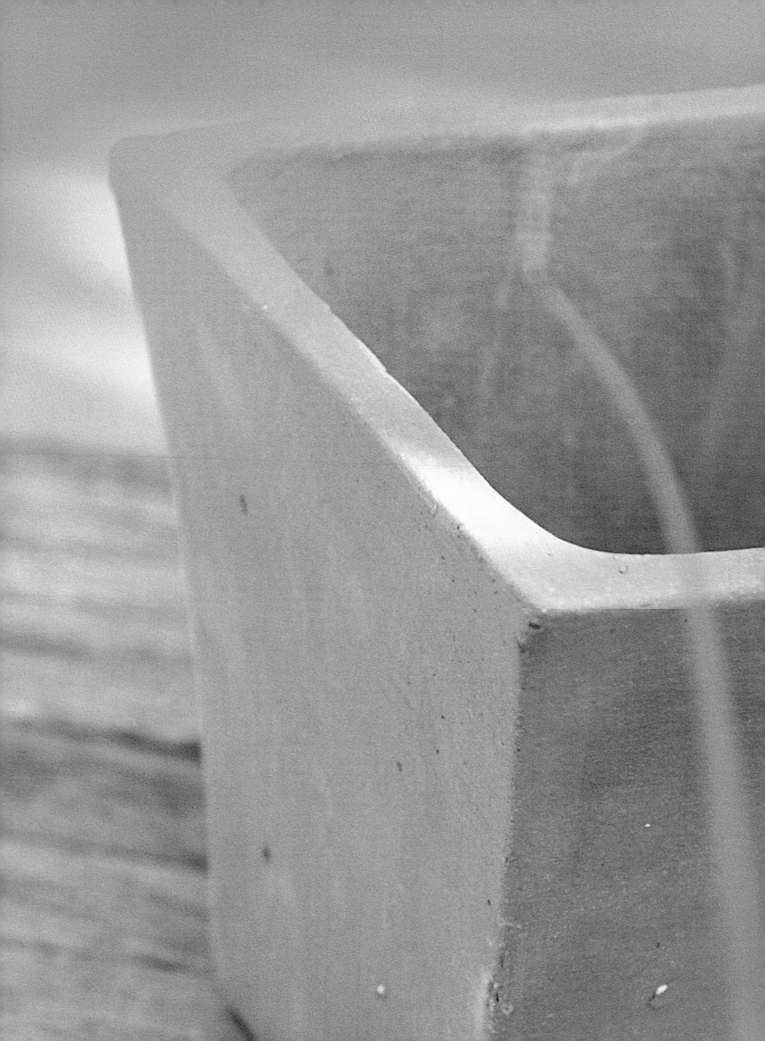

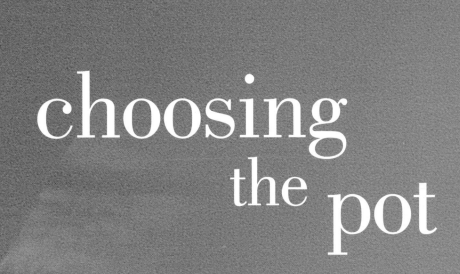

choosing
the pot

picking the right shape

Looks matter when you choose a pot, but you also have to consider where it will go and what you want to plant in it. Here are shapes for every purpose.

▲ Comely big-bellied pots in terracotta and bright glazes provide plenty of space for growing large shrubs, such as bougainvillea.

A front door might call for a hanging basket to provide colour and fragrance at eye level, while a patio offers space for a variety of containers. If your starting point is a plant, rather than a location, choose your pot accordingly: for example, a hydrangea will need a much larger pot than a geranium. If your outdoor space is limited, you may want to plant up one large container, but in a larger location you can combine several pots of varying size and shape to achieve the same effect as a border.

A LOOK TO SUIT THE PLANT

A large pot, because it holds more compost, is ideal for growing an interesting combination of plants. Once planted up, however, it will be difficult to move. To lighten the load, fill the base of large pots with polystyrene beads or bits of broken polystyrene plant trays. Another advantage to using a large container is that the compost is less likely to freeze around the roots in winter as it would in a smaller pot, and it won't dry out so fast in summer.

You need to keep in mind the height of the mature planting when choosing a pot. A dwarf or low-growing plant can look swamped in a heavy container, while a large shrub will look badly proportioned in a narrow pot.

Stability is crucial if you are growing a tall plant, which might sway in the wind and eventually topple the pot. Containers with very tapered bases are particularly vulnerable. The most stable shapes are regular ones such as square pots, taller containers with wide shoulders, or large, round dishes.

To anchor a pot in place, drive a stake into the ground, or into the space between two paving slabs, place the drainage hole of the pot over the stake then slide the empty pot over it.

For a successful display, you need to consider the form and size of the plants you are choosing, the location, and the size and shape of your pot. Tall pots suit trailing plants such as ivy, creeping Jenny and ground ivy, which will hang over the pot edge in soft trails. Such

◀ **Hard-edged, angular planters** in metal and wood lend a sense of form and order to a balcony or terrace. You may have to protect wood from moist compost with a plastic lining.

▼ **Tall, slender containers** such as galvanised metal buckets, chimney pots and elegant Greek amphorae make a dramatic setting for spires of colour and show off trailing plants beautifully.

Sleek and sculptural, simple and functional, or softly curved and glazed: a really beautiful pot will enhance any garden

◀ **Shallow containers** or original hanging baskets make neat homes for small plants such as alpines and bulbs.

pots are also ideal for growing lilies or clematis, which both need a deep, cool root run. Shallow containers such as old sinks and alpine dishes are more suited to the delicate shapes of rockery plants, spring bulbs such as crocus, and low-growing herbs.

Tall and elegant, narrow-necked pots, sometimes called Ali Baba jars, make a curvaceous focus on a patio or if set among plants in the garden. These ornamental pots can look spectacular when filled with trailing stems, wispy grasses, or weeping plants, which

create a cascade of foliage, like flowing water. However, the narrow necks of these pots make it almost impossible to remove a plant that needs repotting. Big-bellied pots present the same problem, but both can be used as cachepots, to disguise a plain plastic pot either set in the neck or placed inside the container. This is helpful if the plant needs to be lifted to a frost-free shelter in winter.

Square containers such as wooden Versailles boxes are also often used as cachepots. Their regular shapes set off topiary shrubs and trees that have been pruned into formal shapes.

◀ **Terracotta and plastic** are the most common materials for pots. Terracotta mellows with age, but is easily chipped or broken. It is porous and drains well, so is ideal for drought-tolerant plants such as Mediterranean herbs or geraniums; other plants will need frequent watering.

When moistened, terracotta keeps plant roots cool in hot weather. Check when you buy that the pot is frost-resistant. If not, you will have to wrap it up, or empty out the plant and store the pot indoors for winter.

Plastic pots are light and portable and are not damaged by frost. Plastic tends to be less attractive than terracotta but can be given a lift with a creative coat of paint. As plastic is not porous, compost does not dry out as quickly as it does in clay pots. This means less watering, but also increases the danger of waterlogging.

▶ **Wood and wicker** have a lightweight appearance, but many wooden tubs are substantial enough to hold large shrubs. Wood is resistant to frost and insulates plants from extreme heat and cold. Prevent rot by treating the container with a preservative that does not harm plants, or lining it with plastic. Stand wooden tubs on bricks to aid drainage: if water collects in them, the wood will rot.

▶ **Galvanised metal containers** look great in modern settings, such as on decking or gravel beds. But metal is a poor insulator so compost and roots may be baked in hot weather or frozen in winter. Metal pots are often made without drainage holes, in which case you will have to drill them; otherwise simply use them as cachepots.

▶ **Glass fibre pots** are lightweight, strong and long-lasting. They are also frost-proof, insulate plants well and come in a good range of colours. The only disadvantage is that glass fibre may become brittle and chip if handled roughly.

▶ Concrete and reconstituted stone pots come in a wide range of shapes. Some have details such as handles and swags; others come in simple geometric shapes suited to modern settings. Both materials are strong, frost-resistant and retain heat. Reconstituted stone looks more natural than concrete, and is both less expensive and lighter than the real thing. However, it doesn't weather quickly, so encourage plants to spill over the rim to soften its look.

Great plants deserve fine containers and there are many beautiful options. Each material has good points and bad, so discover how to find the best partner for your precious blooms.

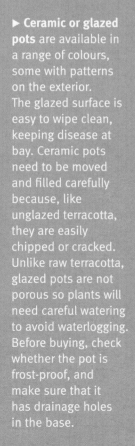

▶ Ceramic or glazed pots are available in a range of colours, some with patterns on the exterior. The glazed surface is easy to wipe clean, keeping disease at bay. Ceramic pots need to be moved and filled carefully because, like unglazed terracotta, they are easily chipped or cracked. Unlike raw terracotta, glazed pots are not porous so plants will need careful watering to avoid waterlogging. Before buying, check whether the pot is frost-proof, and make sure that it has drainage holes in the base.

C hoosing a pot no longer means deciding whether or not you can afford terracotta rather than plastic. Containers are now available in a bewildering array of materials – from galvanised metal containers to bamboo, from glass fibre to glazed ceramic – and there are many ways to achieve a stone effect or bronze finish that don't cost a fortune.

Because there is so much choice, you need to think about the advantages and disadvantages of the material when you are picking a container. Plastic is light, inexpensive and can be treated to all manner of disguises. Wood, terracotta and stone are good root insulators – against heat or cold – and therefore ideal for plantings in full sun or exposed northerly settings.

▶ **A formal collection of pots** acts as a foil for the blowsy borders around the circular front lawn and provides a year-round collection of evergreens that can be dressed up as the seasons change.

▼ **Penny rings the changes** in a wire jardinière, made to fit around the central pole of a marquee at a family wedding. In spring it holds miniature bulbs and in winter, hardy evergreens. One year's summer display was an old-fashioned posy of pinks and daisies; in this display, sedums alternate with geraniums.

◀ **A regiment of neat box balls** stands guard at the front of the house. Rounded rims and moulded ridges add interest to the row of matching terracotta pots without detracting from the simplicity of the display.

▶ **A pair of vast lead-effect glass fibre planters** flank the front door. Thick ivy garlands, made by training a pair of plants along a loop of wire, mirror the mounds of the standard ligustrums, and make an enticing illicit swing for Penny's young grandson.

a
florist's
eye for
design

Pots cheer
up small spaces,
but Penny Snell
believes they
also have a
place in a 'lawn
and border'
garden — and
not just on the
patio. The garden of her
Surrey home is dotted with pots at
every turn: some decorative, some
functional, some planted and others
empty, but all carefully placed for effect.

One year, to welcome winter
visitors, Penny planted a pair of clipped
standard conifers with a cushion of
skimmias beneath, their red berries
contrasting cheerfully with the blue
glaze of the pots, and placed them at the
front door. She didn't expect the ▶

berries to last more than the few weeks of the festivities, but the birds spared them. By June, Penny couldn't bear to look at her Christmas trees any longer, still massed with berries, and moved the pots into the wings for another year.

The garden is very much Penny's own, and her husband is modest about his efforts. "Penny does 98 per cent of the work," he says. "He exaggerates his contribution," Penny retorts. In fact, she cites "Maurice with his secateurs" as the biggest pest in the garden.

A TALENT FOR ARRANGING

Penny is a florist, and wherever there is a table in the garden, it is dressed by an arrangement, such as the shallow wire basket (below right), which fills a table in the yard outside the kitchen. "Normally I plant this with blowzy trailing things," Penny tells, "and every year the basket ends up completely obscured. This year I was determined to see it, so echeverias are perfect – the flowers trail slightly to soften the edges, but they don't have rampant foliage spilling over."

But this arrangement is too big when the table is in use, so Penny substitutes soft mounds of *Selaginella* moss (below, far left). "They need to be kept wet, but I think they're much nicer than mind-your-own-business – they have more guts!" she chuckles.

Some of her favourite pots for the table are the wide terracotta saucers Penny fills with low-growing things. One brims over with the tiny white flowers of *Campanula* 'Elizabeth Oliver'. "It's very pretty," says Penny, "but a nightmare to deadhead, because you end up removing new shoots as well. It's so fiddly."

Another is planted with tiny ferns, "like the ones that grow in stone walls in the Lake District", and mulched with slate. The saucers are perfect for plants like these that need to be kept wet, because they are really designed to go under other pots, so they don't have drainage holes. However, because they are not glazed, water does gradually evaporate, and nothing gets waterlogged.

The kitchen courtyard is a mass of foliage and flowers, all grown in pots. Ferns, a rose, hostas, fuchsias, a conifer, sage and a manger of ivy fill one corner, with smaller pots defining the other side of a path through the yard. Two bronze cordylines pick out the colour of the brick wall and the rusted metal of a cart hanging above them, and in late summer the orange and yellow flowers of a pot of nasturtiums will add to the theme.

> " Normally I plant this with blowzy things and every year the basket ends up completely obscured. This year I was determined to see it. "

▶ **A cluster of gerberas** adds colour to a silvery table display. Gerberas and echeverias grow well together, since both thrive in hot dry spots, and raising the basket brings the low-growing echeverias into the spotlight.

▶ **To dress the table** Penny grows arrangements in all sizes. Tidy mounds (**1**) of the moss *Selaginella* make a short alternative to clipped conifers (**2**), but lowest of all is a saucer of *Kalanchoë*, or flaming Katy (**3**).

Nasturtiums are usually grown trailing from hanging baskets or sprawling horizontally in borders, but Penny is training her plant up a wigwam. In this tiny yard she maximises height to cram more plants in. Climbers smother the walls, including a clematis, 'Etoile Rose', with flowers like pixie hats, and a *Cobaea scandens*, which bears long pale green bell flowers flushed with purple. "It's a terrifically vigorous plant," says Penny, "and more or less grows while you stand and watch it."

KEEP PLANTS HAPPY IN POTS

Penny uses pots to grow tender plants, which she can overwinter in her conservatory, including the extraordinary yellow-stemmed Costa Rican bamboo (below, centre) which stands on the terrace. The plant is more than 1.5m (5ft) high and practically all trunk.

Maurice loathes it, but Penny was captivated by its colour and planted it in a contrasting blue glazed pot to show it off to best effect.

She also uses containers to grow varieties which she has failed with in the soil. Yellow and pink corydalis thrive in the ground, for example, but she can only keep the blue variety, which is her favourite, in a pot.

In the same way, Penny hopes her three-tiered raised sleeper bed of hot coloured plants, such as *Kniphofia*, *Ligularia*, *Penstemons* and *Potentilla*, will transform its spot in the garden, beneath a tree. "The soil there was hopeless," Penny recalls, "and it was shaded and dark." Raising the plants in the bed increases their chances of getting some light but, more importantly, Penny filled the railway sleeper framework with leaf-mould to give the plants all the nutrients they need.

▶ **Pliable twigs** like these – "they're iraqui, from the flower market" – can be twisted and knotted around a bundle of the same to make a simple rustic wigwam.

◀ **A miniature begonia,** *Begonia sutherlandii*, scrambles up Penny's twiggy frame (top) and shares a table with the black grass, *Ophiopogon*, *Selaginella* and a miniature bamboo.

▶ **Penny's newest project** is a raised bed in a poor shady corner of the garden, where nothing would ever grow before.

▶ **The flower market** is Penny's favourite source of plants, such as these gerberas (**1**), bamboo (**2**) and sedums (**3**). But imprecise market labelling means that the names of many of her plants remain a mystery.

▶ **Tiny bi-colour violas** nestle prettily in the top of a chimney pot. Setting the small container inside the rim of the taller pot brings the low-growing flowers up to eye level.

using tall and deep containers

Tall or deep pots provide colour and shape at a good height above the ground. A tall container, or a smaller one raised on a pedestal, offers the ideal fall for trailing foliage plants such as periwinkles, particularly *Vinca minor* 'Variegata' and 'Gertrude Jekyll', which has double white flowers. Other pretty foliage trailers include the softly textured lime-green leaves of *Helichrysum petiolare* 'Limelight', the grey-green form of *Helichrysum petiolare* or *Plectranthus verticillatus*.

Trailing flowers such as lobelia, geraniums, Cascade and Surfinia petunias and creeping Jenny also look great flowing down tall pots. And nasturtiums, particularly *Tropaeolum majus* 'Alaska' with its creamy variegated foliage and orange-yellow flowers, tumble beautifully over the warm terracotta of a Cretan jar.

Chimney pots are often used as tall plant containers. It is neither necessary nor practical to fill them with compost: this only increases the chance of frost damage and encourages

Terracotta or tin, tall pots add structure to any garden and give plants room to stretch their roots. Fill them with tumbling falls of colour, or the drama of soaring spires.

Pink petunias in an Ali Baba urn accentuate Mediterranean blue walls. The metal plant stand gives extra height.

▲ **Succulents**, an unusual choice for a tall urn, trail beautifully down the side with artless informality.

▼ **Galvanised metal buckets** are home in spring to the white blooms of *Allium cowanii*. The strap-like leaves belong to a second allium which will open as the first fades.

▶ **Frail spikes of pink gaura** rise like wisps of smoke through puffs of gypsophila **(1)** in tall and short chimney pots. Later, replace them with yellow rudbeckia and trailing bidens **(2)**.

pests such as ants to nest. Instead, fit a strong wire support into the neck of the chimney to clip around a pot, or choose a flowerpot with a rim that will sit snugly in the top.

A strawberry or herb pot can add welcome height to a kitchen garden. The holes in the side will accommodate trailing herbs, such as thyme and some varieties of mint and rosemary, while the top supports bushier species, such as coriander and parsley.

DEEP POTS FOR COOL ROOTS

Large plants, such as conifers, some ferns, and cacti with deep taproots will thrive in deep containers. Lilies also need a deep run for their massed fibrous roots. Tall terracotta pots, known as 'long toms', which are specially designed for growing lilies, are now widely available.

A deep, wide pot is the best container in which to plant a formally shaped tree such as a standard bay or spiral box. The extra width and depth of the pot makes it possible to underplant the tree, and to add a softening edge. Variegated trailing foliage plants or a single colour of trailing petunias work particularly well. Choose plants with shallow roots, which will not rob the main tree of essential nutrients.

Deep pots are also ideal for growing fruit trees. Apples, cherries, figs, peaches and large fruit shrubs such as blueberries and gooseberries will all thrive for many years in large deep containers. Although growing any tree in a container will have a dwarfing effect, in the case of apples, cherries and pears it is also important to check that the cultivar is on a dwarfing rootstock to start with.

shallow pots for small treasures

Seed pans, wicker baskets and basins make ideal homes for small plants. Choose these containers for succulents and seaside plants, which won't mind if the shallow compost dries out from time to time on hot sunny days.

Bowls and low troughs show off the smaller treasures of the garden, such as alpines, mat-forming plants and low-growing bulbs, to their best advantage. A group of shallow pots of just one type of plant, such as houseleeks (sempervivums), set out on a patio becomes a textured ornament.

Traditional stone alpine troughs are rectangular and about 15-20cm (6-8in) deep. They are expensive, but old stone sinks are a popular alternative – and come complete with plughole drainage. Most plugholes, however, are so large that water and compost will drain rapidly away so it is best to cover them with broken crocks or a piece of fine wire mesh.

Ceramic sinks can be used as they are or coated with a cement mix to produce a more traditional weathered look. If weight is an issue, it is easy to coat a light plastic or polystyrene base with the cement mix or make a mock stone trough (see pages 264-265).

Troughs should be raised off the ground on bricks to improve drainage and to keep the bottom free of slugs and other pests.

Mountain plants, such as alpine pinks – *Dianthus alpinus*, *D. deltoides* and *D. neglectus* – grow well in shallow containers. Thrifts are also good choices, and form softly textured foliage mounds with flower stems rising up out of the clump.

Mat-forming plants such as houseleeks, saxifrages and creeping thymes with their subtle range of foliage colours are well suited to shallow containers, where they spread in mounds and rosettes, as well as in ground-covering mats.

Seed pans, popular wide, shallow terracotta pots, which can be round or square, provide a shapely setting for spring bulbs. Because they are small and easy to carry, they can be brought into position near the house just as the flower buds start to open.

Low-growing bulbs such as crocus and *Iris reticulata*, closely planted and in a single colour, look like jewels set in these shallow bowls. Tulips growing out of a sea of blue forget-me-nots will also provide good spring colour, as will collections of dwarf, multi-flowered and species tulips.

When the spring bulbs have finished flowering, plant delicate pink or white *Cyclamen coum* for autumn and winter pleasure.

◄ **A stone Venus** gazes across a sea of low pots filled with a selection of alpines and small succulents.

▶ **A terracotta box** **(1)** houses a clump of late-flowering 'Angélique' tulips, while a basket **(2)** of low-growing sedums and alpine pinks make a pretty outdoor table decoration. Bonsai trees **(3)** need very little soil for their roots and grow best in shallow pots.

A painted barrel makes an informal home for this easy mix of pale pink bedding daisies, bright peony tulips 'May Wonder' and cerise *Ranunculus*, backed by graceful bleeding hearts and a nodding green hellebore.

improve your
view with a
window
box

A window box, sitting snugly on a sill or fixed to the wall beneath a window, offers the chance to change your outlook with every season and to enhance the façade of your home.

The most attractive window boxes are often those in which the colours are vibrant and the vigour of the plants creates a swirling mass that obscures the box and almost envelops the window it is dressing. But if you are attaching a box below a window that opens outwards, be careful to site it low enough, so that you can still open the window when the plants mature.

Window boxes are long, thin, usually not very deep, and hold a relatively small amount of compost, so they need slow-release fertiliser granules, as well as water-retaining gel or granules incorporated into the mix.

Make sure that a window box sited on the front of the house is securely fixed with brackets or iron restraints. This will keep it safe from theft and will prevent endangering the people walking beneath it.

If you live above other people, or if your window box overhangs a pavement, it may be a good idea to equip the box with a drip tray: it will be no fun for neighbours to be caught under a shower each time you water the flowers.

Try to fix your window box into position before you plant it up – it may be impossibly heavy to move later. If the box is for a ground-floor window it will be easy to work on it from the outside. But if you live

◄ Too pretty to hide, this picket-fence window box has country cottage charm. Creamy white *Asarina procumbens* trail through the slats in contrast with the dark red *Lobelia* 'Fan Scharlach' and chocolate cosmos.

◄ A regiment of primulas lined up along a sill will brighten many a dull winter's day and makes a pretty alternative to a traditional trough.

▶ Plain colour schemes often work best in a confined space like a window box. Here, white begonias and geraniums, with a touch of lilac lobelia, make an elegant summer display.

◄ Strong plants are needed to withstand autumn weather. Here dwarf conifers draw the eye to the glossy pink berries of *Pernettya mucronata* while glowing purple heather makes a miniature hedge.

To make your own picket-fence window box, turn to pages 260-261

▶ **A sizzling mass** of bright fuchsias, geraniums, mimulus and nasturtiums screens this window from passers-by as effectively as a net curtain would.

Troughs laden with flowers offer a bright and cheerful welcome

higher up, you may need to throw the windows wide open and work from inside.

CONCENTRATED STYLE

Even in the confined space of a window box it is possible to create a variety of styles. A limited palette of one colour plus foliage plants – for example, a rich red geranium with ivy – would provide a vibrant, yet formal style and will have most impact when viewed from a distance. Pastel petunias, with lobelia in complementary colours, and trails of fuchsia, suggest a more relaxed, country style.

Silver and grey is a deservedly popular colour combination for foliage in window boxes. Add a white or cream variegated ivy or white-flowered lobelia to add highlights to a cool contemporary display.

For a north-facing window use ivy, box or busy lizzies, which all thrive in shade, as well as ferns, and cyclamen. In full sun try the floriferous diascias in a range of pastel colours.

◀ **A formal stone trough** with its winter display of clipped box can be livened up instantly in spring by tucking a few bright polyanthus in at the front.

pots to make a big impact

For a really strong statement, nothing beats a big bold container. It doesn't even have to be planted up: shape and colour will create a drama all of their own.

Big pots make their own architectural statement, even when empty, and can be used as focal features just as you might use a piece of statuary to mark the meeting of paths or sight lines in the garden. Big glazed containers look particularly attractive nestled into a group of large shrubs or set among a collection of planted pots.

Substantial pots offer proportions that work well with single statuesque specimens, but can also hold sufficient plants to make a dramatic floral effect. Their depth means that they can be planted in layers so that one plant succeeds another as the season progresses.

Place upright, bushy shrubs at the centre of large plain pots and smaller plants around the sides, with trailing varieties frothing over the edges to soften the line of the container.

If the pots are highly decorated, let their beauty show. Use them for upright, flaring plants which will leave the pot sides visible.

Climbing plants such as clematis look attractive tumbling over the edge of a big, wide pot, but for clematis, try to keep the base of the pot in the shade. Allow the climbers to grow naturally, so that their trails of soft foliage and flowers occur at different levels. Alternatively, you can also use canes or obelisks to support the climbers, and train annuals such as sweet peas and black-eyed Susan into soft-edged pyramids.

Deep pots are ideal for shrubs such as hydrangeas. With formal plants, such as these, and topiary bays or box, covering the surface of the compost at the base of the plant with a gravel mulch gives a stylish and professional finish.

Large pots offer a solid base for flowing plants, such as grasses. When planted with single specimens, especially if positioned in pairs, they will also lend a formal air to a garden. Although big pots make majestic focal points when filled with dramatic plants, they can also be used effectively with dense plantings of low-growing saxifrages or sempervivums.

Big-bellied pots give plants space to stretch out and flourish

▶ **A battered pail** focuses attention on the corkscrew stems of *Juncus effusus* 'Spiralis'. Hang it low, to give a good view of the plant.

▶ **A glowing autumn sumach** makes the perfect place to hang a basket of burgundy-leaved *Heuchera* 'Chocolate Ruffles' and orange violas.

▶ **Trailing campanulas** tumbling out of a moss-lined wire basket harmonise with the droopy green branches of a weeping willow.

hang colour where you need a lift

Suspended anywhere from a door to a tree, baskets of flowers have an old-fashioned appeal. But with the right plants and container, the hanging basket can have a place in even the most modern of settings.

A successful basket can be so luxuriant at the height of summer that the chains and container are hidden and the whole confection seems to be floating on air. Hanging baskets are the most popular garden ornaments and several matching ones grouped along the front of a house or on a pergola have great dramatic impact. But just one carefully considered basket can be enough to add interest to a front entrance. If you are hanging a basket by a door, position it away from head-height.

A basket does not hold much compost and dries out rapidly, so it should be watered at least once a day.

If your basket is out of reach, you will need a long-handled watering device, a bracket that enables you to lower the basket, or a permanent irrigation system (see page 236).

To make your task less arduous, choose plants that will thrive even if water is in short supply. There are numerous drought-tolerant bedding

◄ **A contrasting palette** of blue and yellow stands out against a white wall. The cottage mix of begonias, lobelia, petunias, and trailing bidens softens the hard lines of the door.

► **Densely flowering** busy lizzies grow into a neat shape naturally. Here they cover a plastic pouch.

► **A soft blue verandah** makes a muted background for clustered petunias in sugared almond colours. The extra-long trails of greenery of *Desmodium callianthum* add a touch of grandeur.

◄ **The classic mixture** of white and silver gives this basket its cool simplicity. An underplanting of silvery grey helichrysum frames a froth of *Petunia* 'Ice White'.

plants, which will flower all summer. Begonias, brachyscome, busy lizzies, felicia, geraniums, nasturtiums, petunias and verbena are all suitable.

There are also a number of ways to increase the water-holding capacity of your compost. Select the largest basket possible: the more compost you have, the longer it will take to dry out. Use a moisture-retentive liner for the basket, such as wool, fibre or foam. Cardboard liners are also suitable, and their looks can be improved by covering them with moss. Finally, mix water-retaining gel or granules into the compost.

GREAT PLANTS TO FILL OR SOFTEN THE EDGES OF A HANGING BASKET

Upright plants
- Begonia
- Geraniums
- Heuchera
- Impatiens
- Petunia

Trailing plants
- Begonia x tuberhybrida 'Pendula'

- *Bidens ferulifolia*
- Campanula
- Fuchsia
- Ivy-leaved geraniums
- *Glechoma hederacea*
- *Helichrysum petiolare* (green and yellow)

- Small leaf or variegated ivies
- Lobelia
- Nasturtium
- Scaevola
- Black-eyed Susan (*Thunbergia alata*)
- Verbena
- Viola

Naturally trailing plants can also be encouraged to climb. Wind their stems around the chains of the basket to give your display added height.

Assemble your own hanging baskets, flower balls and flower pouches – see pages 230-233

breathing new life into quirky pots

Be creative when choosing pots. Add excitement to your garden, by re-using worn-out or unwanted objects, from both outside and inside the home, in an unexpected way.

In an informal, relaxed garden or patio, there is no limit to the creativity of the container gardener. Virtually anything can be pressed into service as a plant-growing opportunity by the keen gardener, whether designed for the purpose or not. Even the remains of broken flowerpots can make very effective containers for sedums and low-growing alpines.

Any pot you choose will need to have drainage holes cut or drilled into its base to ensure that the compost doesn't become waterlogged. Alternatively, you can use the quirky container as a cover to hide a less exciting inner pot. In this case the outer container will retain any rainwater, so will need to be checked and emptied regularly to prevent any plants' roots being swamped.

Whatever the container, make sure it is clean, that all paint is removed from any old paint cans and that wooden containers have not been treated with chemicals that damage plants. Clean off any rust from iron containers using a wire brush, then apply a rustproofing paint, such as Hammerite.

You can also use more flimsy containers such as wooden trugs as short-term planters. Line them with plastic so that the wood on the interior of the basket is not damaged by wet compost and tuck in colourful summer bedding plants for a quick effect.

The kitchen is a fine place to raid for suitable containers. Pots and pans can make instant plant pots and teapots are just the right size for a few crocus bulbs: set them near the house for a bright, visible display in spring.

▶ **A culinary theme** links this old kettle with its planting of basil **(1)**, while bright busy lizzies **(2)** shine out of a row of dark lanterns.

◀ **A discarded fruit box** seems to have been colonised by crassula, grasses, *Leucojum*, thrift and thyme. In fact, this is a carefully chosen group of plants, all of which need dry soil.

▶ **New wood rises from old,** as this battered beer barrel is brought to life by a vibrant contorted willow.

China or enamel washbowls are also the perfect shape for holding bulbs. Wire wine racks, found in bric-a-brac shops, are becoming popular as holders for handfuls of small pots, each with a striking individual flower. And even if a recycled container such as a stack of car tyres, a plastic bucket or washing-up bowl is ugly when empty, you can soon disguise it with trailing plants.

There are numerous agricultural items that can be picked up at country sales and transformed into successful plant containers. Feeders for horses, or mangers, make large and attractive basket-type planters to fix to walls, while the long troughs used for chicken feed make excellent shallow homes for creeping thyme or chives.

▼ **The natural look** is best for some containers. This boat with a simple planting of grasses and flag iris set in gravel evokes a sense of nature's colonisation. In such a setting, bedding plants would look too formal.

the pleasures of containers

▲ For a successful colour combination use the wheel as your guide and mix only opposite (complementary) or adjacent (harmonious) shades. Green is the neutral of the plant world, but can still have impact (above, far right).

design a better garden with the colour wheel

Though plants have inspiring scents and shapes, they make their impact with colour. Follow these simple rules to using colour with flair.

▲ **Team green** with bright red (above), its opposing colour on the wheel, for dramatic effect, or with neighbouring yellow (above left) for a more harmonious container display.

Understanding the impact colour can have is a skill. Some people have a natural eye for colour, and mix and match colour schemes by instinct, but most of us have to learn by experimenting until we achieve the desired effect. A good place to start when putting colours together – in the garden or anywhere else – is by studying the colour wheel (left), which is based on the natural spectrum of the rainbow.

Schemes in which the use of colour is restrained are usually more successful than those that combine a riot of different colours and shades. The most memorable plantings often use colours that are next to, or close by, each other on the colour wheel. Such neighbouring colours are sympathetic to one another, rather than fighting for attention, and create naturally harmonious planted arrangements.

A late-summer harmonious arrangement could be achieved by filling a dark burgundy container with carmine red and dark cerise dahlias and placing it in front of a background of maroon-tinged foliage, such as

cotinus. Here all the colours are in sympathy because they are close together on the colour wheel. Another way to achieve harmony is to use shades of a single colour.

For a dramatic look, choose colours that are directly opposite each other on the colour wheel. These contrasting pairs are known as complementary colours, because they work together to create maximum impact. You could mix yellow and purple using daffodils and irises, or orange and blue by putting nasturtiums with lavender.

ADD A SPLASH OF COLOUR

Including a small amount of a contrasting colour in an otherwise harmonious arrangement produces a dash of excitement. The mainly burgundy arrangement described earlier, for instance, would really come alive if you added one or two bright marigolds or orange-centred gazanias to the planting mix.

To achieve the strongest display of pure or saturated colour, pack the container with flowers of similar colours but different shapes. But remember that saturated colour can be tiring after

a while, so an arrangement or collection of pots is often more successful if it is broken up with a paler shade, or muted with a darker one.

To create a really restful effect with your container arrangements, combine different flowers in a range of similar colours and use lots of green foliage to give the arrangement natural balance.

White is a powerful and eye-catching colour – adding a white flower will provide definition in almost any display. But it can be overpowering if used in a block, except in a dark corner. Most white daisies have dark or yellow centres for relief, but you can also soften the stark effect of an all-white arrangement by including green or silvery foliage, or the velvety, richly coloured leaves of a variegated coleus.

Hot colours vibrate in the midday sun and these spring poppies seem to leap from a surrounding sea of silver to create an instant feeling of energy and excitement.

use colour
to get you in the mood

One pot of plants looks hot and sunny, another cool and restful. The versatility of container gardening means you can introduce any colour you please to create exactly the look you desire.

▼ **Cool blue pots** filled with daisy-like blooms pick out the tones of a painted bench and bleached wooden deck to create a restful atmosphere.

Different colours conjure up very different emotions, so decide what mood you want to create before you choose any plants and pots. Bright yellows, oranges and reds will dominate any setting and are described as 'advancing' colours. Blues, mauves and greens are known as 'receding' colours, because they appear to withdraw into the background. If you position a pot of red flowers close at hand and one of blues in the distance, the eye is cheated into thinking that the vista is longer than it really is.

The intensity of natural light also has an impact on how we perceive colour. Hot and fiery colours have impact in the midday sun, while at twilight misty blues and mauves radiate a more subtle glow. White flowers and silver foliage look luminous in shade, drawing the eye. White also glows magically at night, making it the perfect colour for plantings that will be seen mainly in the evening.

MONOCHROME ARRANGEMENTS

A scheme based around a single colour can create a distinctive feel. For example, a combination of bleached timber, silver and grey foliage and white and blue flowers can induce a feeling of peacefulness.

As a general rule, receding colours can be used together in greater quantity than advancing ones. A terrace filled entirely with scarlet flowers might look stimulating but it would soon become tiring on the eyes. However, shades of pink, tempered with touches of cerise and magenta, would be stimulating but never overpowering. Similarly, a splash of an advancing colour, such as yellow, adds a cheerful and welcoming note to any display, outside a front door, for instance, or for a window box in the depths of winter.

▲ **Bright colours look fresh (1)** in the cool light of spring, while lilacs **(2)** suit the soft haze of a British summer. Reds and bronzes glow **(3)** in the gloom of autumn and whites and blues **(4)** echo the crispness of an icy winter day.

▲ **Plant a bouquet in a bucket,** mixing shapes and colour. Here, spires of purple lavender, red dianthus and sunny, daisy-like gerberas combine with tumbling nasturtiums for an expansive effect.

the changing delights of shapes and seasons

One yellow flower can vary widely in shape from another, and each will strike the eye in a different way, depending on the season. Look beyond the basic colour of plants to appreciate the many effects you can achieve.

Flowers offer the container gardener not only colour but also texture and shape. When planning a display, you need to look at the size of the plants, the outline of their flowers and whether the foliage is glossy or muted. Striking a balance between colour, texture and shape can create a beautiful tapestry effect.

You could plant a container to resemble a luxurious bouquet, for instance, using spear-shaped lupins, bell-like campanulas or petunias, daisy-shaped gazanias and the pompoms of alliums or scabious, all in different colours. Or plant an arrangement such as the pots of cool-coloured lime-lovers on page 102, where the colours harmonise but the contrast of different shapes reverberates with excitement.

COLOUR AND SEASON

The effect of light at different times of the year can also influence the look of an arrangement. In spring the soft cool quality of the light suits bright colours – yellow daffodils and red tulips look bright and fresh early in the year where they might look harsh in summer. The pinks, lilacs and mauves so popular in summer containers seem to suit the soft, often hazy light of

a sunny British day. And in the darker autumn months, glowing reds and bronzes are particularly effective.

One of the joys of container gardening is that colour schemes can be changed from one season to another or even during the same season. A bare brick wall seen from indoors during winter could be made attractive with variegated climbing ivies. In summer these could form the background for flowering climbers, such as roses or clematis, morning glory or sweet peas.

Sometimes a shrub creates year-round colour opportunities for a container garden. *Skimmia japonica* and *Viburnum davidii* both have neat shapes and evergreen interest, but also produce flowers in spring and autumn fruits. A pot of creamy crocuses or hyacinths would emphasise either plant's tiny spring flowers. In autumn the red berries of the skimmia could be highlighted with miniature red cyclamen, and the blue viburnum fruits set off with metallic blue pansies or violas.

Lavender is another good choice for year-round interest. It can be teamed with different plants as the seasons change and as the lavender itself shifts from stark silvery foliage to a mass of rich purple blooms (see pages 182-183).

Colours, shapes and textures combine in glorious container displays to lift the spirit, whatever the season

finding the perfect colour match

Creating a successful colour scheme is not just about choosing the right plants. To get the best results you also need to consider where you plan to put the container.

Matching a display to its background can make or mar an arrangement. A familiar background for many containers is the red brick of a house or wall. This harsh tone can be balanced with the complementary greens of evergreens or semi-evergreens such as box or laurel. Or consider berberis and euonymous whose leaves change in autumn from green to burnt orange or pinky red.

Other good plants to use against red brick are hostas (see page 306), which are tailor-made for containers. Their abundant large arching leaves make a strong statement particularly in urban spaces that yearn for rich foliage.

Lighter brick, pale weathered timber and rendered cement painted in pastel tones all suit displays with pale foliage, and with flowers that contain some degree of white. In sunny positions, white flowers tinged with apple green, creamy yellow or blush pink look wonderful against a foil of silver, grey or blue foliage.

◄ **A display made for its spot,** this milky, terracotta pot, the pale stone step and weather-beaten door, and delicate white marguerites are all in perfect harmony.

Shadier locations look fresh and bright with gold-variegated and lime-green leaves, and with stronger tints of buttery yellows or salmon pinks.

THE COLOUR OF THE CONTAINER

It is important to match the style and colour of the pot to the background, as well. The façade of a smart, red brick town house would look elegant accompanied by lead window boxes filled with dark green evergreens that would look out of place against a white-painted cottage.

If you want your pots to work against a variety of backgrounds, choose neutral coloured containers, such as creamy stone or soft, weathered terracotta. Vivid glazed pots often look wonderful on their own, but it can be hard to match plants to them without the flowers being overpowered by the colour of the glaze. If you do want to fill a colourful container, the best solution is to choose the pot first, then select the plants.

If you are using garden furniture or a feature such as a trellis as a foil for your containers, you may want to paint them first. A colour that has been softened by a touch of white, such as lavender or a bluey grey, or one with some black in it, such as a dark smoky green, makes a more suitable background for flowers and foliage than hard, clear colours.

49

◄ **A spiky cordyline thrives on a spiral staircase,** hinting at the roof garden beyond. The steps lead to the top level of the roof, a crow's nest of a corner tended by another of the resident Buddhists and crammed with an eclectic mix of plants, trinkets and holiday souvenirs.

high above the city streets

Pause to look up from the busy streets of east London, and you may just spot the spikes of a cordyline jutting into the sky. This is the only hint from outside of the rooftop garden at the London Buddhist Centre. Here roses bloom alongside damson trees, magnolias flourish in spring next to azaleas, camellias and rhododendrons, and pots and troughs of bedding plants blaze in dense rows all summer long.

The garden is a haven amid the city bustle for the 35 Buddhists who live at the centre, and has been tended for the last 14 years by Paramabandhu. Because the garden is on the roof, everything is grown in containers, and ▶

► **Stepping in from the street** is like passing through an enchanted gate. The running water and cool simplicity of the planting scheme in the courtyard – all pale blues, pinks and whites – create an instantly tranquil effect for visitors to the centre.

◄ **The garden begins,** for the Buddhists who live here, at the top of a flight of steps from the entrance courtyard. A bright mural transforms a blank neighbouring wall and sets the scene for the colourful planting around the main eating area.

51

▶ **To create a green screen** between the eating area and the rest of the roof garden, Paramabandhu planted irises with long strappy leaves in the two 'ponds' and tall white Shasta daisies around them.

▲ **Intense colours enrich the 'jewel box',** including the flowers **(1)** and twisted stems **(2)** of a *Tradescantia*, and the *Clematis* 'Perle d'Azur' **(3)**. This was previously just a place to keep the bins, and the planting is still developing.

◀ **The plants in the two 'ponds'** are mirrored by the pot plants surrounding them. There are water irises and herbaceous irises, water lilies and arching garden lilies, as well as water mint and culinary mint.

◀ **In the eating area, blue, red and yellow flowers** represent the 'three jewels of Buddhism' and remind the Buddhists of the beliefs of their religion. Yellow represents the Buddha and enlightenment; blue, meditation and the teachings of Buddhism; and red, the Buddhists themselves.

> " My **vision** for this area is a kind of jewel box, but I haven't quite **achieved** it yet. "

in spring, trays of plants, bags of compost and pots are strewn about as the new displays are potted up. "We eat and socialise out here, and use the space to meditate," Paramabandhu explains, "so I focus on summer colour, because the garden isn't used much in bad weather."

Take three steps down from the top of the stairs and you enter a sunken courtyard. "My vision for this area is of a kind of jewel box, but I haven't quite achieved it yet," Paramabandhu confesses. Blues, purples and reds predominate, with acers, a red

camellia, clematis, the geranium 'Mourning Widow', lupins and a *Thalictrum delavayi*, a Hampton Court flower show find.

This is also where most of the roses grow. Their new foliage glows a deep russet before turning green, and before the deep magenta blooms emerge.

Paramabandhu buys fruit trees with a restricted rootstock, intended for container living, but with roses, he steers away from pot varieties. "I like the size of ordinary bedding roses and find they do really well in largish containers. I buy good-quality

David Austen plants, but don't give them any special treatment, and they all flower every year."

A PLACE TO SOCIALISE

One of the most colourful parts of the garden is the eating area, where a clash of red, yellow and blue flowers surrounds a table. "Because this is an eating area, I don't worry about using scented plants," Paramabandhu tells me, "The food smells." So most are annuals chosen for their colour.

Most are also compact species that will live in pots small enough to fit on the surrounding

"It would be nice to have more terracotta pots, but the roof would probably fall in."

◄ **Cool whites calm the mind** and create a serene place in the main pink and white area of the roof for meditation. Here, a bench backed by a haze of fluffy astilbes faces an inspiring statue of the Buddha.

▲ **Heavy pots** rest on the sturdiest parts of the roof, such as the steps (top) and edges; elsewhere, plastic pots are the rule. Black dustbins (above) hold large shrubs and are hidden behind bushy plants, such as this astilbe.

low wall and still leave room to sit at the table. There are scarlet geraniums, yellow nasturtiums, yellow lilies for their striking shapes and lobelia. "The lobelias were supposed to be blue, but some flowered a pinky purple – you can't rely on them."

Next to the bright eating area, the main area of the roof is a sugared confection of pink and white. Between the two is "the obligatory water feature" – two enamelled sinks. The smaller sink is encrusted with lichens, but the larger pond is a more recent addition. It had been used in the

basement of the building and was about to be thrown out when Paramabandhu spied it. More bath than sink, it is a mighty size and even empty of water it is incredibly heavy. "Unfortunately," Paramabandhu grins, "I had a broken arm when we moved it."

WEIGHTY CONCERNS

Although the 'ponds' work perfectly where they are, they could not go anywhere else on the roof. Here they sit on top of a strong external wall – one of the few areas of the roof that can bear their weight.

In fact, all the heavy pots follow the pattern of the walls below. "It would be nice to have more decorative terracotta pots, but the roof would probably fall in if I did," Paramabandhu muses.

"I used to have a huge bed of roses along one wall and a large wooden trough with a white wisteria spreading along the fence, but one day the person in charge of the building realised what was on the roof. Apparently the roof has wooden supports and just isn't built to take that kind of weight, and he made me take it all down."

the good grouping guide

While a single container can create a focal point, several pots grouped close together can completely transform a bare patio or balcony. Make the most of the flexibility of containers to achieve the effect you want.

What makes container gardening so very versatile is that you can grow several plants in one large pot, or arrange a group of planters side by side to become an integral part of the garden design. And if you have a passion for a particular type of plant you can build up a container collection.

The pots could each hold a different variety of hosta or lily, for instance, or several species of grass. Or you could gather together a number of tiny plants, such as alpines which would look small and insignificant on their own, into a group that demands attention.

Alternatively, you can group a collection of different plants to create a particular effect, such as a traditional border, or to add a pretty cottage garden look to a bare terrace.

Rearranging a group of pots as flowers fade in one and come into bloom in another also enables you

to refresh the look of a container garden again and again. This is particularly true of spring bulbs, which have a short season compared with summer pot plants such as busy lizzies. Using containers, you can add a new bowl of blooms to replace an old one from early March to late May to keep the display constantly fresh and pretty.

Putting a group of containers together also provides scope for experimenting with the effects of combining colours and textures. If you are not confident about whether the combination of plants you want will look good together, put them all in separate pots and shuffle them until you achieve a pleasing result.

If your chosen plants have different heights, it is obviously best to place the taller ones at the back and the shortest ones at the front, arranging the others so their sizes are graduated in between. If you want to group very low plants together, you may need to

place them on a tiered stand, which maximises limited space, or on a table to lift small leaves or tiny flowers closer to eye level.

FAMILIES OF POTS

If you are adding containers to an existing group then they need to be sympathetic to the atmosphere already established.

As a general rule, it is wise to choose one style of container from a source which enables you to add to the collection with ease. Visit garden centres or potteries where you can pick out pots, and arrange and rearrange them until you create a pleasing group.

If you want to achieve a tight arrangement, square or rectangular shapes can be butted up closer together than rounded shapes. Sharp angles also create a modern style, whereas curvaceous shapes have a more traditional appearance. Flat-backed wall pots are also useful containers if space is short, because they sit tight against a wall.

▶ **A line-up of evergreens,** an olive, a bay, a box and a lavender, extends the path of a rustic fence creating a living barrier between two areas of a terrace. The tallest plant, positioned at one end, anchors the grouping.

▶ **Square-edged containers** can be grouped more closely than round pots. The clean angles and shiny metal have a modern feel that works well with this crisp purple-and-white scheme.

▶ **Group plants on a table** to draw attention to a special collection. These hostas, all at different stages of development, make an attractive display and are also lifted clear of hungry slugs and snails on the ground.

◄ **Clipped or conical,** conifers are ideal for a formal evergreen planting. This neat row of three small trees on a table (left) are snipped into lollipops with shaggy feet. Two conifers in tall, elegant glazed pots (below) stand guard on shallow steps.

pots and plants
standing to attention

In the grand gardens of the country house, containers were used to mark the junction of a path or the ends of a terrace. Often shaped like Grecian urns and planted with clipped trees or trailing foliage, they created a formal look that can still be used to add structure and shape.

When an elegant and restrained formality is required in the garden, the relationship between plants and containers is crucial. Plants that have a strongly defined shape all complement the traditional formality of Versailles planters, pedestal urns and classic terracotta. Try tightly clipped box or yew fashioned into cones, balls and spirals, or one of the many narrow, cylindrical dwarf conifers. A strongly shaped flowering plant, such as a chrysanthemum ball, can make the same formal impact as a box ball, with the added pleasure of a bright colour.

A sense of formality is further emphasised when containers of a uniform style are arranged in an organised or symmetrical layout. A line of matching pots with identical plants, or duplicate containers and plants placed to frame a front door, an opening in a hedge, or to mark the start or end of a path work well.

A pair of period urns at the top or bottom of a flight of steps is a device frequently seen in elegant Italian gardens where they are planted with fountain-shaped cordylines or neatly pruned camellia or azalea. They work equally well on the smaller steps of a terrace or back garden.

TIMELESS GEOMETRY

A single pedestal urn makes an imposing focal point in the centre of a formal parterre – a popular garden feature in the 17th century, which is now enjoying a revival. It consists of a bed of small geometric compartments, defined by low hedging and filled with either permanent or seasonal planting, to which containers add authenticity.

In modern settings, geometric planters made from galvanised metal create a chic formal style planted with clipped lavender, rosemary or santolina. A toning stone mulch adds a crisp finishing touch. Contemporary zinc and glass-fibre planters are relatively light and ideal for formal low hedging plants on, say, a roof terrace or balcony where weight is an issue.

Choose trailing foliage and delicate flowers for simple charm

Battered wire baskets look especially charming in an informal setting and are the prettiest way to display cascading varieties.

◄ **A ragged silhouette** works perfectly in this informal planting. The trailing plants, *Bidens*, Indian mint and petunias, almost hide their colour-washed terracotta pot.

Create the impression of nature running wild to give your garden a relaxed, spontaneous look. Choose containers with worn finishes and plants with soft outlines for happy informality.

take it easy
in the garden

W hether you live in the town or country, you can create an exuberant and relaxed style of container gardening that gives an atmosphere of unrestrained nature.

The effect to aim for is one of spontaneity, so that the container looks as if it has been planted haphazardly – though it takes careful planning to make this look beautiful, not messy. The overall shape is crucial: informal designs need to look generous and expansive rather than neat and tidy.

◄ **Simple stencils** have been used to decorate these three terracotta pots, brimming with tufted *Lampranthus spectabilis*.

And while a variety of colours can look wonderful, it is usually better if they harmonise. Informal displays are a great way to emphasise the texture of an arrangement – for instance, by using daisy shapes and bells, spires and soft trailing plants all in the one pot.

The best time to assemble such a display is when the plants are small and can be packed tightly into the pot. If you wait until they are large enough to see the flower buds, they will have bigger rootballs and the container will accommodate fewer of them.

CASUAL CONTAINERS

The most successful containers for informal arrangements have a neutral finish allowing the plants to shine whatever their colour, shape or size. Unlike formal settings, in which plant and pot have a clear relationship, informality can lead to the pots being almost invisible, because they are either clustered in a random group or hidden by tumbling greenery.

Curvaceous terracotta pots have a romantic, relaxed appearance and their surface improves with the patina of time, which mellows and softens the colour. However, the harsh red of new machine-made pots may be softened instantly with a coat of pale stone paint or limewash. Terracotta is a great medium for experimenting with paint techniques such as colour-washing, dragging or stippling. These give a broken finish, and provide colours and tones that harmonise or contrast with flowers and foliage. Or you could try using stencils to add a border of leaves or flower motif to plain flowerpots.

Wood can also be used effectively in an informal garden – half-barrels may be stained in natural shades or their slats painted to echo the colour scheme of the plants. Wooden crates and old fruit boxes make attractive homes for herb or vegetable gardens.

Salvaged sinks, stone troughs and galvanised tubs all make terrific wide, low-level planters for a profusion of trailing plants and are great for scattering seeds of annuals that will give a delightfully free effect.

Find out how to decorate pots on pages 256-257

▶ **Carefully placed accessories,** like this Japanese lantern, set the scene for a display of oriental plants. Here, a feathery acer in a pot sits on a deck of weathered wood.

▼ **The flaming red foliage** of this bonsai Japanese maple stands out against a garden bench painted in a slate grey that almost matches the tree's pot. The wispy foliage has a light, cool effect, but the vibrant colour is unmistakably hot.

cool
oriental
styles
and hot
exotic
drama

The Chinese and Japanese have been growing plants in pots for centuries. Their containers are usually earthenware with plain or decorated glazes and are planted with trees and shrubs. Pines, bamboos, acers, evergreen azaleas and camellias are all good subjects for an oriental display.

For an authentic look, arrange your containers on a low platform or group single specimens on upturned pots to create a variety of heights and display the beauty of each plant. Both wood and gravel make sympathetic settings for a collection of pots with oriental style and are easy to incorporate on a patio or balcony.

Pots with traditional Chinese designs are widely available. They are glazed in mottled blue 'Chun' (meaning sky after rain) or rich earthy shades and decorated with birds, butterflies and dragons.

Pots imported from Thailand and Vietnam often have an almost metallic glazed finish. Check that any pots you buy are frost-proof and remember to stand them on pot feet in winter.

TURN UP THE HEAT

To achieve a more exotic feel for summer, re-create a Mediterranean look with citrus trees in containers, or flowering shrubs, such as a *Bougainvillea*.

Whatever look you choose, the key is to create a complete design. A single exotic display in an ordinary garden would look bizarre. It is better to include the odd unusual plant in a more homely arrangement, for example, placing a yellow-stemmed bamboo by a pond among other water-loving plants. Or devote a whole section of the garden to the design of your choice.

▶ **From far-flung shores,** this *Aechmea* adds tropical brilliance to a sunny terrace. A tall pot with a steely industrial feel emphasises the silvery blush of the leaves and accentuates the plant's exotic silhouette.

Transport yourself to another land with displays inspired by foreign influences. The oriental look is well suited to containers, since it uses few plants and limited colour. In pots you can also create the perfect conditions for exotics that would normally be unattainable.

be creative
with pots for impact

Punctuate your garden with pots, using colour and positioning to create accents and to add interest and structure to the overall design. Or add impact to a container collection with a single bold splash of a contrasting colour.

▼ **Put a full stop** at the end of a low wall and the top of a flight of steps with a bowl of contrasting flowers. White marguerites tone with the limey shade of the bricks, while the purple blooms stand out.

Y ou can use accents most effectively to add a bright sparkle to a main colour scheme. For instance, if you decide on cool blue and mauve arrangements for your summer containers, a splash of bright orange from a zinnia would provide the highlight. At other times of year – when there are fewer flowers to choose from, and keeping colour in a display is more difficult – a dot of an accent colour will add interest to an arrangement of evergreens.

Do not be tempted to overdo accents: too much of a contrasting colour only succeeds in confusing the eye and bewildering the mind. For dramatic impact, include only a few accent plants, restricting them to about a fifth of the overall scheme at most. To avoid a display looking bitty, it is best to restrict yourself to one accent colour. For example, creamy white or buttery yellows against the background of evergreens.

POSITIONING POTS FOR EFFECT

In formal schemes (see pages 56-57), planted containers make an impact ranged in rows or placed in pairs to flank an entrance or similar focal point. However, a single accent pot, carefully positioned, can act as a pivot in any garden design. Try placing a pot centrally at the edge of a patio and plant it to echo a dominant tree or shrub or a colour scheme farther back in the garden. By adding this accent in the foreground you will create interest with alternative horizons and also emphasise your favourite existing features.

Planting several matching pots with the same combination of plants and placing them along a path or in disparate areas of the garden will lead the eye from one to the next, highlighting and drawing together the areas you have chosen. If you have a large garden, an effective way to do this is to use attention-grabbing glazed pots in a strong colour that will have instant impact, even at a distance.

▲ **A splash of cobalt blue** shows that accents need not be limited to living colour. A sculptural empty pot will draw the eye to the area of a garden in which it is set, particularly if it is a contrasting colour to the plants around it.

◀ **Placed on the corner of a terrace,** two potted hollies, mark the divide between house and garden. Being evergreens, they accent the seasonal changes in the rest of the garden by echoing them in miniature.

63

the perfect place for a pot

Make your containers the centre of attention by framing them in a setting or raising them to a prominent position.

The setting is as important to overall effect as the shape and size of container and the plants it holds. All too often a ravishing display is relegated to an insignificant spot on the floor of a patio. But a little thought and ingenuity can lift almost any container from the realms of the mundane to become a work of art.

Look carefully at your garden, balcony or terrace, and think about both architectural and natural shapes, as well as colour, before deciding where to place a pot. A small pot, simply planted, will have a big impact if it is framed by a terrific view, whether it is a stunning backdrop of blue sea (left), an angular city skyline or the glimpse of a hidden section of garden through an arch.

A useful trick is to raise containers above ground level. Use flights of steps or low walls. Pop a plant in the top of an old chimney pot. Trailing varieties look charming grouped on a rusty wrought-iron table or chair, and car boot sales and clearance houses are a great source of wooden or metal furniture for the garden. Use outdoor paint or stain to tone in with your colour scheme, or leave them untouched for a contemporary distressed look.

A device borrowed from the Victorian greenhouse is the tiered plant stand. These range from elaborate antique wirework jardinières (see pages 24 and 73) rescued from grand conservatories to simple modern metal shelving. Basic wooden greenhouse systems with adjustable shelving can be waterproofed with exterior paint or stain. Or simply commandeer a wooden stepladder and range your pots on the treads.

You can also frame a pot in its setting at ground level. Try standing a round container in a simple circle of stones or on a platform of old tiles – just experiment, and have fun.

◄ **A simple pot is brought centre stage** before a backdrop of the shifting sea. Its 'frame' is a twiggy arch over a gate and an artfully placed stick of driftwood.

▶ **A group of succulents** is given structure and importance by sitting the pots in regimented rows on an old set of painted kitchen steps.

65

One of the main advantages of container gardening is its great flexibility. You can move plants to centre stage when they are in their prime and out of the spotlight when they fade, or you may decide to discard and replace them as you would a vase of flowers.

This flexibility also means that a container display can be dropped in anywhere in the garden to add colour, shape or interest wherever it is needed most. Perhaps a boring corner needs enlivening, or the view from a window is so depressing that it needs a pot or two of colour to cheer it up.

It is a good idea to plant your bulbs in pots, dropping them into strategic places in a border when they come into bud. That way, they are kept safe from scavenging squirrels and spiking garden forks and you can enjoy maximum benefit from the blooms. This idea not only works well for spring bulbs such as daffodils and tulips, but also for beautiful summer lilies. Plant the bulbs in simple black plastic pots and stand them in the border as they come into flower – the black pots will become completely invisible, hidden in the shadows of surrounding perennials.

FILLING A GAP

You can also put a flourishing container into a herbaceous border to hide the gap left when a plant dies back or fails. Position a pot in front of a flowering shrub once its own flush is over or try nestling an empty pot, such as a striking glazed urn or a battered old terracotta favourite, among the dense foliage of a thriving border.

A dreary passage along the side of a house can be cheered up with a well-placed pot or narrow trough filled with bright busy lizzies, while boring utilitarian steps are transformed by placing a small pot on each tread. And containers are ideal for front steps, too, particularly for those town houses that do not have much or any soil to plant in, and where there is limited space between the house and the pavement.

▲ **Pots of living sunshine** march along a low wall, brightening the view from a side window. Dwarf sunflowers are great candidates for small pots.

bring in colourful pots to brighten a dull spot

The beauty of a container display is its portability, which means it can be placed anywhere in a garden to add a splash of colour and interest. Even a strategically placed empty pot can have an impact.

A pot of jewel-like anemones stands in front of a clump of bergenia. Though the bergenia's spring flowers are over, its evergreen leaves provide a glossy backdrop to the anemones' fragile stems.

paint a bare wall with living colour

Plants that climb and plants that trail – a bare fence or wall gives you a great opportunity to be creative with beautiful displays in a variety of different containers.

W here a hard surface, such as paving or concrete, meets a wall, planting in the ground is not an option. But it is a great opportunity to let your imagination with containers run riot. For the fastest results, start at the top of the wall and work down. Try using several hanging baskets filled with trailing plants and suspended from a series of brackets fixed to the wall.

One well-planted basket is always pretty, but a whole group – at least three, but as many as space will allow – can be really spectacular. Position the brackets so that the plants in the upper baskets have room to grow, but stagger the arrangement so that when they trail over they do not smother those lower down. For the best effect, and to avoid an untidy look, it is a good idea to use similar groups of plants in each basket.

An alternative to hanging baskets is to fix a collection of containers to the wall supported on brackets or screwed

Camouflage a bare fence with a collection of foliage plants, such as the purple sage and trailing ivies used here. Small pots sit snugly in wire loops hooked over a trellis.

Find out how to fix brackets to walls – see pages 268-269

to the vertical surface. Iron mangers, which hold a large number of plants, can look superb but they are quite expensive. Window-box troughs, wire half-baskets, drilled flat-backed terracotta pots, and even small pots in ornamental wall holders can all be just as effective.

Whatever the receptacle, make sure that it is firmly attached to the wall or fence: even a small pot will be heavy when it is full of compost and fully grown plants, and thoroughly watered. Try planting these containers with permanent displays of clematis, ivies or jasmine. Remember that what grows up will also trail down to provide a valuable long-term screen.

GROWING UP

Covering a wall or fence from the bottom up is a more traditional, but less instant solution. Climbing plants and freestanding shrubs such as clematis, honeysuckle and pyracantha are as happy in sturdy pots as they are in the ground. Any supports should be in position before the plant is placed against the wall.

Choose substantial pots for your plants: not only will this prevent the roots from freezing in winter or baking in summer, but it will also minimise the likelihood of your needing to repot, which will be difficult once the plants have attached themselves to the wall or been trained on supports.

Use a good-quality, soil-based compost, such as John Innes No.3 and dress the surface with an attractive mulch – which also helps to stop water loss.

A row of leafy
bamboos hides a bare fence and gives this garden an exotic jungly feel. Maximum coverage has been achieved by raising the pots on a wooden platform and placing them close together.

▶ **Everything must earn its keep** in Sheila's tiny plot, so lasting foliage plants, such as euphorbias and hostas, and shrubs with stamina, like the *Hebe salicifolia* in the centre of the paved area, play a large part.

◀ **A limited colour scheme** will create an impression of space. Sheila explores the full range of shades in her palette of green, white and yellow, mixing shapes and textures for variety.

an **oasis** in the **heart** of the **city**

She was a novice when she moved in, but Sheila Jackson has transformed her back yard into an urban haven. The concrete paving behind her city-centre basement flat is not quite 8m wide and 5.5m long (26x18ft), but is crammed full of plants. One corner has a bed of soil, but pots and planters provide most of Sheila's gardening opportunities.

With such a small space, Sheila soon realised that the only way to grow is up, and the house wall and garden fences are all but obscured by scrambling clematis, correas, forsythias, jasmines, pyracanthas, roses and a vine. Many of these stretch several metres from their copious plastic buckets, now hidden by other pots, and screen the rumble of ▶

" I'm always reminding people, 'green is a colour, too'. "

▲ **In a small garden** too many large plants would be oppressive, so Sheila needed more imaginative ways of adding height. A saucepan stand tower of Chinese bamboo steamer baskets filled with creeping sedums and alpines and topped with a spray of blue grass (*Festuca glauca*) is an inventive solution.

trains on the railway line that borders the plot. They also help to create the impression of a garden much larger than its true size.

Two roses float like clouds at the back of the garden, where they bridge the gaps between four chimneys, each 1.5m (5ft) tall, taken from the roof of the house. The small-flowered 'Félicité Perpétue', now 25 years old, mingles with the more open blooms of 'Cooper's Burmese' in a froth of white.

The simple white dots of the roses set the scene for the whole garden. "In a small space it is often best to follow a simple colour scheme, so that as the eye travels around the overall impression is of harmony, not jolting contrasts," Sheila advises. Her artist's eye – she

worked as a costume designer and is an accomplished water colourist – helps her to make the most of her palette. Whites from warm cream to almost blue are combined with a full range of greens and yellows.

A low wall around the garden's planted area offers a perch for several containers, but other arrangements are lifted by being placed on an upturned pot, or on bricks. Sheila's advice for using bricks in the garden is to get them from old storage heaters found in salvage yards: their deep ridges, or fins, give them an attractive shape and, because they have been fired, they are resistant to fluctuating temperatures, Indian summers and harsh winter frosts.

Raising a pot can offer a new perspective on a familiar plant. The spray of blue grass, *Festuca glauca*, at the top of the saucepan stand shimmers in the sunlight in a way it never would at ground level, and the tiny pink flowers of the sedum planted beside it catch the eye when they are at head height.

A TASTE FOR THE UNUSUAL

In the centre of the garden a retirement gift – a three-tiered wire jardinière – houses a generous collection of pots that changes with the seasons. On the bottom tier in summer, common pansies sit alongside a *Kleinia tomentosa*, a strange-looking silver plant with fleshy 'fingers', which Sheila inherited from a friend's conservatory. "He always had trouble growing it," she says, "but here it has been no problem. It just needs to go in for the winter."

> "I think I have more of a **botanical streak** than a horticultural one. I have a **Chinese hosta** which has an **extraordinary** fragrant flower in September."

▼ **Swirling spines** make this Chilean *Puya chilensis* an inspired choice to top Sheila's wire jardinière, where it echoes the stand's structure. Blue flowers shoot out on an arm-length spike in summer.

◄ **Exotic souvenirs** can be found all over the garden. A string bag **(1)** for a *Polygonum* 'Pink Bubbles' was once a Yemeni camel muzzle, while a curious stone **(2)** in a pot of sedums reveals fossils from the Sahara.

This odd-looking specimen is not alone in the garden. "I think I have more of a botanical streak than a horticultural one," Sheila says, and, as you explore, her collecting habit soon becomes apparent. Among a medley of hostas now so old Sheila claims to have forgotten what most of them are, is a Chinese variety, *Hosta plantaginea* 'Grandiflora', which grows only in full sun, producing an extraordinarily fragrant, white flower in September. But it's not just the plants which come from far afield. Mulching her pots, rocks from the Sahara sit next to less exotic holiday mementoes gathered by her great nieces and nephews.

ORDER IN THE JUMBLE

Keeping things small is Sheila's perennial challenge. "In all my years of gardening," she says, "I still haven't learnt how big things grow."

> "In all my years of gardening I still haven't learnt how big things grow. I dare not buy a gunnera, and I'd love a Crambe cordifolia, but friends keep telling me 'No!'"

But big-leaved plants with mighty proportions are among her particular favourites, and fill gaps all over the garden.

As well as the many hostas and a huge *Fatsia japonica* at the side of the house, she has a shady corner of ferns and a bank of dark-leaved perennials including *Heuchera* 'Palace Purple', 'Persian Carpet' and 'Chocolate Ruffles' and an umbrella plant, *Darmera peltata*, whose rhubarb-like leaves change colour through the year from light green to bronze in autumn, and can grow to almost twice the size of a dinner plate.

Another monster leaf belongs to the *Rheum*, or ornamental rhubarb, but still Sheila hankers for more: "I dare not give in and buy a gunnera… and I'd love a *Crambe cordifolia*, but friends keep telling me, 'Sheila, you can't have one!' It's true: it would be far too big."

▲ **Wrought-iron panels** contain a medley of pots in the same way as a border edging. At first Sheila repainted every year, then realised that the whiteness dominated the garden. The rusty weathered look is more sympathetic.

◄ **Big bold foliage** is one of Sheila's passions. Here a lime green *Darmera peltata* flourishes with its feet in the 'pond': a washing-up bowl in a wicker hanging basket. Behind it the mighty leaves of a *Rheum* catch every ray of light that reaches this dark corner.

▼ **With no room for a greenhouse,** Sheila built a frame onto her bedroom window – an ingenious way to shelter seedlings and tender plants, but still allow light into the house.

Swaying bamboos and palms give this dappled verandah a jungle atmosphere. The battered white chair hints at faded gentility and the days of the Raj, and looks quite irresistible.

hide away in a secret garden

Curl up in a bower of greenery with a good book or a close friend and enjoy a sense of privacy rarely achieved outdoors. Clever container planting can be used to create your own personal space in the open air.

There is something very special about a hideaway in the garden. It may be a place to read or snooze on a sunny afternoon, or somewhere to share a drink or meal with a friend on a balmy night. Whatever the purpose it needs to feel comfortable, sheltered and private. A sense of being enclosed can be achieved using plants alone or with containers in combination with screens or other garden structures.

ROOM FOR THOUGHTS TO ROAM

Before deciding where to site your secret garden, think about when you will be using it. Are you aiming for a south-facing suntrap or do you prefer less intense dappled light? Perhaps you want somewhere to unwind after a hard day's work and watch the sun go down?

You may like to base your plan on a ready-made feature such as a twiggy bower (left), a wrought-iron rose arch or a wooden trellis-work gazebo. But that is just the framework – what will personalise your space is the planting.

Containers allow you to continue a style of planting from the garden, such as the potted bamboos that complete the planting circle around the jungly verandah on the far left.

You might site your hideaway in a sunny part of the garden surrounded by a colourful border and choose to echo the perennial planting round about with tubs of scented lilies and marguerites inside. Pots of climbing roses, honeysuckle and wisteria could also be trained over a framework, offering increasing privacy as the years go by.

As the sun goes down, candlelight gives a bower a magical theatrical feel – somewhere to share a bottle of wine and even a midsummer night's dream.

the soothing
splash
of
cool water

◄ **A spray of water catches the light** and adds a sparkle to this display. Choose water-tolerant species, such as *Houttuynia* and *Oenanthe* (variegated water dropwort) for the fountain container.

For an instantly tranquil effect, nothing beats a water feature. Make a lily pond in a half-barrel or stand a tinkling fountain, splashing the leaves of waterside plants, on your patio and enjoy the calm.

Dappled sunlight reflects from the rippled surface of a container pond, glinting silver and gold as the water moves.

intact. Plastic containers may be an easier option, since they tend to be sold with holes marked, but not punched out. Old wooden beer barrels make excellent ponds when they have been waterproofed on the inside with a sheet of tough pond liner.

WATER-LOVING PLANTS

It is possible to make a very attractive, contemporary-looking water feature for your garden without including plants (see pages 270-271). But there are many beautiful species that will thrive in watery conditions.

Plants such as the *Houttuynia cordata* 'Chameleon' and *Oenanthe javanica* 'Flamingo' in the fountain bowl (top left) are happy with their roots in water and with their foliage being splashed. *Lysimachia* and *Mimulus* will also stand up to being splashed – *Mimulus* are often found by streams – but grow best if they are not actually standing in water.

Any successful pond needs at least one oxygenating plant, and a surface-floating plant to cast shade (see pages 270-271). *Cotula*, *Lobelia*, *Phalaris* and *Ranunculus* serve a more decorative purpose.

◄ **A spreading dwarf water lily** and tall cyperus are happy here in their blue glazed pond. Raising a container pond off the ground on pot feet or upturned flowerpots will help to keep it from freezing in winter.

▲ **A half-barrel makes a perfect pond,** deep enough to grow water lilies and wide enough to accommodate a good balance of different plants. You could even include a couple of fish in a tub this size for their flashes of gold.

Even the smallest garden has space for a pond or other water feature in a pot. Moving water adds interest in a garden and makes a welcome change of appearance in a bank of greenery.

The first thing you will need is a watertight container. Most stone and glazed terracotta pots have drainage holes already drilled in them, but aquatic centres and large garden centres may stock them

To install a water feature or plant a barrel pond, turn to pages 270-271

twinkling
in the
twilight

Create a fairytale atmosphere by using lights in the garden. Position them where they will turn the spotlight on to your container displays as evening falls.

Light up your garden by hanging lanterns from shepherds' crooks, dotting candles on tables and low walls, and twining strings of fairy lights around trees or shrubs.

Fine summer evenings make the garden an inviting place to be. If you don't want to head indoors as soon as the sun goes down, a few carefully positioned lights will allow you to linger for as a long as you like.

Battered old flowerpots make charming holders for nightlights, shielding the flickering flame from wind and casting a terracotta glow. Line them up along the edge of a path for a magical effect, or tuck them around the base of planted containers to illuminate your displays. Candle holders can also be suspended from trees or hanging baskets (see pages 214–215), where they will sway in the breeze.

Larger candles can be incorporated into your displays (right). Use them in simple arrangements where there is no danger of wafting foliage being set alight and always keep a close watch on the candle. Surrounding it with a ring of stones will help to prevent hot wax dripping onto your plants.

OUTSIDE ELECTRICS

Electricity provides more reliable garden illumination and has the added benefit that lights can be set with a timer switch to come on automatically. However, using electricity outside can be dangerous, so seek expert advice if you are unsure.

Always buy low-voltage lights with a transformer designed for outdoor use, and keep the transformer inside. A safe alternative for a temporary decoration is to use battery-powered strings of fairy lights.

◄ **Lights lead the way** down a garden path. A pair of conical box trees is dotted with large-bulbed electric lights that come on every evening to mark the top of a flight of steps, and candlelight torches follow the path towards a twilight hideaway.

◄ **A subtle glow** creates a gentle mood. On a fine still night a fat candle (far left) will cast a golden light, while clustering electric lights at the base of a shrub has a similar 'low-light' effect without the flames.

▶ **Brave the wintry weather** and enjoy the fireworks on bonfire night in a candle-lit garden. Drop tea-lights into empty flowerpots or glass holders to create decorations that will not be blown out by the November wind.

▼ **There is a wealth of different mints** to choose from, but they all tend to be invasive. So if you want to enjoy, but control, them plant each variety in a separate pot.

▶ **A group of fresh young herbs**, including chives, coriander, oregano and flat-leaf parsley, starts to flourish in the sun.

herbs to enhance your kitchen and garden

◀ **Pinch out the growing tips** to keep plants like this purple basil vigorous and bushy. This will give you a more expansive display, and many more leaves to add to your cooking.

If you like to cook with herbs but do not have much space, you can still grow them using pots and window boxes. Their beautiful foliage makes a pleasing alternative to summer flowers and their scented leaves have a sensory impact.

Gardeners have treasured herbs for their wonderful properties.

A window box decorated with lead flashing looks soft and pretty and brings its cargo of herbs within easy cutting distance.

The best herbs for containers are those you use regularly but in small amounts; when you want large handfuls of parsley for a fish sauce or basil to make pesto, it is better to buy a bunch than to strip the leaves from an entire plant.

As a rule, herbs look best in traditional pots. Ceramic, terracotta, stone, lead or wood will all add to the tranquil feeling that herbs give to an area. Make sure the container has lots of drainage holes before you start to plant it and position it near a sunny seat if you want to enjoy the fragrance.

To grow a collection of culinary herbs in a very small space, a strawberry or herb pot is a good choice (see pages 190-191). Depending on size, it will hold four to eight herbs around the sides and up to three in the top. When you are planting several herbs in a single pot, choose varieties that do not grow too quickly and avoid mint, which can overwhelm a mixed container in a matter of weeks. All mints are better confined to individual pots.

Before you pot, consider the shape of the plant and the colour and texture of its leaves. Most culinary herbs have variegated forms, or varieties with leaves in gold, silver-grey, blue, purple or cream as well as green. It is easy to find herbs that look beautiful and still retain all their flavour.

Tall herbs, such as angelica, fennel and lovage, make an impressive display planted one or two to a pot and placed where they can make a bold statement. They need a pot big enough to balance their height, and heavy enough to remain stable in windy weather.

Some shrubby herbs, such as rosemary and bay, make sizable plants and can be trained into pyramids, balls or informal half-standards. Once established, they will not need to be repotted for several years.

GROWING TIPS

Herbs grow best in well-drained soil, so add one part sharp sand to four parts compost, or add a core of grit (see page 230). Plant herbs in late spring or early summer and give them a balanced liquid plant food weekly from six weeks after planting. Annual and biennial herbs such as basil, dill and parsley, need to be replaced every year, but even perennials, such as mint and sage, taste better when they are young, so it's worth renewing them after three or four years.

GREAT HERBS FOR CONTAINERS

- **Basil** cinnamon; liquorice; lemon: lettuce leaved; Minette; Red Rubin; Thai; sweet basil
- **Chives** traditional; garlic
- **Parsley** Curlina; plain leaved; moss curled
- **Lemon balm** common; variegated (*Melissa officinalis* 'Variegata'); golden (*M. officinalis* 'Aurea')
- **Oregano** (pot marjoram) golden (*Origanum onites* 'Aureum'); variegated (*O. onites* 'Variegatum'); compact (*O. onites* 'Compactum')
- **Sage** common; purple (*Salvia officinalis* 'Purpurascens'); golden (*S. officinalis* 'Icterina'); tricoloured (*S. officinalis* 'Tricolor')
- **Thyme** bushy form: garden thyme
dwarf and creeping forms: gold variegated (*Thymus* 'Doone Valley'); lemon-scented golden (*T.* 'Bertram Anderson'); woolly grey thyme (*T. pseudolanuginosus*) wild thyme: (*T. serpyllum*)

If you would like to make the lead window box yourself, turn to pages 262-263

Strawberries can be grown in all manner of containers. To enjoy fresh berries over the longest period, either grow perpetual fruiting varieties, which allow you to pick small quantities of fruit all summer long, or plant early, mid season and late varieties separately. This method allows you to harvest more fruit at any one time, but takes up more space.

The best way to start is to buy pot-grown strawberry plants in spring: five strawberries are plenty for a hanging basket and ten for the average 35cm (14in) pot. Plant them immediately in soil-based compost and they will produce a modest crop in their first year. The second season should see a bumper crop, followed by a slightly lower yield the third summer. Then start again with fresh stock.

Careful watering and feeding are essential. If you are to reap a good crop, you must never let the compost dry out, particularly when the fruit is forming and ripening; if you do, the bulk of your crop will drop off the bush almost immediately. Water well then leave the pots for up to three weeks, until they reach the point of drying out. Be careful not to overwater them during the winter months.

Blueberry bushes and redcurrant bushes will also thrive for many years in large containers. And rhubarb is another great, if unexpected, pot plant, with its wonderful architectural foliage. If you have room in the pot around the fruit bush, you could add almost any decorative bedding plant: the effect will be spectacular.

GROWING TIPS

Most soft fruit thrives best in a soil-based compost: John Innes No.2 for strawberries, and John Innes No.3 for red, white and blackcurrants and for gooseberries. A rhubarb crown needs a good-sized tub or a 60cm (24in) pot. The stems can be pulled until early July; then it should be allowed to grow unchecked to build up reserves.

All soft-fruit bushes need to be watered copiously and fed regularly with a liquid tomato fertiliser, starting when the fruit begins to form and continuing until it is gathered. Blackcurrants are especially attractive to birds and the bushes will need some form of protection.

Blueberries are unusual pot plants. These delicious fruits need a lime-free, humus-rich compost and are more successful if replanted every two to three years.

juicy, fruity and on your doorstep

Fruit grows very well in containers, so if you yearn for the taste of a just-picked strawberry or blackcurrant, here is how to grow your own.

▶ **Redcurrant 'Redstart'** is a bushy plant and needs a container to itself. The glowing berries will lend drama to any position until picked for summer desserts.

◀ **Pot-grown strawberries** won't yield as much fruit as those grown in the ground. The pleasure lies in producing them on your own doorstep – and enjoying the flowers as well as the fruit.

PRUNING FRUIT BUSHES

Gooseberries and red and white currants should have the side shoots from the main branches shortened and the leader tipped in early autumn. With blackcurrants, take out about a third of the branches at the base of the bush each year to encourage new wood to develop. Pruning the bushes may be done as soon as the crop has been gathered, or left until later in the season.

enjoy a fruit tree all the year round

▶ **A container-grown orchard** of fruit and nut trees down the side path of a suburban house needs far less space than trees planted in open ground.

Who doesn't relish an apple off the tree? It is surprisingly easy to grow a fruit tree in a pot. Plant one and savour blossom in spring, fruit in autumn and frosted winter branches.

Fruit trees make great specimen plants for the patio. They look equally good on their own, or underplanted with other fruits, such as strawberries, or with small flowering bedding plants.

Most types of fruit tree are suitable for container cultivation, given the proper care and attention. Apples, apricots, cherries, figs, nectarines, peaches, pears and plums may all be grown as bushes or standards, or trained as fans and espaliers against a sunny wall.

When buying fruit trees choose varieties that have been grown on a dwarfing rootstock and are suitable for growing in a restricted area. And keep an eye open for cultivars that have been specially raised for patio culture; new varieties are being introduced all the time with today's smaller gardens in mind.

When planting a fruit tree, you may need to group more than one variety to ensure cross-pollination and guarantee a good crop. Alternatively, choose a self-fertile variety: these always have the term 'self-fertile'

within their name, such as the plum, 'self-fertile Victoria' or the pear 'self-fertile Conference'.

Instead, you could plant a 'family tree', where two or more varieties of a fruit tree, capable of pollinating one another, have been grafted on to the same rootstock. Family trees provide an excellent way of producing more than one kind of a particular fruit without cultivating several plants. A family apple, for example, could give you an early eater, a late eater and a cooker all on one tree.

CARING FOR TREES

When you are planting a fruit tree, use a large, stout container – at least 60cm (24in) in diameter. Your young tree may look lost in such a large pot when you first plant it, but it will grow quickly and will need lots of space to develop.

Wood, stone or imitation stone tubs are preferable to ceramic pots, which may crack as the plant's roots expand. Plastic is not ideal for long-term planting either, as it does not offer enough insulation against extreme temperatures. Plant up your

container in its intended finished position: once it is filled with compost and the tree, it will probably be too heavy to move with ease.

Place plenty of crocks in the base of the pot and plant your tree in John Innes No.3 compost, which contains enough fertiliser to get the sapling established in its first season. Be careful not to bury the rootstock in the compost or the tree could lose its dwarf character.

Stand the pot on feet or bricks to keep the drainage holes clear. This will also stop water from pooling underneath and turning to ice in the winter, which could damage the roots. Finish with a thick layer of mulch to prevent the compost from drying out.

During the tree's first season, water moderately. Once established, it will dry out more rapidly and should be watered thoroughly at least once a day in hot weather. Every spring, sprinkle on a slow-release feed and water it in well.

Once the fruit starts to form, feed every week with a tomato or other high potash liquid fertiliser until it is ready for picking.

▲ **A young peach** produces a small but precious crop of fruit. The shallow pot is quite adequate for the roots at this stage and will help to keep the tree's growth within bounds.

▶ **Catching the early summer sun,** green lemons start the slow process of ripening. The lemon tree can spend summer outdoors, but must be moved into a conservatory for winter.

PRUNING FRUIT TREES

Container-grown apples and pears should be pruned in late summer or early autumn by shortening back the side shoots made that season to three or four leaves (see below). Fruiting spurs will eventually form at these positions.

Apricots, cherries, figs, nectarines, peaches and plums grown in pots as bushes or as short standards are best left unpruned — although you may want to trim off some of the shoots to maintain the plant in good shape. In the unlikely event of a branch dying, it should be cut back to healthy wood immediately.

►**From path to conservatory** and deep into the garden, fruit trees, lavender, day lilies, runner beans and a flowering *Abutilon* 'Ashford Red' flourish in pots all through this rampant garden.

► **Every detail counts: (1)** Red Devil apples crown a pot-grown tree. **(2)** Snail and sea shells provide a safe topping to supporting canes. **(3)** Peas planted to scramble up a pear tree tumble over the edge of the container.

▼ **An artist's eye** reveals itself in the way the silvery patina of the terracotta pot links the delicate pale flowers of *Fuchsia* 'Annabel' to the soft metallic tones of the old milk churn and the garden bench.

a passion for growing

Elsa Day has only a modest back garden yet it contains an orchard, a vegetable plot, a stream and masses of intermingled plants ranging from abutilons heavy with flowers in summer to hydrangeas, bamboos and cosmos. Her secret is that so many of her favourites are in pots.

"What I like about growing things in containers is that they don't take up so much room" Elsa explains. "If the plants were in the ground, they would need lots of root space and I wouldn't be able to fit them all in." ▶

▲ **A slender papaya tree** soars above the dense planting of the garden. Elsa built up the sides of its container with bits of broken pot so that she could add more compost for weight and stability. Getting it back into the conservatory for winter is a two-person job.

Elsa's chief pleasure is in the actual business of growing and almost anything will start her off. A mysterious plant in the conservatory grew from a bit of stem she found on the floor of the London college where she teaches print making. An acacia tree came from a seed she picked up in Madeira. "I find it a challenge to grow from seed. I just want to see what happens. It can take a long time, but when it grows, it is such a thrill."

Along the side of the house a walnut, a sweet almond and an espaliered apricot tree rub branches with a nectarine and an apple tree in pots, and a grapevine and tayberry. Turning into the garden the procession continues with another apple, a pear, a young peach bush and a crab apple on a table.

Elsa has two conservatories: one is a permanent home to tender plants such as a baby orange tree and a dark-flowered datura (*Brugmansia*). The other is Elsa's workshop, but in winter she packs in her abutilons, fuschias, geraniums, baby banana trees, the acacia and a mimosa that is just getting going. "I once had to cut a few feet off the top of the papaya to get it in, but it grew back."

▲ The fruit harvest includes pots of strawberries set on a stepladder (above left) so the sun can reach and ripen each one **(1)**, a young lemon tree brought outdoors for summer (above) and a velvety peach **(2)**.

▲ Vegetables on parade spring from a row of fire buckets picked up at a sale. Every year Elsa grows summer crops of tomatoes **(1)**, peppers **(2)** courgettes **(3)**, beans and salad leaves from seed. She also grows potatoes in a stone pot near the kitchen door. "It's ugly but no one sees it."

◄ Glowing purple aubergines ripen on the sunny terrace. After years of service, the paint on the vegetable buckets has started to peel.

Her gift for growing shows in the way each of her plants thrives in its container, such as the 15 sky-blue heads of agapanthus soaring out of one modest-sized pot. "In winter I put a woolly jersey stuffed into a plastic bag on top, then cover the whole lot in bubble wrap" she says tenderly.

"I have found most things live quite happily in the container. If something looks dead, I always keep it a year and 99 times out of 100 it will put up a shoot. The nut and fruit trees are in 22 inch pots in a mixture of homemade compost and multipurpose.

I add some 'Dug' fertiliser – it's organic and very smelly – and I water them every day and sometimes twice. That is absolutely vital.

"The advantage of a container garden is that you can move the pots about. If the place they are in isn't good for them, move them to a better one; and when a container is over you can put it out of sight. I can have a new garden every month." Elsa's creative instinct is always alive. "Next year I am going to plant a lawn in a box," she says. "I will make a square box on wheels so I can have it by my chair on the terrace to put my bare feet on."

"I find it a challenge to grow from seed. It can take a long time, but when it grows, it is a thrill."

▲ **Delicious peas and beans** can easily be grown in pots. Whether trained up a support or left to trail decoratively over the edge, they bring you flavour in a snap.

► **Tumbling cherry tomatoes** (this variety is 'Sweet Million') look pretty partnered by nasturtiums and French marigolds. The marigolds will also help to keep aphids away.

easy vegetables to get you started

Nothing compares with the taste of freshly picked vegetables – and you do not need a lot of expertise to grow them. Beans and peas, tomatoes and salad vegetables are quite easy to raise in pots. Place them near the kitchen door for easy access.

▶ **Trailing cherry tomatoes** can be grown in hanging baskets as well as pots – to make a display that is pretty to look at and tastes wonderful.

Tomatoes are one of the most adaptable container plants. You can grow dwarf or bush varieties in window boxes, hanging baskets or around the edges of pots. Bush tomatoes are happiest in grow bags or pots at least 30cm (12in) across; one 45cm (18in) in diameter can accommodate three plants.

Tomatoes grown on a single stem as cordons will need tying to a stake as they grow. Or position the pots near a wall or fence and tie the plants to a fixed trellis.

This is probably the best way of training the long stems of a cucumber, too, although some outdoor varieties, such as ridge cucumbers, can be left to trail over the side of the pot.

Both tomatoes and cucumbers will thrive only in warm weather conditions and are nearly always killed by frost. If you are growing from seed, this can be sown direct into the pots outdoors when the temperature starts to rise in spring and there is no further risk of frost. But you may find it easier to raise seedlings indoors or buy young plants. Again, plant out after the last frosts.

Use soil-free compost, place the containers in full sun and water carefully: young plants need sufficient water to keep the compost just moist – any wetter and they may rot.

If you are training cordon tomatoes, pinch out the side shoots as they appear. Bush tomatoes and cucumbers should be left to grow naturally, leaving the side shoots intact. Harvest tomatoes regularly once the fruit is ripe. Cucumbers should be gathered young to maintain a steady supply.

You can also raise salads in pots to pick regularly through several months of the year if you choose cut-and-come-again varieties. Pick off a few leaves at a time and allow the centres to grow on to supply a succession of new leaves.

The most important things to remember are watering and feeding. The compost should never be allowed to dry out and, once the crops start to develop, a weekly feed of a general purpose liquid or soluble plant fertiliser should be applied to keep the plants growing strongly.

GROWING FROM SEED

You can grow vegetables from seed in soil-free compost and there is no need to add a drainage layer. Many vegetables can be sown directly into the compost in spring, although they may need protection from birds, cats and snails. You can also sow pinches of seed into small pots or plugs in a cold frame or on a light windowsill for earlier crops.

When they are big enough to handle, thin out the seedlings before moving them into pots. Vegetables in containers can be grown closer together than those in the open ground; although the plants may be smaller, the yield will be similar.

Flavour bursts through the warm skin of a container-grown tomato freshly picked from the truss.

If you want to grow tomatoes in the greenhouse, turn to pages 250-251

grow
something
a little
more
exciting

Many varieties of vegetables that once demanded a hot house, now grow happily in pots on a sunny patio. And with their architectural foliage, or mixed with flowers, they offer looks as well as great taste.

▲ The crimson stems of Swiss chard 'Bright Lights' are pretty as well as edible. Team them with bright summer flowers such as colour co-ordinated French marigolds (*Tagetes*).

▶ Shiny green peppers hang temptingly from their stems, ready to enhance a host of summer dishes. In a few weeks' time they will ripen to red or yellow, according to variety, to add yet more colour to the display.

▲ **A new aubergine** pushes out from the flowerhead into the sun. You no longer need a greenhouse to grow many of these formerly exotic vegetables.

◄ **Courgettes start to emerge** from their flowers. This variety is 'Tristar', which produces dark green, pale green and yellow courgettes all on the same plant.

CARING FOR YOUR VEGETABLES

- **Use a soil-free compost** and stand the containers where they will get maximum sun.
- **Water carefully** throughout the growing season. The young plants need sufficient water to keep the compost just moist – any wetter and they may rot. As the plants mature, watering should be increased. Be careful not to let the compost dry out or the flowers and fruits may drop.
- **Feed your plants regularly** with a tomato fertiliser once the first fruits start to develop.
- **Do not prune:** aubergines and peppers should be left to grow naturally, leaving the side shoots intact.
- **Harvest** aubergines regularly once the fruit is ripe. Pick green peppers when large enough, or leave them on the plants to ripen and turn from green to red or yellow.

Although they look good in traditional warm terracotta, summer vegetables also lend themselves to containers such as glazed ceramic pots in strong colours, which give a fittingly Mediterranean feel to these crops.

Some vegetables, such as aubergines and sweetcorn, grow on striking architectural plants and look terrific in individual pots. But they can also be combined with other attractive vegetables such as baby beetroot, dwarf beans or salad leaves. And for a softer visual effect, underplant them with flowers: edible ones such as pot marigolds, pansies and nasturtiums are particularly apt.

The size of pot you choose will depend on what kind of vegetable you are growing. Some of the bushier, more compact sweet and chilli peppers, for instance, will thrive in containers about 20cm (8in) in diameter. But each plant of big leafy vegetables such as aubergines, courgettes, pumpkins and squashes will need a pot at least 30cm (12in) across. And vegetables that will grow tall, such as climbing beans and sweetcorn, need large, heavy-based containers, both for steadiness and successful cropping.

Some of these vegetables, such as aubergines, will need staking, although bushy varieties may need only a few split canes pushed in around the base to hold the plants upright.

stylish pots add a touch of humour

▶ **Pot-grown courgettes** are best grown singly. This pot is angled, which allows the sun to reach the heart of the growing plant.

Vegetables can make a design statement as well as providing a home-grown harvest. Have fun with your pots and your planting, and provide a visual feast for your patio as well as an edible one.

A group of well-chosen pot-grown vegetables can produce a stunning display, since many common vegetables have surprisingly pretty foliage. The feathery leaves of carrots, tall dark plumes of blue sweetcorn and green-maroon foliage of beetroot are as pleasing as those of many herbaceous perennials.

You can also have fun when planting vegetables in containers. Forget the neat drilled lines of the kitchen garden. When vegetables are going to be grown in full view – on the patio or balcony, for example – you can experiment with original ways of growing them.

The dramatic foliage of a courgette always commands attention, but it looks doubly arresting leaning tipsily out of a slanted ceramic pot in a vibrant colour.

Beans are another plant that container gardeners can have fun with. Both beans and peas are easy to grow in pots and offer pretty flowers before the crop ripens. Dwarf and green beans can be left to sprawl over the side of a pot. Climbing beans, peas and mangetout will need support.

The traditional solution is to grow them up a wigwam of canes – one for each plant – pushed firmly into the compost. But for a more entertaining effect use a small pot-grown tree, or a sturdy sunflower, as a living support for your crop. Keep picking peas and beans when young, to maintain a steady supply.

Sweetcorn is another vegetable whose stately looks recommend it to the patio. As you will want to grow at least three cobs, giving four to five heads each, it will need a substantial tub. Don't be tempted to remove the secondary shoots that appear at the base of sweetcorn plants; they are essential for healthy development and stability. The cobs are ready to eat when the sap in the kernels is the colour and consistency of milk.

When growing more than one kind of vegetable in a tub, select types which develop at the same rate and are either harvested a few leaves at a time, like spinach or Swiss chard, or are harvested at the same time, such as quick-maturing carrots, baby beetroots and mini-turnips. That way the ornamental look of your planting will not be spoilt.

GROWING ROOT VEGETABLES

You can grow root vegetables in all sorts of containers. Round and baby varieties of carrot need only a few centimetres of compost so may be cultivated in troughs and window boxes; a long, tapering variety will need a deeper root run, such as a half-barrel.

Choose varieties that mature quickly, such as the carrot 'Early Nantes 5' or beetroot 'Pronto' – so you can raise a second crop in the same season. Or choose carrot 'Autumn King', which takes all summer to develop, giving you the maximum display of foliage.

◄ **Peas need support,** but it doesn't have to mean making a cane wigwam. Here a pear tree in a pot makes a living support for a climbing mangetout.

▲ **Blue sweetcorn looks dramatic and decorative** and the flowers of the runner beans tumbling over the edge in front add a contrasting colour. Sweetcorn roots need a large container like this half-barrel.

▲ **For something different** plant a sunflower in a heavy pot and sow a runner bean with attractive flowers (try 'Painted Lady') separately. When the bean seedling is 8cm (3¼in) tall, plant it alongside the sunflower to use as a support.

plants
for
special
places

◄ **For delicate dots of colour,** heathers will oblige all year round. In the wild, this Scots heather, or ling, grows on exposed heaths where there is no shade, so you can grow it successfully in full sun.

▶ **A blue-flowering hydrangea** will turn purplish or pink if it is growing in a limey soil. Plant one in a pot of acid compost for a wonderful display of clear sky-blue blooms.

▶ **On a miniature scale,** lewisias, like large rhododendrons, are hardy alpines. They grow best in an acid compost. Their delicate flowers are borne on long stalks from spring through summer.

a place to grow
acid-loving
plants

Cushions of springy heather, vivid rhododendrons and sweetly scented azaleas look wonderful, but need special soil. The answer is to grow them in containers, giving them the acidic growing conditions in which they thrive.

▲ **In cold winters,** *Pieris formosa* needs protection, so grow it in a pot, where you can wrap it up.

▲ **The shell-pink flowers** of the hardy dwarf rhododendron, 'Cheer', bloom in clusters in spring.

Many of our best-loved garden shrubs, such as rhododendrons and azaleas, gaultheria, heathers, kalmia and several heathland berries, require very particular soil conditions in order to thrive. These plants grow naturally in peaty or boggy locations, particularly in areas with high rainfall, and in soils rich in leaf-mould. All these conditions give soil an acid quality, and such plants will struggle where the soil contains chalk or lime, which are alkaline. Many of these plants, such as heathers, belong to the family Ericaceae, and they are often referred to as ericaceous.

Other garden favourites, such as magnolias, pieris, skimmia and even lupins, will tolerate a little lime but not much, and some shrubs grown for autumn colour, including coryopsis, enkianthus, fothergilla and witch hazel (*Hamamelis*), only produce a really good show if grown in lime-free, humus-rich soil.

If your garden has chalky, alkaline soil, containers offer the perfect opportunity to grow plants that dislike this. In a pot you can give acid-loving plants the conditions they love. Using a lime-free compost is absolutely essential when growing acid-loving plants in containers. Most proprietary composts contain some lime, so you must choose one that is labelled as an ericaceous compost. Many of these are largely composed of peat, but if you are concerned about the damage to the environment caused by cutting peat, you should be able to find a compost made with an acid peat substitute.

Ericaceous composts are fine for temporary use, but for a permanent planting their nutrients will soon be exhausted. Instead, use a mixture of two parts (by volume) of moss peat or an acid peat substitute to one part of good, fresh weed-free garden soil. This mixture will suit most acid-loving plants and will sustain good growth for much longer than compost alone.

WATERING THE POTS

Because tap water is alkaline it will, eventually, have an effect on lime-hating plants. Even if the plant is growing in an acid compost, its leaves will gradually turn yellow, it will cease to thrive and will ultimately die. Ideally, container-grown ericaceous plants should be watered with rainwater or distilled water (such as that produced by dehumidifiers).

If you do not have a water butt, and your only water source is the tap, add a splash of vinegar to the watering can before you dampen your acid-loving plants. You can also water container-grown acid-lovers with a specially formulated ericaceous plant tonic from time to time to give them an added lift.

COMPOST WISDOM

- **Check the label** on the bag to be sure that its contents are suitable for acid-loving plants (it will probably say 'ericaceous').
- **The amount of plant food** the compost contains should also be stated. Some have enough food for six weeks, others for six months. Start liquid feeding when compost food runs out.
- **Avoid buying bags of compost** that have water seeping through the ventilation holes. This indicates they have been stored in wet conditions, which may have caused deterioration.
- **Store composts** at home in a cool dry place to maintain the balance of nutrients.
- **The shelf-life** of compost is only about six months. Spread any that is older than this over the garden and buy fresh.

◀ **On a crisp autumn day** look out on the bright cheering berries of a golden pyracantha. A piece of trellis can be mounted in a container to make climbing plants movable.

I
n a sheltered garden, acers make ideal potted shrubs. Position them away from the buffeting of strong winds and where you can enjoy their early spring and autumn foliage from the warmth of the house. Other good choices are *Magnolia stellata* and the evergreen *Magnolia grandiflora* 'Exmouth': both provide attractive flowers and foliage, and keep a neat, interesting shape.

The frilly foliage of the dwarf *Robinia pseudoacacia* 'Lace Lady' will be a show-stopper in a small garden or courtyard. This little tree makes a big impact with its well-proportioned branches and beautifully textured leaves. For a similar effect, and the bonus of late spring flowers, plant a *Coronilla valentina* ssp. *glauca*.

Evergreen shrubs will complement a procession of seasonal flowers in tubs. For added interest, choose ones with striking variegated foliage, such as *Euonymus fortunei* 'Coloratus', *Pittosporum* 'Garnettii', and *P. tenuifolium* 'Purpureum' or 'Silver Queen'.

Another good choice is a camellia whose evergreen foliage shines brightly all

make an impact
with large shrubs

Just one substantial plant, carefully positioned, can make a big difference in a small space. Many large shrubs will thrive in roomy containers to give year-round pleasure.

◄◄ **A camellia earns its keep** (far left) with its glossy evergreen foliage, but the rich blooms of this *Camellia japonica* 'Rubescens Major' are a delight on a dull winter afternoon.

◄ **For a few glorious weeks** in summer, move a flowering rose (left) to a prominent position in the garden, where its fragrant blooms can best be appreciated.

year round. White, pink, red or two-tone flowers appear from late winter to mid spring. Be careful where you site a camellia: the early morning sun can damage frost-encrusted buds and flowers, turning them brown.

For a less traditional look, choose a sculptural specimen. Plants with spiky foliage, such as yuccas and the windmill palm, *Trachycarpus fortunei*, will give any patio an exotic feel.

ROOM TO GROW

The key to a long life for large shrubs grown in containers is to give them a little regular attention. Once

a year, lift off the mulch and the top 5cm (2in) or so of the compost, top-dress with fresh compost and reapply the mulch.

If you notice that a container shrub is failing to grow strongly or is not flowering well, it probably needs repotting. If you don't have room for a larger container, then you can prune the plant's roots, add some fresh soil and put it back into the same pot.

If repotting a shrub into a larger pot, limit the increase in diameter of the new pot to within 5-10cm (2-4in). It is hard to regulate the moisture level when a

pot is over large and you risk parching or swamping the plant it holds.

Always give a plant a good soaking before removing it from its pot, and have its new pot ready with crocks and compost in the base. Carefully ease the shrub out of its old pot and tease off some of the soil around the rootball. Position it in its new pot and fill around the sides until the compost is about 5cm (2in) below the rim. Water the compost thoroughly so that any air pockets disappear and add a layer of mulch to conserve water and suppress weed seedlings.

REPOTTING AND ROOT-PRUNING

If a container-grown shrub is not thriving you can often revive it by repotting it or pruning its roots.
• **Repotting** will encourage bushy new growth, but be careful not to shock the plant by moving it into a pot that is too big.
• **Root-pruning,** which involves trimming the roots and putting the plant back in the same pot, will limit the growth of your plant.

lime lovers welcome here

Want to grow carnations but don't have the right soil? Create the perfect conditions in a container.

Some plants, although they will tolerate a wide range of soil types, do best and last longest in alkaline soils rich in lime, and in full sun. If your soil is acid, boggy or shady, you will enjoy more success with the lime-lovers if you grow them in pots. In the wild, many lime-lovers grow in

PLANTS THAT PREFER CHALKY SOIL

- **Annuals and biennials** alyssum, poppies (*Papaver*), sage (*Salvia*), scabiosa, viola, ornamental cabbage (*Brassica*).
- **Bulbs** anemone, crocus, iris, narcissus, scilla, tulip.
- **Perennials** alyssum, anemone, aubretia, daisies (*Bellis*), campanula, lily of the valley (*Convallaria*), carnations and pinks (*Dianthus*), peony, rudbeckia, saxifrage, verbascum, veronica, yucca.
- **Shrubs** berberis, box (*Buxus*), cotoneaster, daphne, escallonia, hebe, honeysuckle (*Lonicera*), lilac (*Syringa*), olearia, osmanthus, rosemary, viburnum, weigela.

▲ **Silver and purple lime-lovers** are gathered in harmony. The tiny purple flowers of the hebe and the silvery buds of sage (*Salvia farinacea* 'Strata'), in the smaller pot are echoed by spires of Russian sage (*Perovskia* 'Blue Spire') and silver sea holly in the larger one.

▶ **A small pot of pinks** will add the heady scent of cloves to your patio. All they need is the slightly alkaline compost they prefer.

open, free-draining areas, such as the chalk downs or alpine meadows. They include flowers such as clematis, delphiniums, peonies, stocks and wallflowers, and shrubs like arbutus, broom, buddleja, choisya, daphne, holly and juniper. Many alpines and grey or woolly leafed, 'Mediterranean' plants are also lime-lovers, and all these plants can be successfully grown in pots.

Bulbs and herbaceous perennials can be combined in all manner of arrangements. And low-growing grey-leafed plants, and junipers, can look great when they are close-planted in one container as a collection.

However, shrubs tend to look best if they are planted singly. If carefully pruned and trained, they will thrive in their container for several years without replanting. If you feel you would like to liven them up with a little extra colour at different times of the year, you could

▲ **A clematis may grow better** in a container, where you can give it limey soil.

add some pinks or perennial wallflowers to the container.

CHOOSING THE RIGHT COMPOST

Plants that will last only one season, like annual dianthus, ornamental kale, wallflowers and ten-week stocks, will grow happily in general-purpose composts, all of which have lime added during manufacture to balance their acidity.

Soil-based compost also contains lime, and will support good growth for the first few months after potting. In permanently planted containers you should always use a soil-based compost – preferably John Innes No.1 or 2 for smaller plants, and John Innes No.3 for established ones.

If your tap water is soft, you will also need to apply an annual top dressing of garden lime each spring to permanent plantings: allow 55-115g (2-4oz) for each container, depending

on its size. Remember that lime is a soil improver, not a plant food, so the container will still need fertiliser. However, you should not mix lime and fertiliser together as this can cause a reaction which will release some of the plant nutrients into the air. To be on the safe side, wait a month after liming before top dressing with fertiliser.

WATER WITH CARE

Plants that are happy in chalky soils can usually tolerate fairly dry conditions. Indeed, they are more likely to be killed by waterlogging than the occasional drying out. Add a good drainage layer to the bottom of your pots and raise them off the ground.

Regular, careful watering to maintain damp, but not soggy, compost is the best policy. Hard water is best for these plants, as it helps to maintain alkalinity. But if your tap water is soft, or if you use rainwater, which is always soft, the lime will gradually be lost from the compost. In this case you must replace it by adding garden lime to the compost once or twice a year.

▶ **The winter flowers** of *Viburnum tinus* bring cheer to the darkest months. This vigorous evergeen shrub grows best in chalky soil.

▶▶ **Sunny wallflowers** (far right) make perfect companions to many spring bulbs. Although tolerant of most soils, they prefer a little lime.

plants that like it wild and wet

Some of the most delightful plants need cool moist conditions if they are to thrive. And luckily you don't have to live near a bog to enjoy their beauty – you can create a scaled-down damp patch quite easily in a container.

▲ **Plumed pink astilbes** make a handsome display set beside a garden pond.

▼ **Bamboo** likes to get its feet wet: here it grows with another moisture-lover, gunnera.

When your natural garden conditions are hot, dry or free draining, you can still provide the conditions that many moisture-lovers, such as filipendula and ranunculus, prefer by creating a miniature bog garden or riverbank in a container. To get the best out of moisture-loving plants, start by using the biggest container you have room for, as this will stay damp longer and will not need constant watering. Bog plants, like marsh marigolds (*Caltha*) and gunnera, look particularly good in large half-barrels; otherwise choose any container that will retain moisture well.

Most moisture-loving plants will grow perfectly well in a good-quality, soil-free compost, as long as it does not dry out. But soil-based composts will retain moisture longer between waterings, especially if you add water-retaining granules to the compost before planting up (see pages 236-237).

MAINTAINING MOISTURE LEVELS

For moisture-loving plants, free drainage is not particularly desirable, provided that water does not stand in the container indefinitely. This means that you do not need to put a layer of drainage material in the base, although it is still a good idea to stand the tub on bricks or similar supports so that the holes in the base do not become blocked.

Because moisture-lovers soon lose condition – the leaves wilt and turn brown and the plants die quickly if they become dry, even for a short while – automatic watering (see pages 236-237) is ideal. It means they will never dry out accidentally and will still cope unsupervised during a wet spell – when other plants may be drowned.

Most moisture-loving plants also prefer shady or partially shaded conditions so try, if you can, to stand the container under a tree or in the shadow of a wall. And you can help to keep your plants in tip-top condition by adding a liquid feed to the watering can weekly or fortnightly during summer.

◄ **Purple irises**, the beardless variety *Iris sibirica* 'Shirley Pope', and shuttlecock ferns both grow best in damp and shady conditions.

MOISTURE-LOVING PLANTS

Your options are not restricted if you want to grow plants that prefer damp and shade. You could opt for a bold effect with just one giant gunnera or *Rheum* (both resembling huge rhubarb) or *Rodgersia* (rather like a large filipendula), or you can choose from these groups:

• **Grasses and grass-like plants**, such as Bowles' golden grass, (*Carex* 'Evergold'), miniature bulrush and sweet flag (*Acorus calamus*), or the bamboo-like *Arundinaria viridistriata*.

• **Moisture-loving flowering perennials** such as giant cowslip (*Primula florindae*), globeflowers (*Trollius*), hemp agrimony (*Eupatorium cannabinum*), and purple loosestrife (*Lythrum salicaria*) will give you the impression of a pond margin.

• **Shrubs** such as box elder, dogwood (*Cornus*), ornamental elders (*Sambucus*) and willows (*Salix*), also prefer moist conditions and can be grown in containers.

thin rations for rockery plants

Alpines and succulents actually grow best in poor soil. Pots are the perfect way to provide these typical rockery plants with conditions to suit, and will help to draw attention to their often tiny features.

Under normal garden conditions, where the soil has been improved and fed over the years, alpines and succulents will grow tall and lanky, flower poorly and die prematurely. But where there is low soil fertility and free drainage, they grow strong and stocky, and produce abundant flowers. Here, perennial species, such as aubretia, candytuft, gentian, pinks (*Dianthus*) and saxifrage, will live to a ripe old age.

In their natural habitat, alpines root in rock crevices or pockets of gritty soil, so in pots most prefer a coarse compost, but one which holds a certain amount of moisture. Succulents, such as lampranthus and sedums, often grow in little more than rocky debris in the wild. Houseleeks, or sempervivums, earned their common name because they will even grow when 'planted' between the tiles of a leaking roof. There, they spread their tightly packed rosettes to plug the hole.

PLANT IN A SHALLOW CONTAINER

Alpines do not need deep soil or compost, so sinks, seed pans, shallow troughs and the like make ideal containers. Whatever pot you use, it must be free draining, so be sure to provide plenty of holes and a good layer of drainage material in the base.

▲ **In a hard-to-water spot,** echeverias make a perfect drought-tolerant choice for a hanging basket.

▶ **A mountain collection** of alpine pinks and stonecrop (*sedum*) would make a pretty decoration for a garden table.

The leaves of many alpines will go brown and rot if they touch wet compost, so it is a good idea to cover the surface with a 2.5cm (1in) mulch of coarse grit, granite chippings or gravel. Including a few large craggy stones in the arrangement will add to the alpine effect. You could even plant a sempervivum in a stone with a hole in it, or in an empty shell for a seaside theme.

Fill the container with a proprietary alpine compost. This will contain a mixture of loam, peat or peat substitute and sharp sand, or grit, to ensure that the plants' roots do not become waterlogged, plus just enough fertiliser to get the plants off to a good start. Alternatively, you can make your own mix of one part topsoil, one part sieved leaf-mould or peat substitute, and one part grit or fine pea shingle.

Most alpines are not drought tolerant, but equally they hate waterlogging. This means that the compost must be kept reasonably damp, particularly during the growing season.

For really healthy specimens, give your plants a weak liquid feed as they begin their growing season. Choose a feed with a fertiliser suitable for flowering plants, but avoid one containing a high level of nitrogen, which will encourage straggly growth.

▲ **Tiny succulents** look terrific grouped together in lots of miniature pots.

POOR SOIL IN A NATURAL ENVIRONMENT

The tough conditions that suit alpines are also perfect for many of Britain's native wild flowers, which thrive on roadside verges.
• **Bring the countryside to your patio,** and attract beneficial insects, by growing plants like baby blue eyes (*Nemophila*), love-in-a-mist (*Nigella damascena*), and poached egg flower (*Limnanthes douglasii*).
• **Don't use multipurpose compost** or your wild flowers will grow leggy with lots of foliage, but few blooms. Use an alpine mix instead and keep feeding to a minimum, and you will be rewarded with sturdy plants and a profusion of flowers.

◄ **A seaside flower** which dislikes the cold and wet, *Asteriscus* grows as an annual in a basket of free-draining compost.

► **A natural arrangement** of tall alliums and pink wallflowers thrives among the succulents in this shallow trough.

◄ **Top a tall slender pot** with a crown of houseleeks. Their pink-tinged rosettes glow like a flaming torch.

first impressions start at the front door

Foliage and flowers soften the hard textures of masonry and paving, and show a welcoming face. Planted containers are the perfect solution for a year-round welcome.

It is all too easy to devote your energies to the back garden and ignore the front of the house, hurrying past to get indoors. But, whether your ideal is roses round the door or a more formal effect, it is good to give your front door a welcoming look. Here, pots come into their own, providing a flexible garden that you can change and keep fresh with the seasons.

SELECTING A STYLE

Your choice of containers and plants will be determined, in part, by the architecture of your home and the style of the front door – although, if you live by a busy road, you may be wise to consider pollution-tolerant species, such as cranesbills, geum and *Veronica*.

The formal doorways of many town houses call for a symmetrical design, and a pair of plants in matching planters is often the best option here. Choose conifers or lollipop bays for all-year effect, fuchsias or standard marguerites for a light summer touch. Square terracotta pots or Versailles planters work particularly well.

Alternatively, you might be guided by colour, choosing a scheme that tones with the door itself, opting for all white,

Aromatic plants give visitors an old-fashioned scented welcome and perfume the house when you open the door. Fill summer pots with regal lilies, try scented hyacinth and narcissi for spring, or encourage honeysuckle, jasmine or roses in pots to scramble around the door.

◄ **A stark white city doorway** is softened by this informal group of terracotta pots and urns bursting with joyful spring colour. The haphazard arrangement is stunningly held together by a huge weathered pot of early geraniums.

► **Warm autumn colour** welcomes the visitor to this front door. A bronze-leafed berberis and a stunning weeping cotoneaster, laden with a berry feast, are underplanted with brilliant red cyclamen.

▲ **Pinks and blues** are used to charming and unpretentious effect. A blue galvanised pot echoes the glossy door, while a creamy band painted round the top of a terracotta pot picks up the colours of the tiles and grout.

or using foliage with different textures, shapes and hues. If you have no porch, you can create pillars of flowers instead. Place half-barrels filled with summer bedding on either side of the door and suspend hanging baskets above them. Then train annual climbers such as canary creeper to grow up strips of trellis fixed to the walls behind the barrels.

SAFE AND SECURE

Containers are vulnerable to theft, so you may wish to consider using less expensive glass fibre or plastic items in a front garden. Alternatively, secure planters with chains and rings set into the wall, or deter thieves with a stake driven through a drainage hole in the base of the pot (see pages 268-269).

◄ **Festive frills** brighten a front step at Christmas. Metal gift tags swing in a wintry breeze and fairy lights twinkle in the lower branches of this evergreen, lighting the way to the door and adding sparkle to a crystalline mulch of crushed glass.

▲ **Matching pairs** of sculptural plants in urns dressed the entrance to many a stately home. Here, a pair of standard fuchsias in steel boxes provide a modern interpretation of a traditional decorative style.

living sculptures of topiary

Carefully clipped evergreens will add grandeur or whimsy to any garden. While balls and pyramids recall the glories of Versailles, birds and animals have a lighter touch.

Trees or shrubs clipped into interesting or decorative shapes make attractive formal and informal features in the garden. Although the art is often associated with hedging and large scale projects, topiary can be very successful in pots.

The best plants for topiary are bushy evergreen shrubs with small leaves, which is why box, juniper and yew are so often chosen. But any vigorous, well-branched plant will work: both holly and rosemary make interesting alternatives. Complicated shapes involve patient training which can take many years to fill out – reflected in the high prices charged for a spiral box or lollipop bay at garden centres. A fast-growing plant, such as privet, will give you a quicker end result, but will also need trimming more often than box.

A simple container adds emphasis to a small topiary shape, and allows you to position a plant for best effect. To add distinction to a front porch or to define the edges of a patio, use topiary in Versailles planters. These traditional wooden containers were first used at Versailles, France, in the 17th century, when topiary was a staple of the formal French garden (to make your own, see pages 258-259).

Topiary shapes help to punctuate a garden: a box ball in a terracotta long tom makes a stylish full stop that will draw attention to a particular point in the garden or patio – to accentuate the meeting of paths or the entrance to a garden room. A pair of pyramid bay exclamation marks will frame a perspective, while an evergreen Portuguese laurel (*Prunus lusitanica*) shaped into a cone, will give a formal touch to an elegant front door or bay window.

With patience and skill, topiary can be cut or trained into any shape you like: your imagination is the only limit. Clip your house number in box or make or buy a shapely frame for a climbing or trailing plant, such as honeysuckle, ivy and *Muehlenbeckia*, to scramble over. Deer, rabbits, stars, birds or chairs will add a quirky note to a garden design.

Clean and simple geometric

▲ **Frame a focal point** with a symmetrical arrangement. Pots of white tulips and topiary pairs make a feature of this statue.

◄ A dusting of **snow** or a glint of frost will accentuate the crisp lines of topiary. Here, a pair of lollipop box trees is repeated closer to the house and mimicked in miniature by ornamental cabbages.

KEEPING SHRUBS IN SHAPE

- **Cut back hard in spring**, when growth is most vigorous. New leaves will soon fill out any bare patches.
- **Clip little and often** to achieve a dense shape in the shortest time.
- **Use florist's wire** to hold difficult shapes, such as animal tails, in position.
- **Tie in new shoots** often when training a climber over a frame.
- **Make a template** of the intended shape and size of your topiary (below) as a guide for training and trimming your shrubs.

shapes create a sense of order in the garden

◄◄ **Topiary birds** in a family group makes a charming portrait in front of a bare wall. Wire frames give the birds their shape; ivy cloaks them in green.

◄ **The strong lines** of a grand entrance demand an unfussy planting. A pair of standard box balls in simple terracotta containers provide the perfect solution.

◄ **Cut large designs**, such as this spiral, in yew: it is slow to grow, and so keeps its shape well.

Shape it yourself – all you need to know about pruning topiary, see pages 242-243

◄ **Using just one colour** gives a sense of unity to a pretty country patio. Palest pink roses tumble from terracotta pots and clamber over a graceful bower, creating an intimate setting for this pretty seating area.

spread beauty over the terrace

Where the house meets the garden, groups of container plants form a bridge between the two. Here people can relax and enjoy balmy summer days and candle-lit evenings.

Summertime is the season when a terrace comes into its own. Your patio may be part of a bigger garden, or a paved courtyard may be all you have. Whatever its surroundings, an area of brick or stone paving, gravel or decking can become a welcoming haven with carefully chosen and cleverly planted containers.

As a general rule, the most successful groupings combine one or two large pots with various smaller containers. Too many little pots distract the eye and make for a disjointed effect.

A big shrub or tree creates a focus and is a good starting point for a terrace design. They also look good viewed from inside on a winter's day, whether covered in pretty evergreen foliage or with their bare branches outlined in frost.

A sunny terrace is a great place for scented plants – the warmth will enhance their scent and the blooms will attract lazy humming bees and bright butterflies. Herbs do especially well in sunny corners – thyme, marjoram, rosemary and sage have aromatic leaves that will scent the air if you brush against them.

Try adding a trellis to a tub and grow summer jasmine (*Jasminum officinale*) up it. The mock orange blossom (*Philadelphus* 'Beauclerk') emits a heady citrus scent in the early evening while an even richer fragrance is given off at twilight by the white trumpets of the tobacco plant (*Nicotiana alata*).

You can achieve a stylish look by choosing just one or two colours for your plantings, or using similar pots. But don't be too strict – a cool theme of blues, lilacs and mauves, a warm theme of reds, yellows and oranges, or a mix of the palest pastels and whites will all give a sense of unity.

Bring sunlight to a shady patio with greeny yellows, whites and glossy foliage planted in warm terracotta pots. Cool corners can be enlivened with ferns and variegated ivies, and the cheerful colours of busy lizzies, which thrive in shade.

A PATIO KITCHEN GARDEN

One of the prettiest as well as most rewarding patio plants is the tomato, and it is easy to raise in a grow bag. To prevent your colour scheme being spoilt by the bag's garish print, hide it in a log-roll box (see pages 258-259). Strawberry planters are always pretty,

▲ **Enjoy yourself:** your patio is for relaxing as well as for gardening.

and you could grow a tangle of runner beans and sweet peas up a wigwam of canes in a sunny corner. If you have enough space, a dwarf fruit tree in a pot will add structure as well as giving you an autumn treat.

MOVE THOSE POTS

One of the best things about containers is that they are not static. If one plant looks miserable, change it for another that is bursting with health; as an arrangement passes its best, hide it behind another that is starting to bloom. Move the pots to suit your mood, the occasion and to maintain maximum year-round interest.

A sheltered patio also makes a good summer home for container-grown conservatory specimens and house plants. Abutilons, agapanthus, citrus trees, cordylines, tender fuchsias and geraniums, olive trees, most palms and tree ferns will provide an exotic contrast to the hardier plants that surround them.

◀ **In a city garden** the owner has made the best use of the walls by hanging pots of brilliant red geraniums. On the ground are tubs of lobelia and petunias in softly co-ordinating colours.

▶ **A glorious blue urn** gives weight to an informal arrangement of fragile angelonias, penstemons and 'Million Bells' petunias. The colour is carried through to the chair beyond.

add a
touch of style
and
glamour

Exotic-looking architectural plants bring a sense of theatre to even a small space, and they are surprisingly easy to grow in containers. For an elegant look, think bold and beautiful.

Large architectural plants in containers provide instant style statements, and nurseries now stock an increasingly wide variety to choose from, including agave, arbutus, cordyline, fatsia, phormium and yucca. Unusual plants such as the tree fern, *Dicksonia antarctica*, or the cycad, *Cycas revoluta*, with their fascinating foliage, are impressive plants that need no fussy underplanting or companions. For a similar but floral effect choose the trumpet-shaped, double and scented blossoms of datura, *Brugmansia* x *candida* 'Knightii'.

Movement adds an extra dimension to container plantings, and for willowy, free-flowing movement, ornamental grasses are a perfect choice. *Pennisetum alopecuroides* 'Hameln' makes a soft but distinctive shape, and in winter its wispy foliage and spent flowerheads will glisten with frost.

Hebes, which originate from New Zealand, offer a wide range of fresh evergreen foliage. Choose from rusty brown, grey, silver or apple green, or deep bottle green, variegated yellow green and pinkish shades. Furthermore, its flowers, in a range encompassing white, pink, mauve or light blue, offer

◀ **A dramatic tree fern,** *Dicksonia antarctica*, brings a tropical look to this wooden verandah. A roll of bamboo conceals an unattractive pot and the gravel mulch reduces water loss.

◄ **Make a bold statement** with four pots of agapanthas **(1)** standing sentry on a flight of stone steps or a striking cordyline **(2)** spraying proudly out of a tall pot in a pretty border.

summer and autumn colour. Hebes can be low-growing, dome-shaped or erect. These low-maintenance shrubs thrive in large containers.

If you have a spare large pot in which you want to establish a plant for architectural impact – a box or bay, perhaps – you can avoid the expense of buying a large plant. Spend less on a smaller one and you will only have to wait a few seasons until the plant is the right size for the pot. Keep the plant in its original pot and sink this into the soil of the large container. As the plant grows, you may need to repot into a container of intermediate size, before allowing its roots the freedom of the large container (see pages 228-229). Tuck annuals around the edge of the larger pot for a decorative effect until the plant has matured, and add an ornamental mulch of bark or shingle to hide the rim of the smaller pot.

◄ **The aptly named cloud tree** (*Luma apiculata*) grows in a huge 'missionary boiling pot'. The stylish mulch of vivid blue chippings helps the plant to retain water.

WINTER CARE

• **Hardy plants in pots,** such as bamboo and phormium, do not need moving indoors in winter, but their roots should be shielded from harsh frosts. Wrap the pot and plant with plastic bubble wrap and cover with seagrass matting or bamboo screening, cut to size. These materials add further insulation and look good too.

• **Frost-tender plants** like tree ferns, cycads and datura need the shelter of a greenhouse or conservatory during winter. If your patio is on ground level these plants are relatively easy to move using a plant dolly (see pages 268-269).

◄ **Cool colours shimmer** in hot settings. This collection of lavenders gives the impression of a traditional bed bordering a path, while the silver pots and foliage echo the sun-bleached wood.

taking it easy in the sun

Plants from hot countries like Australia, Mexico and South Africa, are able to withstand drought and continuous heat, so they make carefree choices for sun-baked containers.

One of the most important principles for successful container gardening in a very hot or sunny place is to choose the largest pot you can accommodate. Sun-loving annuals will grow profusely throughout summer if they are positioned to catch the light at its brightest, but they will need watering two or three times a day if they are planted in tiny pots. The exceptions are pelargoniums and nasturtiums, which will flower more generously in the stressed conditions of a small pot with poor soil.

Fat-leaved succulents such as echeveria, and many of the euphorbia and sedum families, revel in hot sun and dry compost by storing water in their leaves. And plants with narrow, spiky foliage, including yuccas and many tropical palms and grasses, retain their own moisture well.

Mediterranean plants which have pale grey aromatic foliage, including helichrysum, lavenders, rosemary and santolina, are perfectly adapted to long periods of scorching sun and drought as they have a high level of oil in their leaves, which reduces water loss. A standard bay tree looks good with a culinary underplanting of thyme and both plants prefer a light, well-drained chalky soil and a sunny position.

To give plants their best chance of survival on sun-drenched balconies and hot patios, reduce the amount of water that they lose from the pot by topping it with a thick layer of mulch. It will also add an attractive decorative element.

There are numerous options to choose from (see pages 226-227), which may be co-ordinated with the colour of the pot or the style and colours of the plants. Pebbles will create a seaside atmosphere with silvery metal or weathered terracotta pots set on bleached timber decking. Crushed recycled glass, the colour of green and amber rough-cut semi-precious stones, will enhance the subtle colours and rosette shapes of sempervivum.

A sunny patio will inevitably be used far more in the summer months. Provide some welcome shade with a vertical planting of fast-growing climbers, supported by a twiggy or metal obelisk, or trained around the open structure of a pergola. You need to choose plants that will flourish in containers basking in full sun: morning glory, climbing nasturtiums, passionflowers, sweet peas and the Chilean glory vine (*Eccremocarpus*) will romp away in these conditions.

Alternatively, you can make the most of spring sunshine by selecting climbers such as wisteria, which produces chandeliers of fragrant flowers followed by dense summer foliage. Or you could choose fragrant summer-flowering shrubs, such as clerodendron and many of the viburnum family, which will reflect the waning sunlight later in the year and produce brightly coloured fruits in autumn.

A clutch of hot pots livens up a south-facing wall. **(1)** Brightly coloured petunias and geraniums thrive in this blazing location.

Shades of gold from **(2)** dahlias, french marigolds and rudbeckia mingle with whirligig heads of osteospermum to light up a trough.

A bougainvillea (3) trained as a standard is the classic Mediterranean plant. The gravel mulch reduces water loss.

SUN-LOVING PLANTS

These plants will thrive in the scorching heat of summer.
- **Annuals** *Cosmos bipinnatus*, gazania, morning glory, opium poppy (*Papaver somniferum*), nasturtium (*Tropaeolum majus*)
- **Bedding and patio plants** *Bidens*, *Diascia*, *Helichrysum petiolare*, marguerite (*Argyranthemum*), *Portulaca grandiflora*, *Senecio cineraria*, tobacco plant (*Nicotiana*), zinnia

▼ **Delicate and mysterious,** the orchids on the table – the tall, slender *Cambria* hybrid and the *Paphiopedilum* below it – lend an exotic air to this sunny conservatory.

▶ **Re-create a border** with a bank of summer bedding plants in pots. A flowering geranium has been grafted onto a tall stem of a fast-growing 'Unique' variety to add height.

the restful pleasures of a conservatory

Bathed in natural light and protected by glass, a conservatory can make a wonderful setting for container plants and will allow you to enjoy the sense of being outdoors whatever the weather.

Conservatories may be simple glassed-in patios, or grand affairs with brick walls and fanlights or a cast-iron frame. Whatever their style, they are a delightful blend of house and garden, and make the perfect setting for containers that bring a little of the outside in.

Before you fill your conservatory, think about growing conditions. If the room is south facing, you will need to avoid delicate plants that will fry in the sun – unless you don't mind shutting out the heat and light with blinds. Equally, if the conservatory faces north and is not heated, there is little point dreaming of a tropical paradise.

Cooler conservatories can look stunning filled with plants that normally thrive in the garden, such as clematis and hydrangeas.

With regular deadheading and feeding they will provide you with colour and fragrance for much longer than they would outside.

SOME LIKE IT HOT

If your conservatory is a south-facing sun trap, make a virtue of it. Opt for plants that relish the heat and extreme dryness. Tropical natives, such as bougainvillea, geraniums and plumbago will all scramble up baking walls or around window frames if you give them something to cling to. Fix up a trellis inside your conservatory, painted to blend in with the walls, or strings of garden wire or raffia, or give new life to a junk-shop find, such as an old wrought-iron gate.

Several daisy-like garden flowers, such as gazanias, mesembryanthemums and osteospermums, are native to hot dry climates and will be quite happy in your hothouse, as will Mediterranean herbs, like sage or thyme. You could cultivate a collection of spiny cacti or succulents with thick fleshy leaves, which also enjoy arid environments.

Many plants that only survive outdoors in the summer months will have a cheering effect inside from autumn to late spring. Abutilons, bougainvillea, tender fuchsias, olives and lemon trees will all continue to thrive if overwintered in a conservatory.

Even if your conservatory is sited on a north or east-facing wall, its glass construction means that it will still be

light and will suit most indoor plants as long as it is kept warm in winter. If there is no heating in the room, choose hardy shade-loving foliage plants such as ferns, ivies, spider plants (*Chlorophytum*) and the Victorian conservatory favourite, aspidistra.

Hostas look terrific with a collection of ferns in a cool conservatory – where they are safe from slugs – but for summer colour blowsy hydrangeas are hard to beat. During the colder months, winter bedding plants, like pansies and polyanthus, are a good choice teamed with tender exotics, such as amaryllis or poinsettia. You can also make the most of the sheltered conditions to force bowls full of fragrant spring hyacinths in time for Christmas.

◄ **Conservatory plants** need just as much care as those outside. Deadhead and prune regularly for a lasting display.

indulge a passion for tender plants

The conservatory is a room to enjoy, so fill it with plants that offer something extra special: a delightful scent, rare and exotic flowers, abundant glossy foliage, or plump tropical fruits.

Plant enthusiasts often devote containers in conservatories to indulging a passion – for cacti, lilies, or orchids. But specialist plants need special care, and orchids, in particular, are sensitive and fragile. They have to be kept warm, so your conservatory needs to be heated in winter, and they require constant humidity. You can buy slatted staging with a built-in moisture tray which does the job perfectly.

Scented plants will give your conservatory a sensual appeal. Jasmine, grown indoors, flowers from late spring filling the room with its delightful heady perfume. For year-round perfume, choose plants from the citrus group which flower continuously. Just one waxy white bloom from an orange

or lemon tree is enough to sweetly scent a garden room. The baby orange (x *Citrofortunella microcarpa*) also produces masses of tiny oranges from late summer, while the Meyer's lemon is the best lemon tree for edible fruit, again fruiting from late summer. You could even grow plants from pips.

KEEP IT HEALTHY

Pests love the warmth, dampness and ready supply of food offered by plants in warm conservatories. A room jam-packed with plants may look terrific, but if any one of the plants becomes infected the problem will spread very quickly to the others.

Whitefly, scale insects, red spider mite, mealy bug and powdery mildew can all proliferate and cause problems. Frequent deadheading, snipping away

▲ **Wall to wall geraniums** – from the table top pots of bedding plants to the climbers – is the way to indulge a passion.

▶ **A troupe of ballerina flowers** smothers the hanging basket this tender trailing fuchsia is planted in.

◀ **The waxy flowers** of *Hoya carnosa* (**1**) will fill an entire house with their scent at night. The fragrance of lilies (**2**) is best appreciated at closer range.

1

2

▶ **For sheer exotica,** nothing beats an orchid, such as this fragile-looking *Paphiopedilum*.

◀ **The blue potato bush,** *Solanum rantonnetii* 'Royal Robe', is related to the potato, but its red fruits are poisonous.

▲ **Desert cacti,** such as this *Mammillaria zeilmanniana,* will thrive in a hot south-facing conservatory.

dead leaves, cleaning the pots, windowsills and floors regularly and ensuring adequate ventilation will all help to prevent problems arising.

Check plants carefully for signs of infestation before you buy them, to avoid introducing pests or disease (see pages 244-247). Treat new plants to a spray of pesticide if in doubt. Ready mixed pesticides in spray-guns, designed for indoor use, are ideal for conservatory plants. If you notice any signs of disease, isolate the affected pot until the problem clears up.

in the dappled light of a shady corner

It is a common misconception that only foliage plants will thrive in shade. In fact, a wealth of flowering varieties prefer a cool and sheltered spot out of the glare of direct sunlight.

Woodland plants are a natural choice for a shady position, since they have evolved to survive beneath the tree canopy in the wild. If your patio is sheltered by a deciduous tree or large shrub, spring varieties, such as crocuses, daffodils and primroses will do well in the dappled light that filters through before the dense covering of new leaves has formed. When the branches are bare again in autumn the spot will be perfect for colchicum, cyclamen, hellebores and Japanese anemones.

Summer-flowering plants that can cope with a lack of light are harder to find, but the herbaceous perennial geranium known as cranesbill is a versatile choice. It grows in a range of habits from prostrate and spreading to upright and clump-forming and with a choice of colours including pinks and reds, blues and purples and shades of white. *Geranium phaeum* not only has exquisite dark purple flowers but it can tolerate the deepest shade. Don't confuse these old-fashioned geraniums with the newer annual zonal pelargoniums, which are often called geraniums, but which need full sun.

If you want to grow plants to add interest to the area beneath a tree, using containers often gives better results than planting directly into the ground, where the new plants have to compete with the tree for water and nutrients.

A PLACE TO SIT

A shady corner is the obvious place to create a seating area, to enjoy an alfresco meal out of the glare of the midsummer sun, or to relax with a book and a glass of wine. Busy lizzies and fuchsias are superb for creating bright colour in gloomy surroundings. Choose varieties with white flowers to fill the space with a luminous glow at twilight.

Many white-flowering plants have blooms that are deliciously scented, and their perfume is most powerful in the late afternoon or early evening, when they attract pollinating nocturnal insects. Tobacco plants and lilies both thrive in pots and make a strong fragrant impact, especially if arranged with pots of bright green hostas, whose scented trumpet-shaped flowers open in the evenings from late summer to early autumn.

CATCHING THE LIGHT

Many large-leaved plants can tolerate shade because their wide surface area makes the most of the available light. Hostas are a typical example, and are particularly well-suited to being grown in containers, where their juicy leaves can be protected from the ravages of slugs and snails.

A collection of foliage plants with contrasting textures will make a striking display. Try combining broad-leaved hostas with the delicate filigree shapes of lush ferns or the arching stems of a bamboo. All these plants will grow happily in shady spots provided they are never allowed to dry out.

If there is space for a really large container placed near a tree or a shaded wall you can provide support for a climbing hydrangea or one of the many evergreen ivies whose mottled white, gold or cream leaves will lighten the darkest corner. Many variegated shrubs will revert to plain green if deprived of sunlight for a long time, but ivies retain their interest.

► **Nodding spires of pink foxgloves** tower above a bed of shuttlecock ferns (*Matteuccia struthiopteris*). A fallen log in the garden inspired this woodland arrangement of shade and moisture-loving plants.

GREAT PLANTS FOR SHADY PLACES

- **Annuals** busy lizzies; lobelia; mimulus
- **Bulbs** *Allium hollandicum* 'Purple Sensation'; cyclamen; lilies; snowflake (*Leucojum*)
- **Flowering plants** astilbe; buttercup or crowfoot (*Ranunculus lyallii*); escallonia; phlox (woodland perennial varieties); Solomon's seal (*Polygonatum*)
- **Foliage plants** fatsia; heuchera; hoheria; hosta; ivy; Japanese painted fern (*Athyrium niponicum*); lungwort (*Pulmonaria*); spotted laurel (*Aucuba japonica* 'Variegata'); stripy bulbous oat grass (*Arrhenatherum elatius* ssp. *bulbosum*); variegated ground elder

◄ **In a shady border,** creamy yellow petunias and a pale-edged hosta glow in a matching 'big-top' striped barrel. They help to illuminate and draw attention to the ferns and alchemilla mollis growing there.

Luminous petals and leaves that catch the light shine in shady spots

◄ **A green fountain** of fern fronds spurts from an old drainpipe hopper, lifting an otherwise dark corner.

▲ **Basking in a shaft of light,** these hostas make the most of every ray of sun that reaches their shady niche.

Pots of red, white and blue – geraniums and lobelia – look bold and colourful while gold-and-green variegated leaves focus sunlight into this shadowy stairwell.

ideas that give a lift to the basement

Pots brimming with attractive plants can transform a basement. Whether it's a shady courtyard or a sunny stairwell, you can still create a pretty view.

▲ **Be creative with space** by sitting a pot on every step and hanging them from the walls to fill a narrow basement with colour and scent.

D eeply shaded places, such as basements, where there may be little visible sky, or stairwells, where there is barely enough space on the ground for a doormat, let alone a collection of pots, provide a challenge for the container gardener. But pots and planters can bring much needed life to what might otherwise be a dull area.

A SHADY SITUATION

Even a site in full shade can make a hospitable home for plants if you give them some reflected light. Painting walls in a pale colour and positioning mirrors cleverly can help enormously, not only increasing the available light in the space but also making your basement feel more spacious.

For scent and colour in spring, fill pots with bulbs and put them in the least shady spot. Rotate them if necessary so that each container gets a ration of sunshine. In summer fill troughs and baskets with busy lizzies, which grow happily in shade.

Fuchsias and trailing begonias also do well in a shaded or semi-shaded position. You could choose colours that come from a single palette – all deep pinks, perhaps, or all pastels and white – or opt for a range of colours that complement one another.

If you want to bring some living sunshine into a dark spot, try planting gold and orange monkey flowers (*Mimulus*) and pansies. Mimulus is best treated as an annual in shade – it will flower successfully in the first season, but not as well thereafter.

Foliage plants usually do better than flowering plants in a sunless spot. Try bergenia, fatsia, holly and ivy or cheerful golden variegated shrubs, such as eleagnus and euonymus. Be careful not to overwater plants in shady basements – you cannot rely on the sun to dry off any surplus. Regular removal of dead flowers and leaves will help to prevent fungal infections.

Decorate a sunny flight of steps with sun-lovers such as geraniums and sempervivums in flat-backed pots that lie flush against balustrades and walls. Wall baskets – similar to hanging baskets but only half the width – are especially good for mounting a display where space is tight. Because they dry out quickly, keep them well watered.

If your basement can be seen from indoors, then think about the view through the window. A city basement might be warm enough for an evergreen such as a yucca or a palm to survive outside all year round. A single specimen can add dramatic focus to the view in a small space, and make a green backdrop for seasonal plantings.

EASY WAYS TO CHEER UP A BASEMENT

- **Fix trellis to the walls** and use wire loops to hang an ever-changing gallery of small pots from it (see page 267).
- **Choose evergreens**: many are happy in sheltered positions, and the more exotic palms and yuccas add tropical spice.
- **Train climbers up balustrades** for a decorative stairwell. Try evergreen honeysuckle in shade; wisteria prefers the sun.
- **Plant trailers in troughs** hung from banisters and walls and allow them to tumble, covering masonry or trellis.
- **Nurture your plants** by watering and feeding regularly – and if yours is a city basement, wipe foliage clean from time to time.

▶ **On the brightest of days,** the white balcony bakes in the sun like a Mediterranean terrace. Leading off the living room, this is a much-used vantage point over the garden. Another is the basement kitchen, so Catherine has to consider how her plantings will look from several different levels.

growing
in **sun**
and
shade

▲ **Nearest the house** a collection of succulents (right) gathered around a mossy statue forms a year-round display. In summer, lilies and marguerites add height and floral interest.

► **The leaves of blue-green plants** cast a silvery light in a shady corner, soften the hard paved edge of the pond and create a barrier to keep people from falling in. "I usually have more hostas, but this year they've been eaten down to stumps by the snails."

Every turn of the path in Catherine Horwood's garden presents a fresh challenge. Hot and dry, dark and damp, she has tackled them all. Catherine has divided what was a ribbon of lawn into rooms – "since the children grew out of needing somewhere to play" – each with its own character. And to bring the garden into the house, the Horwoods added a conservatory and balcony over the flat roof of the basement kitchen.

In summer, this is a glorious sun trap. "I'm passionate about scented plants," Catherine enthuses, "and the balcony is an obvious place to concentrate on ▶

127

scent. I've experimented with colour and tried trailing plants up there, but the lavender is brilliant, because it looks good all year round. In the summer, its flower stalks poke through the railings and smell wonderful when you brush past – and when the flowers are over you can clip the plant into a nice domed shape for the winter."

The balcony looks down on a circular bricked area. "This bit of the garden has to look good from three levels of the house: the basement, the balcony, and the bedroom at the top, so it's an important part to get right." An archway through a hedge leads through to the rest of the garden, but this hedge and a towering ash behind it cut out the afternoon light to the area, making it shaded and damp – "the original lawn here was always mossy".

The rings of bricks frame a statue of a reclining woman and a group of succulents, which Catherine augments each season. She makes a big effort here in spring, because this is the part of the garden they can see from the house, when they'd rather be inside than out. "I go mad with tulips and daffodils, and all the camellias are in bloom, too." In winter there is a backbone of evergreens, with box balls, hollies and yew. "I like their shapes, and the holly balls look lovely in the mornings, when there's a frost on them."

An even shadier spot is the basement outside the kitchen. Steps lead down from ground level, with pots crowding in from the

▶ **Where space is tight,** such as on the basement steps, Catherine grows well-behaved plants, such as tidy succulents, in wall pots. Many of the pots have flat backs and snuggle up close to the wall; others have wire loops to tie them back.

" **I'm passionate** about scented plants. The **lavender** on the balcony is brilliant, it looks good **all** year round. "

▶ **From the kitchen sink** the view is of a forest of pots. Old cisterns make space-efficient containers in narrow places for wall shrubs like this pyracantha, giving the roots room to spread without obstructing the steps.

edge of each tread (see below, left). Shafts of sunlight nudge down into the area and white walls, steps and balustrades help to lighten it, but Catherine's main aim was to improve the view from her side window. Pictures and ceramic tiles give a Mediterranean feel, but plants provide the main interest and Catherine is growing a pyracantha in a toilet cistern to 'green' the wall.

THE BENEFITS OF PLASTIC

The white lilies that add height to the summer arrangement around the statue, arch out of simple terracotta pots, but they also stand tall in the borders around the garden. Here their long stems lead back to plain, black plastic plant pots that are all but invisible behind the other plants. This simple trick of dropping a lily into a gap also solves some of the common problems with planting bulbs in the ground.

Catherine finds that her bulbs get eaten or – if they survive the slugs – spiked by her fork, but by keeping them in pots at the back of the garden she can bring them into the limelight when they bloom. In fact, she finds that plants often do better in plastic pots than in terracotta ones, because they don't dry out so fast. They are also much easier to move once a plant's finest flush is over, so whenever a pot is not going to be on prominent display, Catherine uses a plastic one.

Beyond the arch in the hedge, the garden is very dry. The house is on a hill, so the neighbouring garden on one side is higher than the Horwoods' and on the other it is much lower. Rainwater drains straight through, so an irrigation system was the only way to feed the flowerbeds without spending hours watering every day in summer.

It was easy to extend the pipes into many of the pots to ease the task of watering, but when Catherine goes away she simply moves the pots that aren't linked into the system close to the edges of the borders, where the spray from the pipes will reach them. "I did have most of the pots linked up, but we had a flood in the basement so I had to disconnect the ones very near the house." Instead

Catherine's staple plants there are drought-resistant succulents, that will survive periods of neglect in summer.

Despite the dry ground, snails are a constant problem, and Catherine goes out every morning with a bag of salt to collect them. "It's no good just moving them, I'm afraid," she says, frankly, "because they come back. You have to be brutal. I see them sometimes clambering over the wall from next door, and it's as if they're saying to the others, 'come on chaps, over here!'."

" The beauty of pots is that I can take my favourites with me when I go away. They're like my children."

◀ **In a secluded spot** at the back of the garden Catherine goes wild, "with all the colours I'd never dream of having anywhere else". This is where she grows beds of flowers for the house, and the clashing colours come together in this stone urn.

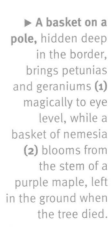

▶ **A basket on a pole,** hidden deep in the border, brings petunias and geraniums (1) magically to eye level, while a basket of nemesia (2) blooms from the stem of a purple maple, left in the ground when the tree died.

◀ **Look up** as you walk round the garden and you find lots to admire at eye level, such as this whimsical chicken wall pot overspilling with *Kalanchoë pumila*.

what a difference a shape makes

Upright or rounded, spiky or feathery— plants come in all sorts of shapes and sizes. Choosing a container that will match the plant can make all the difference.

◄ **The stiff fleshy leaves of an agave** lend definition to the soft textures found in a mixed border, and need a deep pot to anchor them.

Creating a happy union between a plant and its container takes careful planning. You need to think about the colour, size and shape of the pot and the plant or group of plants you intend to grow. You can grow almost any plant in a container and any vessel that can hold soil may be considered, but for the best effect, choose a shape of container that will enhance the form of the plant.

Trees and shrubs need a container that stands at least a third of the mature height of the plant. Not only does this present a well-balanced appearance, it also provides stability, particularly if the tree is on a roof terrace. Trees and shrubs in containers will have their growth restricted by the mere fact that they are constrained within a pot, but it is still desirable to provide them with a container wide enough to allow a healthy root system to develop for two or three years, before re-potting may be necessary.

A standard bay or rose tree has its shape maintained by regular pruning and, since there are no lower branches, these shapes look better in a

▶ **Ball shapes** are hugely satisfying, whether made by a sunny high-rise chrysanthemum, or the clipped discipline of box. For these strong outlines, a plain, undecorated pot looks best.

The play of sunlight on a plant's foliage reveals hidden textures

▲ **Strong outlines** like those of a neat conifer are accentuated by frost and draw the eye in an otherwise drab winter garden. Team the clean lines of the plant with a simple geometric pot.

▶ **The wispy shapes** of dwarf pampas grasses (*Cortaderia selloana* 'Pumila') flutter on a terrace. Matching plants look best in different sizes of matching pots.

slightly narrower pot, with the bare compost covered by a decorative mulch.

Solid round box balls, and mound-shaped plants such as hebes or small slow-growing conifers, can look very effective planted in square pots, and a collection of matching pots in varying sizes creates a pleasing continuity. This look is most effective if the plants they contain also match. They could all be varieties of a single species, such as

different azaleas, dwarf acers or fuchsias, or a collection of herbs such as thymes and sages.

Plume-shaped grasses or slender bamboos can look like wisps of smoke if they are planted in chimney pots or other tall cylindrical containers where the foliage will rustle in the breeze.

Short spiky grasses, and low-growing succulents such as sempervivums and echeverias also look very effective in tall angular

containers, where they form a neat crown and can be seen more easily.

Big, broad-leaved shapes such as castor oil plants and hardy palms, and the fountain-shaped outlines of cordylines, need to stand in a position where there is plenty of space so that their strong silhouettes can be fully appreciated.

Trailing ivies, lobelias, petunias and verbenas all need to be placed in a raised position so they can

hang freely and they are perfect for pots hung on a wall, or for hanging baskets.

Combinations of contrasting foliage can also look dramatic: try feathery ferns with broad-leaved hostas, or spiky agave with tropical palms. These arrangements offer masses of lush green in daylight; and if you conceal an uplighter at the base of the plants, the leaf shapes will cast some fascinating shadows at night.

nothing succeeds like a tree

You might be surprised to learn that you can grow a tree in a pot. For success all you need is a decent-sized container and the right compost.

A tree will add structure to a collection of pots, and provide year-round interest in a garden. Choosing the style of tree you want is the first step.

You may appreciate the constancy of an evergreen, or prefer watching the seasons take effect on a deciduous tree. Perhaps you want flowers in spring and autumn fruit, or a tree for the terrace in summer that will cheer up the conservatory in winter. On a south-facing patio, a tree can offer welcome shade, while on a balcony or roof garden it could provide screening.

Trees with unusual or interesting foliage attract attention. The yellow-gold new leaves of *Robinia pseudoacacia* 'Frisia' in spring offer shimmering colour and gentle movement in a breeze.

Dwarf acers and maples have spreading foliage in arresting colours, ranging from the softest pinks to bright crimsons and oranges. The red-barked dogwood (*Cornus alba*) comes into its own in winter once its leaves have fallen, revealing brilliant red stems.

A SHAPELY SILHOUETTE

A tree with a strong shape will provide a focal point to a patio or terrace. There are five main tree shapes to choose from: the spreading umbrella or tiered shape of a typical acer; a round-headed standard; a cone or pyramid; a tall, thin columnar shape, like a pencil cypress; and the popular weeping shape.

For an unusual outline and soft blue foliage try the weeping cedar, *Cedrus atlantica* 'Glauca Pendula'. Many conifers also offer a wide choice of shapes, sizes and colours and will grow well in containers.

◄ **Spring blossom** is one of the most cheering sights of the new year. This standard morello cherry unfolds its delicate white blossom in April, and in late July will be laden with delicious fruit.

◄◄ **An acer spreads** its umbrella-like branches of feathery foliage widely, so position the pot where the tree will have room for growth.

◄ **Drooping branches** lend a genteel air to this weeping Kilmarnock willow (*Salix caprea*). Growing trees in containers will help to keep them small.

Some trees can be clipped, trained or grafted to create an interesting shape. For example, the slow-growing, compact Japanese holly (*Ilex crenata*) has box-like foliage which can be shaped into a ball or cone.

FLOWERS AND FRUIT

Trees can produce fruit, too, even in containers. The morello cherry (*Prunus cerasus*) will bear fruit even in a north-facing position. Train it against a wall as a fan so that its branches are warmed by the heat from the wall and any available sun.

A container orchard of pear 'Terrace Pearl', peach 'Terrace Amber Dwarf' and nectarine 'Terrace Ruby Dwarf', will give spring blossom and, in a warm sheltered site, a good crop of autumn fruit. If space is tight, try the Ballerina and Minaret series of columnar apples and crab apples, which do not spread.

For a Mediterranean feel, grow a fig or an olive tree. But remember that, although olive trees enjoy summer outdoors in a sunny location, they need to be moved into a frost-free place for winter.

GROW A MINIATURE FOREST

Even if your space is restricted, you can still enjoy the pleasures of trees by keeping bonsai.
• **Forest trees,** such as this blue spruce, larch and beech (left to right) can look charming in miniature.
• **The most successful species** are hardy trees with naturally small leaves, flowers and berries. Hawthorn, hornbeam, juniper or spruce are all good choices.

Make light work of moving heavy pots with a plant dolly: see pages 268-269

plants that love to be beside the sea

Climate and conditions at the coast present a challenge to the container gardener. But choose carefully and you will find a host of plants, such as tough hebes, that flourish in exposed sites.

The two main problems facing seaside gardeners are the damage that can be done to leaves by buffeting wind, and the deposits of salt that sea breezes drop on to plants and into their containers. On the other hand, most coastal sites have a milder winter climate than inland locations, so that plants that would not be hardy in other areas, such as cordylines and the dwarf fan palm (*Chamaerops humilis*), will thrive. Sun-loving plants such as gazanias or African daisies, will also overwinter at the coast, while in colder districts, they only survive as annuals.

When planting shrubs at the coast, use a large pot and a weighty, loam-based compost such as John Innes No.3, as this will provide extra stability. Strong winds will also strip plants and pots of moisture, so it is a good idea to add a thick layer of mulch.

FOLLOW NATURE'S LEAD

A good starting point for the seaside gardener is to select plants that are native to coastal environments. Look out for species with 'maritima' or a variant in their scientific name, such as sea holly (*Eryngium maritimum*), sea kale (*Crambe maritima*) and thrift (*Armeria maritima*).

More substantial shrubs to grow in seaside containers include the daisy bush (*Olearia* x *haastii*), which is resistant to strong winds and salt spray and bears fragrant, white, daisy-like flowers in mid to late summer. The Mediterranean sun rose (*Cistus*) and rock rose (*Helianthemum*) are also summer flowering in sunny sites.

For interesting foliage, junipers fit the bill: the leaves of *Juniperus* x *pfitzeriana* and *J. sabina* range in colour from almost yellow through bright green to silvery blue. On the bleached wood of a deck, the sword-like leaves of New Zealand flax have a suitably contemporary silhouette, topped by spikes of tropical-looking flowers in late summer.

HARDY ALTERNATIVES

Most common garden perennials are unsuited to cultivation near the sea. The foliage becomes scorched by salt and the whole plant is quickly killed by a build-up of salt at the roots. Tall and slender-stemmed plants are also easily snapped by strong winds.

However, there are a few sturdy exceptions. In early spring, the bell-shaped pink flowers of elephant's ear (*Bergenia cordifolia*) reflect the typically thin coastal light, while summer colour will come from the purple flowered bloody cranesbill, red-hot pokers (*Kniphofia*) and sea hollies, with their silvery blue thistle-like flowers. All the smaller varieties of day lilies also grow well in pots.

The bright displays seen in parks and on roundabouts in seaside towns are proof that it is also possible to grow a wide range of annuals and summer bedding plants in coastal locations. Plant a hot summer arrangement with red and yellow Californian poppies and yellow horned poppies, surrounded by silvery-leaved *Asteriscus* with its yellow flowers and the low-growing succulent, the Livingstone daisy.

While all the plants mentioned here are tolerant of salt-laden winds, it is wise, after a storm, to hose down the foliage and to soak the pots until water runs through the bottom. This will flush out salt that has been deposited, but will also leach out nutrients, so ensure the plants are well fed afterwards.

▲ **Low-growing succulents** of a table centrepiece shrug off salt.

▶ **Daisy-like flowers** soak up the sun in open sites. *Asteriscus* is a classic sun-loving seaside plant.

▶ **Sleek modern lines** link the fountain of spiky leaves from this phormium with its straight-sided vase-like container.

▶ **Cool white** geraniums, snapdragons and statice echo the tone of the rocks and the sea.

▲ **Seaside summer sun** will bring out a rosy blush at the growing tips of a variegated *Fuchsia magellanica*.

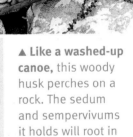

▲ **Like a washed-up canoe,** this woody husk perches on a rock. The sedum and sempervivums it holds will root in very little soil.

▲ **The hot reds and yellows** of this sun plant, or *Portulaca grandiflora*, are revealed only when the sun shines. On grey days the flowers stay shut.

Silvery foliage reflects light to help to protect plants like lavender and the yellow-flowered santolina from the scorching sun. Thin spiky leaves of the dwarf fan palm (left) keep its water loss low.

room at the top for a garden

Flat-dwellers who long for a plot to tend or gardeners with a wish for a secluded retreat can add a new dimension to their living space by using their roof. Create a garden with a view, high above the city streets.

Even the smallest area of flat roof can become a garden with a few carefully chosen and planted containers. But before you transform yours into an urban oasis, consider a few practicalities.

The most important thing to establish is whether your roof will bear the weight: this will mean having a structural survey. You can reduce the weight of your pots by using plastic or glass-fibre containers instead of terracotta, and for drainage, crumbled polystyrene instead of broken crocks. However, a tall plant, particularly in a windy spot, may need to stand in a heavy pot to prevent it from blowing over.

Good drainage is also crucial. In high summer, containers on a sun-baked roof will need watering every day – but a roof terrace covered in puddles will not entice you outside.

Think about access to the roof, too. Will you be able to move pots, compost and large plants up there?

◀ **Create a 'real garden' feel** by adding a few large shrubs – a bottle brush, say – and a tree, such as an acer, and grouping pots in a 'path and border' formation.

▼ **A limited palette** of green with white hydrangea, lobelia and petunias, carried through in the furniture and paving, can make a small area seem more spacious.

▲ **Country plants**, such as foxgloves nicotianas, pansies and violas, soften the contemporary look of this roof's decking, sweet peas and other climbers screen out the city skyline.

Can you fit an outside tap or irrigation system, or will you need to carry full watering cans up awkward steps?

PLANTS IN HIGH PLACES

Most roof gardens will need some screening, either from the elements or from overlooking buildings (see pages 138-139). Tall, wispy bamboos and grasses offer privacy without blocking out light, while trellis panels cloaked with climbers make a more sturdy windbreak.

If you are lucky enough to have a great view, frame it with a pair of sculptural plants. But if your outlook is less appealing, create focal points within the garden by including a few dramatic specimens to draw the eye.

Even in a limited space, a few substantial shrubs, such as a large-leaved fatsia will add interest and scale.

Long strappy leaves can be shredded by strong winds, but many trees and shrubs, including cotoneasters, elaeagnus and mahonias, are more resiliant and make excellent roof-garden plants.

Resist the temptation to position all your pots around the walls. More creative arrangements, such as banks of plants at different levels, will make a much more interesting display and can help to make the space seem larger than it is. Following a theme or simple colour scheme can also help to create an illusion of space.

Few roof gardens are large enough to store more than a few pots of bulbs out of season, so it is important to plan carefully. A bench that doubles as storage space can accommodate the few tools the container gardener needs.

Make every plant earn its space on the roof. Choose long-flowering varieties and plants with something to offer after their flowers have faded. The pure blue blooms of Chinese plumbago (*Ceratostigma*) make it a brilliant choice for summer colour, and its leaves glow a brilliant red in autumn. Choose as staples plants that will provide interest all the year round and use evergreens as a backdrop for showy seasonal specimens.

Do not let the height of your garden deter you from experimenting with exotic or tender species. Heat rises from buildings and will give warmth to a sheltered roof garden even in winter.

137

safe behind a green screen

Whether you need protection from the sun, shelter from wind, screening from neighbours or to block off ugly views, it's surprising what a tub or two of concealing foliage can do.

Nearly every outdoor space has some corner that would benefit from being closed off or sheltered. Whatever the problem, pots of vigorous plants can solve it easily.

Large containers, or a raised bed, are the most suitable choice for growing large screening plants or climbers. For climbers, you will need to erect a support system for the plants to scramble over. Attach a series of stakes or a trellis to walls, balcony rails or to the pots themselves before the plants are in position.

For an evergreen screen to hide a garden eyesore, try the chocolate vine, *Akebia quinata* (below, far right). Ivies and the evergreen *Clematis cirrhosa* also offer foliage cover in winter, and with this clematis, pale, fragrant bell-like flowers.

In a sunny site, a pot of passionflower, such as the purple and white *Passiflora caerulea*, will be vigorous and hardy and provide flowers and fruit.

Cast welcome shade in a suntrap with *Campsis* x *tagliabuana* 'Madame Galen', a flowering vine (below, far right). Another climber, the grapevine, *Vitis vinifera* 'Purpurea', makes a radiant claret-red screen for summer, turning rich purple in autumn. Alternatively, the slender leaves of the Coyote willow (*Salix exigua*) will fan gracefully out of a large tub into a grey-green screen.

To provide shade on a structure such as a pergola, an archway or a bower, put a half-barrel or other large container at the base of each upright and plant one specimen in each.

A pergola with four uprights would look flowery and elegant with four toning wisterias. Four ornamental

▶ **Rippling stems of bamboo** trap and filter the wind to give protection to an outdoor seating area. The rustling of the grass also adds a soothing sound to idle summer days.

◄ **For a screen that you can change at whim,** hang a collection of pots on a trellis. Whether you choose all one variety of plant, or a mixture, you can change them over season by season, so the screen always looks vibrant.

► **Grapevines are fast-growing** and easy to train into shape. Here two vines are woven together at the top to provide an intriguing screen that shields the far part of the garden from curious eyes. Later in the year the vine leaves will offer glowing autumn colours.

grapevines, for fruit and foliage, would also provide good cover. Both lose their leaves in late autumn, but only after making a colourful seasonal display.

GROWING A WINDBREAK

For protection from the wind in exposed gardens, or on a roof garden or balcony, a screen of living bamboo will act as a filter, reducing its force. And because the bamboo stems move with the breeze, the container is unlikely to topple over.

Other good windbreaks are the tough seaside foliage plants, such as escallonia, *Griselinia littoralis*, and tamarisk. Willows can also act as windbreaks, their slender branches sifting the wind like a bamboo, and they will not grow too large confined to a container.

You may need to anchor or weigh down containers in windy sites as the plants' top growth will make them susceptible to blowing over. For overall stability, choose wide containers with upright, rather than sloping sides. Give the pot a heavy base by using gravel or broken crocks for drainage, and mulch the top with pebbles.

FLOWERING SCREENS

Screens can provide beauty as well as protection. The delicate flowers of jasmine **(1)** will wrap a seating area in perfume. Exuberant trumpets of *Campsis* x *tagliabuana* 'Madame Galen' **(2)** help to keep a hot spot shady in late summer. And softly coloured flowers enhance the chocolate vine **(3)** in spring.

139

theatrical flair for a balcony

This tiny space can be given dramatic good looks with very few containers. To have the best seat in the house, bring on the pots and enjoy heavenly scents and flamboyant colours.

A balcony is a privileged, private space where you can find a refuge, just a step away from the demands of daily life. However, it also has its own microclimate, so raising plants on a balcony poses a special set of challenges.

When you raise a pot up onto a balcony, you are putting it into more stressful conditions, without the shelter from wind, rain and sun that can be found at ground level. So when you are choosing plants, it is important to pick those that will be able to withstand the prevailing conditions.

If you want to plant a screen, for instance, choose plants like roses, which have strong stems, rather than a honeysuckle, whose soft tendrils will be blown adrift in a gale. If your balcony faces the sun, or is largely in shade, choose sun-lovers like geraniums, or shade-lovers such as hostas and busy lizzies that will enjoy these conditions.

FIT PLANTS ONLY

On a small balcony, every plant must earn its keep. In a garden it does not matter if one section is quiet provided another is in bloom, but where there is only space for a few pots, each must flourish.

This doesn't mean the tubs have to be a riot of nonstop colour. Quite the

▲ **Inviting tones** of pink verbena and petunias, with a dash of purple, give a bedroomy languor to this little oasis.

▶ **A formal city balcony** is softened by simple pots of daffodils, wallflowers and primulas in harmonising shades.

opposite. In a restricted area, harmony is all important: you do not want to confuse the eye with a mixture of jarring colours. But you must keep your plants in prime condition, and be ruthless about removing any that are looking poorly.

When planning a balcony from scratch, choose the furniture first so you know how much space is left for plants.

If you choose to have a screen along the front, decide whether you want something permanent, such as a climbing rose or a row of evergreens, or whether

▲ **Using too many colours** jars in the tight space of a balcony. This spring planting of daffodils and wallflowers charms because the colours echo each other.

you would prefer to have large pots of mixed flowers which you can change around when needed.

Remember you don't have to start a screen at the bottom. You can attach a trough or window box from the top rail of your balcony and fill it with trailing plants: this will give you privacy in a very short time.

THE VIEW BEYOND

Because you will often look through your balcony from the window, it is best to choose plants from a narrow palette of colours to avoid confusion with the view beyond. A group of pots

planted with a themed mixture of soft pinks, whites and purples might look wonderful in a leafy setting, while a city balcony is a good location for formal evergreens like box and bay. Pruned into clear shapes, their symmetrical lines will echo the geometric lines of the surrounding buildings.

Since balconies are for sitting out on, remember to consider scent when you are choosing between different varieties of the same plant. Hyacinths and wallflowers in spring, lavender and lilies in summer, will fill your balcony, and the adjoining room, with fragrance.

▼ **The exuberant design** of courtyard tubs is left behind as the garden rises through increasingly formal balcony plants.

▶ **Faced with a strip of weeds (1),** Sally and Oliver asked a garden designer for advice. They laid down the bones of her zigzag design with pots **(2)** as the first step in their long-term plan **(3)** to create an illusion of width in the garden.

①

②

▶ **Big leaves and easy maintenance** were Oliver's requests, while Sally was looking forward to learning about plants. But both agreed on colour, preferring autumnal russets, like the permanent collection of foliage plants on the patio, to summery pinks.

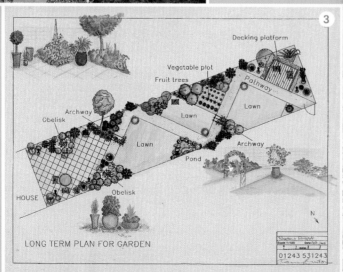
③

Decking platform

Vegetable plot

Fruit trees

Pathway

Archway
Obelisk

Lawn

Lawn

Lawn

Archway

Pond

HOUSE

Obelisk

N

LONG TERM PLAN FOR GARDEN

Scale 1:100
01243 531243

starting
with
a **blank**
canvas

When Sallyanne and Oliver Greenwood moved house, they wanted to enjoy the last few rays of summer before the decorating began. They moved in September, to find a garden full of well-established weeds. Their first priority was to make it usable, but they faced some design challenges. "The garden is really long and narrow," Sally explains, "and we didn't know where to start to give it structure." Whatever they did, it would have to look good from above, as well as at ground level, because their living room is on the first floor. Their house is the middle one of three, and ▶

▼ **Working from the plan,** the first job was to mark out the zigzag path with string as a guide. The plants were positioned then a final sweep tidied the patio, leaving time for a celebratory drink.

143

▼ Baskets make pretty containers for herbs and strawberries in the 'allotment' area. The crab apple, top-heavy with fruit (left), toppled over before a mulch of cobbles was added.

▼ **The tallest plants,** such as these fruit tree saplings, line up along the wire-fenced boundary to give Sally and Oliver some privacy from the next-door garden.

▲ **Deep colours and bold shapes,** such as begonias and a *Canna* (right) give definition to the far end of the garden. Drifts of cobbles give the impression of a hard surface, but the pots will stand on the grass until the decking is in place. Even bare, trellis adds height and interest.

"I can't wait to get out there now and get into it and start to potter in my veggie patch."

the builders left only wire fences between the gardens. "The first thing we did was to put up a fence on our boundary, but the neighbours on the other side haven't done anything yet," Oliver points out.

Working against the clock before autumn set in and with their savings depleted from buying the house, Sally and Oliver decided to use pots to set down the skeleton of the design and give them instant colour.

Using pots meant that they could group the few plants they had more densely than they

would in the ground to create focal points to draw attention away from the bare areas.

The far end of the garden catches the evening sun and eventually decking will provide a sturdy base for a couple of chairs or a hammock.

To add impact to this distant corner they used plants with bold shapes and strong colours. They also put them in striking pots, such as one with a turquoise glaze, and an elegant grey Ali Baba jar which holds a *Canna*, standing like a beacon in the corner. A spreading *Fatsia*

▲ **A pond was high on the wish list** for the garden, and a varnished half-barrel makes a simple potted version. Grasses and *Crocosmia* cast light shade over the water and squares of decking make a dry and stable base for the wooden barrel.

> " We love the patio with all the pots, and our friends all say how much wider the garden looks now. "

▲ **A pair of conifers echo** the slender proportions of the house and punctuate the edge of the patio. The collection of dark foliage plants is lightened by dots of contrasting yellow and blue.

japonica, glowing pink *Hydrangea macrophylla* 'Altona' and carmine red begonias flank the *Canna* and mark out this furthest triangle.

Nearer the house is Sally's vegetable patch, including a flowering cherry, an apple and a crab apple. Putting the saplings in pots means that Oliver and Sally can move them until they are happy with their position before planting them in the ground.

Diagonally opposite is the 'pond', where the path turns again to meet the patio. Many of the most decorative pots are grouped here, since these plants will live permanently in their containers. Galvanised metal and plants with a metallic quality, such as russet *Heucheras* and silvery lavenders give this corner a contemporary edge. This is emphasised by scatterings of slate and pale stone, while autumnal chrysanthemum balls and glazed blue terracotta spheres add colour to take them through to winter and beyond.

"We love the patio area," Oliver and Sally enthuse, "and the pots have transformed the garden. Our friends all comment on how much wider it looks."

▶ **If you don't have matching pots** create a feeling of unity in a group with accessories. In this corner of the patio, white mulch, slate chippings and two marble balls bring together a collection of foliage plants at different levels.

containers
for
every
season

a fruitful year in the container

january

Wrap pots in bubble wrap during very cold spells to prevent the compost from freezing solid.

Check compost moisture content; if over-wet, unblock drainage holes if necessary. Compost may dry out during dry spells, so be prepared to water.

Cover half-hardy plants with horticultural fleece or old net curtains during frosty weather. Do not use polythene, which can cause rotting.

Plant fruit trees and bushes in large pots or tubs.

february

Buy potted bulbs if you did not plant in autumn.

Wash pots and disinfect them.

Order plug plants from catalogues.

Scrub slippery paving with an algicide.

Sow bedding geraniums indoors in a light place.

Cover new shoots with fleece or similar on cold nights.

march

Plant lilies, herbaceous perennials, shrubs, strawberries and other soft fruit.

Divide herbaceous clumps and pot smaller pieces in fresh compost.

Sow tomatoes, other vegetables and bedding plants on a light windowsill or in a greenhouse.

Repair, clean and paint trellis and other wooden supports.

Top-dress permanent tubs with slow-release fertiliser.

Cut back fuchsias and re-pot.

april

Start feeding containers.

Plant alpines, herbs and slightly tender shrubs.

Plant containers with vegetable seedlings sown last month, or sow in situ.

Deadhead spring bulbs and plant summer ones.

Sow polyanthus and primroses for next spring.

Pot-on seedlings and plug plants and sow seeds of hardy annuals.

In a greenhouse, make up summer pots and hanging baskets, and sow beans, courgettes, squashes and sweet peas.

may

Increase watering, especially during warm or windy weather.

Cut back yellow leaves of bulbs, or lift clumps from containers.

Plant hanging baskets for instant effect. Put in a sheltered place to establish for a week before hanging in place.

Start picking salad leaves.

Check for pests and diseases, and act if necessary.

Sow biennials like Canterbury bells and wallflowers.

In late May, plant out half-hardy bedding plants and vegetables.

june

Deadhead all flowering plants regularly.

Protect ripening strawberries from birds by covering with fleece. Pick ripe fruit regularly.

Increase watering of new plants as they grow.

Start harvesting quick-maturing vegetables.

You've done the **hard work** – it's time to reap the **rewards**

▼ wrap containers

increase watering ▶

▲ buy potted bulbs

▲ sow tomatoes

▲ sow polyanthus for next spring's pots

▲ deadhead regularly

garden

july

Make successive sowings of quick-maturing vegetables.

Keep a lookout for pests and weeds and tackle problems as soon as they arise.

Tie in new shoots of climbers.

Clip herbs and topiary to maintain shape.

Sow winter-flowering pansies or order plug plants.

august

Buy pot-grown chrysanthemums and other late-flowering plants for autumn colour.

Feed and water all containers regularly.

Prick out pansies and other spring bedding seedlings or buy plugs and pot on.

Clip herbaceous perennials as they fade.

Start harvesting apples, pears and plums.

september

Finish liquid feeding and reduce watering as temperatures drop and days shorten.

Plant bulbs for spring flowering.

Remove summer bedding plants as they fade.

Empty and clean pots and plant up with spring bedding and winter pansies in fresh compost.

Trim hardy shrubs to keep in shape.

Treat decking and other timber areas with an algicide before they become slippery.

october

Move half-hardy shrubs and perennials into a greenhouse or conservatory for winter protection.

Lift half-hardy bulbs when the foliage dies back and store in a cool, dry, frost-free place.

Plant hardy shrubs and conifers.

Put up arches and pergolas.

Clean canes and store in a dry place over winter.

Empty planters used for growing vegetables and clean thoroughly.

november

Move permanent tubs to a more sheltered position if necessary.

Order seeds from catalogues for next year.

Tidy established roses and plant new rose bushes and bare-root shrubs.

Remove dead leaves and tidy up herbaceous perennials.

Check paths and patios for uneven slabs or bricks. Relay if necessary and clean with an algicide.

december

Cover tender plants with fleece during cold spells.

Insulate pots with bubble wrap or old carpet.

Garland pots with fairy lights for Christmas cheer

Plant holly and ivy and Christmas tree-type conifers in pots for outdoor seasonal decoration.

Treat icy paving slabs with salt or paving de-icer.

◄ tie in new shoots

▲ start harvesting tree fruits

▲ plant spring bulbs

◄ clean and store canes

▲ order seeds

▲ plant conifers

flowers that herald spring

Bright, fresh-flowering tubs bursting with exuberant blooms chime with the sense of renewal that comes with warmer weather and lengthening days.

What better way to greet the arrival of springtime than with a glorious display of sunny, yellow narcissi and luminous creamy white hyacinths? Bulbs prefer a well-drained, moderately fertile soil that is kept moist but never waterlogged. So whatever container you choose, it must have lots of drainage holes and be lined with plenty of crocks.

The pretty pale daffodil 'Ice Follies' (right) produces creamy white petals around a pale primrose cup, which turns white as the flower matures. At around 38cm (15in) tall, these form the focal point of the display. Depending on how large your container is, arrange five, seven or nine bulbs in the centre (odd numbers look more natural than even numbers). If you would prefer a scented variety, choose 'Cheerfulness', or the very new 'Martinette', which is slightly shorter.

For maximum impact, only mix varieties that flower at the same time as one another. Here a circle of smaller daffodils, *Narcissus* 'Hawera' has been placed around the central group. They grow to just 20cm (8in) tall and bear from two to six lightly fragrant, canary-yellow flowers on each stem. Finally, dot several white or cream hyacinths in among the smaller narcissi.

The multiflora hyacinths used here are closer in character to the wild species than many other cultivated varieties and produce several stems of loosely arranged flowers to create a very natural effect. As hyacinth bulbs are more expensive than narcissi, save money by planting them only in the front half of the container.

This display was planted in a traditional wooden half-barrel painted with two coats of weatherproof paint. White paint helps the pale petals to make an impact, where a stronger colour could overpower them. If the half-barrel is to be a permanent feature with changing plantings – by a front door, say – choose a colour that co-ordinates with the paintwork.

HINTS AND TIPS FOR BEAUTIFUL BULBS

- **Buying** Most bulbs sold in autumn are foolproof. If you buy them in advance, keep them in a cool place. Choose bulbs that have no visible shoots and whose outer skin, or tunic, is intact. Avoid bulbs kept in a warm place, where they may have been sweating in their plastic bags.
- **Planting** Plant daffodils by September so that they develop a strong root system. For a good display, plant bulbs very close together, or even touching. The golden rule for effect is to fill the container – don't leave gaps because the result will be less attractive. Bulbs should be planted at a depth of approximately twice their own height, with their pointed noses uppermost.
- **Compost** Use John Innes No.1 with a little multipurpose feed and a few handfuls of grit.
- **Watering** You are unlikely to drown your bulbs as any surplus moisture will drain away.

◀ **Colour holds a group together** as the miniature daffodils are linked to the larger ones through the golden eyes of the polyanthus, and the pink and mauve of the two polyanthus echo with the magnolia blossom in the background.

EXTENDING THE SEASON

Have a longer display in the same pot by starting it off at the turn of the year with early blooming bulbs.

• **Winter** Dwarf narcissus and a creamy white anemone blanda flower in winter. While these bloom, the buds of the later daffodils will begin to push through the foliage, ready to take over where the early flowers leave off.

• **Spring** The arrangement will look as it does below.

winter

spring

◀ **Make a cheerful statement** on a front doorstep with this white tub brimming with daffodils and hyacinths. The varieties have been chosen for their colour and scent.

fresh ways
with polyanthus

The cheerful blotched faces of polyanthus and primulas have an old-fashioned, fresh-from-the-country look, but they can hold their own in today's smart containers too.

▲ **Cool colours shine** in metal containers, as these primroses show. Behind, cream-flowered hellebores add height and the grouping gains added style through repetition.

◄ **Mix the foliage** to give structure to a planting. Here balls of the 'Red Baron' polyanthus are backed by the shapely leaves of *Helleborus orientalis guttatus* and fringed with 'Golden Inge' ivy.

◄ **For a pale and pretty look,** team yellow polyanthus with creamy primroses and drumhead *Primula denticulata* var. 'Alba'.

The pale colours are repeated in the variegated leaves of the spiky liriope and the ivy, while a woolly grey senecio lights up the centre.

The surprise inclusion of a single blue hyacinth adds a flourish to the pastel display.

In the early part of the year, polyanthus and primulas bring a splash of vivid colour to the garden at a time when it is usually quite dull. Both flowers belong to the same family, but spotting the difference between them is quite easy: polyanthus flowers emerge in clusters of colour at the end of flower stalks whereas primulas all flower from the centre of the plant.

It is essential when using small plants like polyanthus to think about how to provide drama and interest.

Start with the pot and choose one that suits the location: a shiny galvanised metal container on decking, for example, or warm terracotta pots for an elegant tiled doorstep. Then select your polyanthus in colours that complement both the container and the location you have in mind.

One way to highlight low-growing plants like polyanthus is to add a focal plant to the group to give it emphasis and to bring out the colour of the smaller specimens. Raising the pot on a table or bench can also give a modest polyanthus much-needed height.

GROWING TIPS

You can buy young plants of polyanthus and primroses from a garden centre or grow them from seed sown in early spring. They can be packed quite tightly together for a profuse display, but in that case you must use a deep container so that the roots can grow down into the compost. If crammed into a shallow bowl without sufficient space for the roots to spread down or sideways, polyanthus will last only two or three weeks. Dead-head the plants regularly and they will flower all spring.

The waving grass, *Carex* 'Evergold', draws the eye to the warm colours of the pink *Primula* 'Betty', set in an antique reclaimed container. Placing the arrangement on a table lifts it to a more comfortable eye-level height.

KEY FACTS

The progeny of wild meadow cowslips and primroses, polyanthus are robust plants, hardy to −15°C (5°F). The flowers can be single, double or hose-in-hose, in which there are two rows of petals one inside the other.

• **Barnhaven** varieties often have speckled flowers held high above the foliage.

• **Gold-laced** polyanthus have single-petalled blooms with golden eyes and a gold edge to a second colour.

• **Charisma** series are large and bi-coloured, with a golden centre.

• **Gemini** series have single-coloured or two-tone flowers with a yellow centre.

a modern setting for old favourites

After the hectic yellows of early spring, brimming with primroses, daffodils and forsythia, the muted shades of mid-spring bulbs soothe the eye and make an elegant choice for contemporary containers.

Cool grey metallic containers have an understated contemporary appearance and a light reflective quality. Their silvery surface acts as the perfect foil for the mauves and purples of these modern arrangements, from the focal point of the tall pale hellebores on the left of the display to the delicate fritillary in the taller square pot.

Hellebores are found naturally in woodlands, but also in rocky and grassy sites, in most parts of Europe and Western Asia. Their growing requirements vary, but these perennial hybrids, *Helleborus orientalis*, briefly known as *Helleborus* x *hybridus*, grow best in a heavy soil and in dappled shade. Given these conditions, they will produce flowers from late winter to mid spring. Removing the leaves will not harm the plants but allows a clear view of the delicate blooms. These winter leaves die and have to be removed anyway, and cutting them off early avoids new leaves being pruned off by mistake.

In the centre arrangement, the shorter container is filled with a delightful new hyacinth called 'Woodstock'. As the blooms mature, they fade to give a paler pinky purple edge to each of the flowers. To contrast with their stiff stems, the hyacinths have been interplanted with snake's head fritillary (*Fritillaria meleagris*), whose nodding heads resemble purple-and-white snakeskin.

For something less austere, try the alternative planting, far right, in which orange and purple make an exciting colour combination. Here the fritillary is joined by a double flowering early tulip, 'Orange Princess'. This sensational tulip has vibrant two-tone petals, and flowers in April at the same time as the fritillary.

▲ **For a pretty finishing touch,** add some colour-themed pebbles.

▶ **Small pieces of moss** provide a pretty mulch: you can usually find some growing in the garden in spring, so you don't need to take any from the wild.

◀ **Tulips are often blown over in high winds,** and they are particularly at risk when grown in containers, or when they lack the shelter of surrounding plants. 'Orange Princess' is an excellent choice for pots and window boxes as it is a relatively short variety, growing to about 35cm (14in), making it less vulnerable to the elements than taller tulips.

USING A DIFFERENT PALETTE

Blue flowers also look good in steely galvanised containers, and you will find the best choice among traditional cottage garden varieties.

• *Primula marginata* (**1**) has evergreen leaves and clusters of lilac flowers.

• *Scilla siberica* 'Spring Beauty' (**2**), a vigorous plant, looks like a small bluebell with its azure-blue flowers.

• *Viola elatior* (**3**) has delicate two-tone petals and more open flowers than the scilla.

a riot of colour in late spring

Holding their heads erect, tulips look great in a pot, on their own or with other spring bulbs. Whether open or shut, their curves and colours always look magnificent.

The passion for tulips dates back hundreds of years. When 'tulipomania' swept through Holland in the 17th century, a single bulb could cost the equivalent of a house in Amsterdam.

Tulips are popular indoors as a cut flower, but they also make a fabulous outdoor display, densely planted in containers. The Greigii variety used in the arrangements on this page is a late-flowering tulip, bringing colour when most spring bulbs have finished. It is a particularly good choice for containers as it not only has stunning flowers, often bi-coloured, but also beautiful leaves, mottled or striped with crimson.

In the arrangement on the right, 'Plaisir' tulip, a carmine-red bloom with yellow edges, and the newer variety 'Treasure', a softer pinky red with creamy edges, grow no taller than 25cm (10in), which suits shallow containers. They are teamed with 'Delft Blue' hyacinths to make a perfect combination. This hyacinth's clear blue flowers are heavily scented and can be grown to coincide with the blooms of the tulips.

If you prefer to focus solely on the impact of these unusual tulips, they can be planted on their own, as they are below. Packed together like this, the short stems hold the blooms upright while the leaves curl prettily over the edge of the pot.

▶ **A carefully chosen pot** can be the making of a display. The fluted edges of this terracotta planter echo the curvaceous shape of the tulip leaves, while the glazed pattern traced on the pot's surface complements the distinctive mottled stripes of the foliage.

early spring

mid spring

late spring

Different varieties of tulip bloom at different times so you can keep a container going for months by mixing them. Choose three colours that will look good together as buds and flowers. Here the colours gradually become more intense.

• **Early spring** White 'Diana' tulips flower first.

• **Mid spring** The pink-edged 'Garden Party' comes through.

• **Late spring** Finish with deep maroon 'Queen of the Night'.

CHOOSING AND GROWING TULIPS

Tulips offer a dazzling choice, with single and double varieties and a huge selection of both plain and striped colours.

• **Pack bulbs tightly** into the container so that they touch for best results. You don't have to leave room for the bulbs to spread as you would if you were planting them in the garden.

• **Support taller varieties** by growing something wiry like a winter heather around the tulips.

• **When flowering is finished,** you can move the bulbs into the garden – they are never as good a second time round. Use fresh bulbs for next year's pot.

157

▲ **Moss and bark chippings** are good companions to woodland fritillaries.

spring flowers from the woodlands

Conjure up the haunting effects of the natural world: a handful of ferns, the subtle colours of less showy bulbs and the sympathetic use of moss and bark brings the wild wood home.

Shade is often considered to be the most difficult aspect to cope with in the garden, yet many bulbs and herbaceous perennials, particularly those whose natural habitat is woodland, positively thrive in this situation. But if you plan to use woodland plants, never attempt to dig them up from their natural setting: always buy them from a reputable supplier.

The arrangement on the near right combines two foliage plants: the delicate fronds of the narrow buckler fern, *Dryopteris carthusiana* and the variegated leaves of ivy *Hedera helix* 'Mint Kolibri'. Both of these can tolerate shade throughout the year. To these low-growing evergreens are added the deep pink flowers of *Corydalis solida* 'Dieter Schacht' and the delicate white blooms of the windflower, *Anemone blanda*, both at their best between March and April.

Adding dramatic height to balance the proportions of the shallow planter, are spires of *Arisaema nepenthoides*. These intriguing looking plants – sometimes called cobra plants or dragon roots – are tuberous-rooted relatives of the arums. They are easy to grow in damp and shady places, though you may have to seek them out from a specialist nursery.

All these plants need a rich organic, well-drained soil that is kept continually moist and they look best arranged in a soft, casual style in plain natural containers. Given a sheltered and shady position, the plants will give a long-lasting display of flowers from early March. Afterwards, the bulbs can be moved into the garden under the shelter of trees to naturalise, while the ferns and ivy can be used in another pot.

▶ This creamy terracotta pot illuminates a dark corner and its generous girth provides plenty of space for plants to grow. Here the ferns, anemones and arisaemas of the main arrangement are joined by pale spring flowers. This mixture is all movement, with nodding flowerheads of snake's head fritillary, *Fritillaria meleagris alba* mingling with delicate *Muscari azureum* 'Album', whose flowers resemble clusters of tiny bells.

◀ Tall striking plants such as the arisaemas, rising like triffids from the container, make a big impact with only a small number. Despite their exotic looks, they are fully hardy.

In their natural habitat woodland plants often flower early in the year, when light can filter through bare branches, before the new leaves block out the sun. So they make a good choice for spring containers.

OTHER SHADE-LOVERS

Many woodland plants are now available from nurseries. These can all be grown in containers: **(1)** Lesser celandine (*Ranunculus ficaria* 'Brazen Hussy'), **(2)** lily of the valley (*Convallaria majalis* var. *rosea*) and **(3)** bluebell (*Hyacinthoides hispanica*).

▲ **A small raised seedbed** in spring (**1**) is protected by twigs of dogwood. In summer (**2**) it provides cornflowers, nasturtiums, nigella and cerinthe for cutting. In autumn, ornamental cabbages (**3**) take their place.

◀ **The garden reveals its form** in spring. The round lawn edged with box gives a feeling of space, while the terrace is crowded with containers. Beautiful pots are also used as a design element: the two pale terracotta urns seem to light up the sycamore.

▼ **The terrace is crowded** with summer pots where the spiky flag irises frame purple lobelia and crimson *Arctotis*. The wind socks were added to replace the blue of delphiniums wiped out overnight by slugs.

a garden for all seasons

One solitary sycamore in a sheet of tarmac greeted Ian Brownhill and Michael Hirschl when they moved in to their suburban garden flat. They had to remove tons of rubble before they hit soil. In the beginning, Ian, who runs a gardening magazine, and Michael, a designer, laid out a conventional lawn edged with narrow borders. Two years later they threw caution to the winds, swivelled the lawn round at an angle and put in a moat along the top, leaving space to extend the patio area. They needed more room because they wanted many more containers. "The first pot we ▶

◄ **As winter nears,** the tabletop group of dormant hostas stands mulched with pea shingle, ready to unfurl in spring (above). The soft colour wash of the nesting boxes, shed and bench creates a harmonious background.

► **Spring-sown *Stipa tenuissima*,** (below) produces feathery panicles in autumn. Then it is joined by harmonious plantings of the striped *Carex phyllocephala* 'Sparkler' and the nodding heads of a *Pennisetum*.

ever had was some daffodil bulbs given to us by a friend" recalls Ian. "We put it in the centre of the patio by the French windows and watched them grow all through the winter until they flowered. There was just weeds and concrete and this container."

From this simple beginning grew a passion that now fills over 70 containers. "If I see a hole, I drop in a pot" says Ian. "Michael has the big picture in mind, while I plant up lots of pots then experiment putting them together."

What makes the garden so harmonious is the sense of colour that underpins the design and changes with the seasons. "In the spring it's pale yellows and creams" says Ian. "Take daffodils; we started off with the normal yellow 'King Alfreds', but we've slowly moved towards creamy white varieties like 'Winston Churchill' and 'Cheerfulness'.

"In the summer we try to make the scheme a bit hotter and more vibrant, although we keep some creams too. For instance, we've got some really strong blue agapanthus coming up and we've mixed in some coppery red *Helenium* 'Moerheim Beauty', so there will be red and blue together and it's going to look stunning. You mustn't be frightened of putting colours together. If you don't like it, you can take it out – you don't have to repeat it next year."

In autumn, the colours darken. "We have some very dark reds such as scabious, canna and chocolate cosmos, and the scarlet leaves

◄ **A collection of saxifrages** is lifted into close-up in an old French wine rack. The garden is full of thoughtful groupings such as this, which have an impact well beyond their size.

◄ **Spring is marked with pale shades.** 'White Triumphator' tulips (far left) are propped up by a companion planting of heather, while leggy pansies (left) are supported by the stiff stems of creamy narcissi.

▶ **Autumn brings bonfire colours** as dwarf acers blaze behind the crimson buds of a dwarf pomegranate. The *Lobelia tupa* in front, grown from seed, will have red flowers too.

"The charm of pots is they're transient. You can try something different every year."

▲ **Summer pots ablaze:** with *Cerinthe major* 'Purpurascens' **(1)**, *Arctotis* 'Killerton Rose' **(2)** and the penstemon 'Purple Bedder' tangled with *Catananche caerulea* 'Alba' **(3)**.

of the acers. But we also plant quite a lot of white cosmos and they will last until October. I think it's important always to have some white as a contrast."

They started off a number of their trees in containers, so that they could move them around for a year or two until they found the ideal position to plant them.

"Also there are still patches in the garden where the soil is very poor so we stand the trees on top of it in pots. Then we wanted some height on the patio and you can't dig into concrete so we put the *Cornus kousa* there in a pot. And we planted a Virginia creeper in a big barrel to cover the side of the house, again because you couldn't plant it through the patio.

"Certain plants, like the gunnera, are kept in check in a container" Ian points out. "They still look architectural, but they're not going to go mad. We bought our contorted willow at the same time as a friend, about five years ago, and she put hers in the ground. Ours is 5ft tall in the pot and hers is 25ft so she's continually hacking it back and she hates it, whereas we love ours.

"The charm of pots is they're transient. You can try something different every year. If a plant doesn't look its best, you just put it round the side of the house and forget it. And if you buy a plant on impulse, and it doesn't go anywhere else in the garden, you can always have it on the patio. There's lots of plants you've just got to have!"

This eagerness to try something fresh can be seen throughout this garden where pots of new plants are crammed into every available space. There are even a few small containers underneath the garden bench, holding treasured rock plants.

They are constantly trying out new species. "A recent survey said that the rose was everybody's favourite flower and, yes, it's great, but there are so many other flowers that are even more beautiful" says Ian. "I'm pleased that plants like coleus and dahlias and cannas are back in fashion: they're beautiful."

If their approach seems like a lot of work, that is the point. "Gardeners want a high maintenance garden because they enjoy gardening" explains Ian.

fresh
ways
with
fuchsias

Simplicity is the key to getting the most out of these beautiful plants, which are at home in both formal and traditional settings.

Many people take a dislike to fuchsias after seeing them crammed together in ranks of clashing colours at flower shows with no thought for grouping either by tones or varieties.

However, look at fuchsias individually, and their delicate beauty becomes unmistakable. This is why they make such good subjects for training as standards, which can be positioned on their own.

If you do want to use fuchsias in a mixed planting, it is best to keep the arrangement simple. Every plant has a different growth pattern, so the fewer species you use, the more likely you are to get them all looking good at once.

ODD NUMBERS BEST

In container gardening you can often group more than one container together for effect. The traditional cottage garden look used three different sizes of pot, or three different heights of planting – it is usually best to use odd numbers rather than even as they are easier to arrange.

The modern minimalist look, however, is for a number of same-size containers and same-height plants standing in a row rather than in a group, such as the 'Tom Thumb' fuchsias (above). These are an early, free-flowering variety with pink and purple flowers that grow only 15-30cm (6-12in) tall.

The 'dot pots' are made from a modern Italian terracotta called Terrachino. Before Terrachino pots are fired the clay is brushed to give them an instant aged

▲ **A modern line-up** of matching 'Tom Thumb' fuchsias forms a discreet hedge to a statue. The raffia bows knotted casually around each pot have the effect of pulling the whole arrangement together.

► **Hanging harmony** is achieved by interplanting two trailing pink 'Border Queen' fuchsias and two dusky purple verbenas – 'Splash' and the smaller-flowered 'Homestead Purple'.

◄ **A cascading standard fuchsia**, one of a pair by a front door, shows how well simplicity works. The soft pinks of fuchsia 'Annabel' look perfect against the white trellis and faded floor tiles.

▼ **White marble chippings** harmonise with the brushed silver surface of the container and reflect light upwards on to the fuschia blossoms.

look. The dot is just a decoration placed around the pot beneath the rim.

The exception to the rule that odd numbers look best is on the doorstep, where a pair of containers provides a balance to the door frame. The standard fuchsias used on the city doorstep (below left) show simple planting at its best. On this traditional tiled entrance, a pale fuchsia looks perfect where a brighter one would have looked brash.

In the hanging basket, just two different plants in variations of pinks and dusky purples are simple and harmonious. The handsome handmade wicker basket is suspended on rope supports, instead of the usual chains, to complete the soft country look of the setting. The basket is lined with plastic sheeting, pierced with holes before planting, to help stop the wicker from rotting.

GROWING TIPS

When choosing a bush fuchsia, look for one with a strong central stem and a good set of branches on alternate sides to give well-balanced, compact growth. If it is leggy and growing out of shape, it will struggle to get back to form.

Hardy fuchsias should be planted in John Innes No.3, which has more trace elements to keep plants going, mixed in equal quantities with multipurpose compost. Annual fuchsias do not need this extra boost.

Because they need moisture, fuchsias like some shade which helps to prevent the pot drying out.

◄ **Shades of mauve** and pink are enhanced by the lilac-grey mulch, which was not only used in the pot but also spread onto the ground at its base.

summer pastels for cool class

Soft colours in gentle harmonies enhance a terrace, a patio or a quiet corner of the garden on sunny days and long, balmy twilit evenings.

▼ **A gorgeous shaggy bouquet** of daisies, verbena and pretty trailing foliage, though carefully planned, looks as though it happened by accident.

Soft pastel colours that would look washed out in a Mediterranean setting make an impact in the softer light of the British summer. The subtle feel of the main arrangement featured (left) is enhanced by choosing plants with an informal shape. The tall centrepiece, *Pelargonium* 'Lady Plymouth', has clusters of small pink flowers which dot the cool pastel arrangement. This pelargonium is grown primarily for its foliage. Its triangular leaves, picked out by their irregular cream margins, provide structure in the pot. Crush a leaf and you will release a delicious minty, rose-lemon aroma.

Placed around the pelargonium are three plants of *Verbena* 'Freefall Purple', a new dwarf variety. These plants branch

▶ **Lime nicotiana** gives this subtle planting its height and structure. Creamy petunias provide the next tier, and these in turn are underplanted with a petticoat of frilly foliage.

outwards as they grow, adding width to balance the pelargonium's height.

Alternating with the verbenas are Swan River daisies (*Brachyscome* 'Jumbo Misty Lilac'). Their leggy, slender stems, fine feathery foliage and pale mauve flowers mingle with the verbena's drumstick clusters of tiny blooms to form a frilly ruff, all but obscuring the grey clay pot.

EXTENDING THE SEASON

- **Early to midsummer** Plant the main arrangement on the left for a frothy summer display.
- **Late summer** When the geranium in the centre of the pot is past its best replace it with *Helictotrichon sempervirens*, a tall blue grass that will keep the cool arrangement looking good until early autumn.

early to midsummer

late summer

Three creeping Jennies (*Lysimachia nummularia* 'Aurea') trail down the side of the pot. Their long stems bear heart-shaped leaves and tiny single cup-shaped yellow flowers.

The daisies will bloom all summer if deadheaded regularly. When the pot has finished flowering, move the creeping Jennies to a damp border, where they will form a golden evergreen carpet.

LIME AND VANILLA

As an alternative to the blues and pinks of the main arrangement, you could try a palette of pale limes and buttery yellows (above).

A dwarf-flowering tobacco plant (*Nicotiana* 'Saratoga Lime'), which has fresh lime-white blooms, forms the centrepiece. This tall upright plant is surrounded by a halo of *Petunia* 'Frenzy Buttercream', a new variety of veined petunia.

Trailing over the edge of the container are the frothy foliage and yellow flowers of *Bidens ferulifolia* and Indian mint (*Satureja douglasii*), whose leaves and tiny white flowers smell minty when crushed.

The bright orangey red terracotta pot was muted with a colour-wash of diluted emulsion paint.

◄ **A bold Vicenza urn** makes maximum impact against a background of evergreen foliage. The arrangement stands in front of a border, in which are planted a few of the same violas (Penny Orange Sunrise 2000) as used in the pot. This helps to create a sense of continuity between the container and the wider garden.

In this striking arrangement, three gazanias are planted between three *Heliotropium* 'Atlanta', another compact plant but one that has dark green foliage and spectacular deep purple flowers.

Effectively softening the silhouette of these two rather erect plants are three *Diascia* 'Red Start', their trailing stems bearing clusters of pinky crimson flowers. Tucked among them are three *Polygonum* 'Pink Bubbles', whose tiny pink clover-like flowers will inch their way around the arrangement and trail down the side as the season progresses.

BOLD AS BRASS

In contrast to the soft, silhouette of the main arrangement is a harder-edged planting (above left). The colours are still hot and bright, but the overall shape is largely determined by the robust foliage of the begonias. These plants look terrific in containers, particularly the large, blowzy, rose-like blooms of the double-flowered varieties.

The Panorama series of begonias, such as 'Scarlet', planted here, are brash, showy, trailing plants, which produce abundant loose double flowers. Together with the violas and snapdragons (*Antirrhinum* 'La Bella'), they produce a riot of clashing blooms all summer long.

The La Bella hybrids flower longer than traditional snapdragons. Their red petals contrast strikingly with their white throats and work well within a hot arrangement.

vibrant colours fill a long hot summer

Contrasting colours, such as crimsons and golds or oranges and purples (see pages 42-43) can be teamed successfully for a really bold, exciting display. Choose the shades you mix carefully to balance the intensity of the hues.

The Kiss variety of the large daisy-like gazania, used in the main arrangement on the right,

Hot colours that shimmer in the sun are the surest announcement that summer has arrived at last. And they will continue to make a bright splash even when other plants have faded.

has a neat habit and prolific flowering which makes it ideal for containers. Its strappy green leaves have the unexpected bonus of an attractive underside,

flashing silvery grey as they move in the wind. But its flowers make the real statement with their richly bronzed orange-red petals and almost black centres.

EXTENDING THE SEASON

• **Early summer** Plant an early poppy, such as the corn poppy, *Papaver rhoeas*, in the centre of the pot and surround it with gazanias and purple lobelia.
• **Midsummer** Put together the main arrangement below, with heliotrope, gazanias and diascia.
• **Late summer** Replace the diascia around the edge of the pot with purple autumn-flowering pansies.

early summer

midsummer

late summer

▼ **Dark purples and oranges** look stunning against lush bottle-green foliage. The terracotta pot, all but hidden by the trailing stems of *Diascia* and *Polygonum*, is big enough to support such an exuberant arrangement.

a subtle blend of harmonies

Shades of blue are easy on the eye and make a restful scheme to soothe and calm the spirit. Add a little mauve, highlights of white and toning foliage, and you have a delightful combination.

Choosing complementary colours for your plants and the settings for your containers will help to create a feeling of space in a garden. Blue is the key to both these summery arrangements, working as the dominant flower colour in the main display on the right, and, in the colour of the pots, as a foil for the paler blooms of the alternative suggestion (below right).

Agastache 'Honey Bee Blue' is the focal point of the planting on the right, its long whorls of soft blue flowers standing like spires in the centre of the arrangement. Three *Scaevola* 'Purple Fan' at the base add width to balance the agastache's height. An Australian native, scaevola will grow outdoors all year round in the warmer parts of Britain and its sprawling habit means it soon spills over the hard edges of pots.

In between the scaevola are six Regatta Series lobelias: three 'Sky Blue' and three 'Sapphire'. This group of trailing lobelia comes into bloom much earlier than other cultivars and flowers reliably throughout the summer.

A MATCH MADE IN HEAVEN

The agastache sets a deep tone for the arrangement, but for a lighter feel pastel shades are ideal. Pure white can be a harsh colour in the garden, but when it is mixed with delicate shades of pink it creates a soft and pretty colour scheme. The matching plantings in the deep blue plastic pots below have a romantic touch reminiscent of a summer wedding bouquet.

Here, a fountain of the palest pink argyranthemum daisies, 'Summer Stars Pink', is dotted with tendrils of arching *Gaura lindheimeri* 'Siskiyou Pink', with its dark pink butterfly-shaped blooms. They rest on a delicate froth of baby's breath (*Gypsophila paniculata* 'Snowflake') and *Sutera* (formerly *Bacopa*) 'Blizzard'.

▲ **Lilac, white and pink** are the sugar almond colours of summer. Plants with slender stems and feathery foliage, such as scaevola, daisies and gaura, allow the pastel shades of their delicate flowers to predominate.

▼ **Pale petals and slender shapes** are given greater definition when positioned in front of a dark, uniform background. A door or wall painted in another complementary colour would also make a perfect setting for these delicate plantings.

◀ **Think of foliage** as well as flowers. Here the blue spires of the agastache are balanced by the blue and purple flowers around the base, while the mint-scented agastache foliage, which dominates the centre of the arrangement, has a toning bluish hue.

fresh ways with patio roses

You do not need a garden to grow roses – smaller varieties flourish in containers so you can enjoy their colours and perfume anywhere you fancy.

You can grow any rose in a container since just confining its roots will have a dwarfing effect, but for the best effect, especially in small containers, choose one of the many patio roses that have been developed especially for the purpose. They are bushy and compact, will bloom steadily all summer as long as you keep deadheading them, and many of them are as fragrant as they are beautiful.

To bring a patio rose up to sniffing distance, try planting it in a table-top container such as the pretty jug (right) so you can enjoy it over tea in the garden. Because patio roses are grown in fields and then transferred to containers for sale – they are containerised, not container grown – this means they have quite a large rootball. If you want to use a small container like this jug, start early with a very young rose which will have a smaller rootball and grow it on.

The narrow silver buckets in the main picture will be almost filled by the rose's rootball, but the depth allows plenty of room for the roots to spread downwards. The trailing campanula is *Campanula poscharskyana*, the best variety for containers because it will keep going all summer and well into autumn. Other popular campanulas, such as Blue or White Clip, do not last as long. Another beautiful pink patio rose is 'Queen Mother', which flowers from May onwards with soft pink blooms that look like a dog rose when they open.

GROWING TIPS

Patio roses are fully hardy. Plant them in 50:50 John Innes No.3 and multipurpose compost. Scrape off the top inch of compost every six months and top-dress with more John Innes, adding a slow-release fertiliser. Do this in spring for the summer and in autumn to see it through the winter.

Patio roses need pruning in mid March or early April to encourage the new growth that will bear flowers. If you are buying one from a garden centre, check whether it has been pruned, otherwise nip off all the tops; if you buy from a nursery, it will probably have been done already. Like their larger cousins, patio roses are susceptible to mildew and black spot and may need spraying.

◀ **A jug planted with roses** makes the perfect centrepiece for a summery tea on the terrace. This sunny yellow patio rose is called 'Rosanova'. It can be grown indoors or outside and soon becomes bushy and free-flowering.

▶ **Perfect roses** need only the setting of a beautiful old terracotta pot to set them off. This is 'Flower Carpet White', a ground-cover rose which is small enough to grow on a patio or balcony.

◄ **With a little ingenuity** you can even grow a rose in a hanging basket. Choose a ground-cover rose with a spreading habit, such as 'Suffolk', and let it tumble in a cascade of glowing colour.

Its velvety petals **heady with scent**, cherished by gardeners and chosen by lovers, the rose represents all the **brave beauty** of summer.

◄ **Silver buckets** stand like a guard of honour at a wedding. Each holds one patio rose 'Lady Love' and some trailing campanula. Formal containers like these look best with very simple arrangements.

KEY FACTS

• **Patio roses** are a cross between a miniature rose and a floribunda, producing a compact variety that is particularly well suited to being grown in containers.

• **Miniature roses** have a denser form and a smaller root system than patio roses. They grow to only around 15cm (6in), which makes them suitable for window boxes. While often kept as indoor plants, many varieties are hardy enough for the outdoors.

• **Ground-cover roses** such as the Flower Carpet and County Series are compact enough to use in tubs. They carry their flowers in clusters and are repeat flowering.

173

a display to last all year

If you have room for only one container, fill it with a clever mix of hardy plants and it will provide pleasure from season to season for years to come.

Plant your all-year-round container to this plan, which shows each plant as it looks at its peak. Assemble the display in early spring, when all these plants will be available, using bulbs that are already sprouting.

- **Summer interest** Allium karataviense (**1**); flowers of Heuchera var. diversifolia 'Palace Purple' (**2**); Hosta 'Blue Wedgwood' (**3**); Lobelia cardinalis (**4**)
- **Autumn interest** foliage of heuchera; houseleek (Sempervivum 'Spring Mist') (**5**); ivy (**6**)
- **Winter interest** Christmas box (Sarcococca confusa) (**7**); Daphne odorata 'Aureomarginata' (**8**)
- **Spring interest** Anemone blanda (**9**); Aubrieta 'Argenteovariegata' (**10**); Bleeding heart (Dicentra eximia) (**11**); Narcissus 'Tête-à-Tête' (**12**); tulips (Tulipa 'Red Riding Hood') (**13**)

Not everyone has the time or space to plant a range of pots and to change them as the seasons turn and plants come into flower then fade.

But there is another option. A large container, such as this stone trough, 65x30x30cm (26x12x12in), can be planted with a range of shrubs, perennials and bulbs (see illustration, above right) just like a garden border. And, like a labour-saving garden, once planted it will produce a changing display over many months and delight you again over the following years.

THE PLANTING RECIPE

Two winter-flowering shrubs, Christmas box (Sarcococca) and daphne, give the display a backbone of attractive evergreen foliage.

Behind them is a row of perennials whose tall flowers easily rise above the shrubs in late spring and summer. The rose-pink flowers of a bleeding heart appear first in spring, followed by the pinky white globes of an allium and the majestic spires of a crimson lobelia towering above the trough in summer (see main picture, right).

Scattered in the middle are the tiny bulbs that look so pretty in spring. There are four blue Anemone blanda and one clump of early red tulips with bluish maroon patterned leaves.

Two bunches of multi-headed daffodils add splashes of bright yellow, one in the centre of the pot and one in the back left to balance the tulips on the right. The new shoots of these bulbs will begin to nudge through in winter, signalling that spring is just around the corner.

The corners are planted with different foliage plants: trailing ivy at three corners, a blue-leaved hosta, silvery aubretia and the spreading rose-pink rosettes of a houseleek. As the planting matures, the houseleek will creep round the edges from the back right.

A magnificent foliage plant, a heuchera, dominates the centre of the trough, with its big, rounded, glistening purple leaves. It also throws up dainty sprays of tiny white flowers on upright stems in summer, turning to stiff seed heads in autumn.

GROWING TIPS

Use a good multipurpose compost for the trough and include a handful of slow-release fertiliser granules when you assemble the display. Prune the daphne and sarcococca after their berries have finished and refresh the top 2.5cm (1in) of compost each spring.

If you would like to make your own stone trough – see pages 264-265

▼ **The display reaches up in summer,** with the towering stems of a scarlet lobelia. All the interest spurts out of the container, with the arching tendrils of the heuchera and lavender buds of the hosta springing from the left hand side of the pot.

▼ **The deep purple leaves of the heuchera** fill the body of the pot in autumn, with the ivies tumbling over the sides. The heuchera's white summer flowers have matured into seed heads that add highlights above the display.

▲ **Daffodils glow brightly** in the centre of the trough in spring. The lilac flowers of a creeping aubretia begin to soften the new edges of the container, while a tulip at the front begins to push out its red blooms.

◄ **Winter flowers** are provided by the Christmas box, with its small white flowers visible in the background, and the daphne in front. Both shrubs produce berries after their flowers and those on the daphne are poisonous.

175

a spire of summer climbers

Think ahead and plant in spring, so that by the time the first frosts have passed you can be well on the way to having a blooming totem pole of colour and fragrance to cheer you through summer.

The most popular variety of sweet pea, *Lathyrus odoratus*, lives up well to its name. *Odoratus* is Latin for 'well-scented', and these flowers have been prized by gardeners for their delicious fragrance for centuries.

Since many modern sweet peas have been bred primarily for their colour, the varieties with the best scent are usually the oldest. However, the newer Spencer Type cultivars used in the two arrangements opposite all have fragrant flowers and are available in every shade and colour, except for yellow.

The sugar almond shades of pale lavender, soft pink and pure white in the main arrangement (centre) make a delicate display, which would work well in a cottage garden setting, surrounded by other pastel blooms.

Sweet pea flowers open in succession, so planting another climber to scramble alongside them will help to ensure that your wigwam blooms throughout the season. To extend the flowering season, morning

▲ **Enjoy the scent of sweet peas** all summer long from just one container. Deadheading or cutting the flowers for the house will encourage new blooms to develop.

glory (*Ipomoea*) makes a perfect companion for sweet peas, as the plants will grow together without one smothering the other. Each morning glory bloom only lasts for one day, but the plant will produce a mass of flowers throughout summer and into early autumn.

In this arrangement the heart-shaped leaves of *Ipomoea tricolor* 'Heavenly Blue' add substance to the finer stems of the sweet peas. As the sweet peas begin to wane, its clear blue trumpet-shaped flowers, with their distinctive white throats, will open.

SAPPHIRES AND RUBIES

For a more vivid display with stronger colours choose sweet peas in the jewel colours of purples, blues and cerises. The column of flowers in the variation (far right) makes a sensual focal point on a bend in a path or at the edge of a patio, where its fragrance can be appreciated as you walk by. The tall arrangement will also fill a gap in a border or balance a group of pots filled with shorter plants.

ESSENTIAL SUPPORT

- **Many climbing plants,** such as sweet peas, can be grown very successfully in containers, but their slender stems will need support. Position the pot by a wall with trellis, or give them a sturdy frame, such as a twiggy wigwam, to scramble up.
- **For a more contemporary look** choose a straight-sided pot, a sleek slate mulch and ultra modern stakes, such as the shiny metal spirals supporting a climbing bougainvillea below.

To complement these darker sweet peas, you could also plant an ipomoea with flowers in a deeper shade than 'Heavenly Blue'. The red or purple common morning glory (*I. purpurea*) would make a good companion.

Both morning glory and sweet pea seeds need to be planted in small pots in spring and germinated indoors or under glass. Once the young plants are established they may be transplanted into their final container, but it is best to keep them protected until all danger of frost has passed. By this time they should also have started climbing up their supports, and will be less vulnerable to damage from the wind.

◀ **Morning glory** earned its name because its flowers open during the cooler part of the day and close when it gets too hot. Some varieties of ipomoea open in the morning and fade in the early afternoon, others open in the evening and close the following midday.

▲ **Add height to a border** and fragrant appeal to the path beside it with a tower of sweet peas and morning glory. A deep pot, such as this giant long tom, is essential for these plants, which put out deep roots. It also balances the proportions of the tall arrangement.

Weave your own cane wigwam – see pages 234-235

A stylish bucket of ivy-leaved geraniums bridges the seasons. The white flowers recall the apple blossom of spring while the pink ones draw the eye to the ripening apples behind.

► **A simple way to group pots** is to gather them into one container. It works particularly well if you can find one as pretty as this old milk crate, loaded with 'Tip Top' geraniums.

►► **A touch of the Mediterranean** is easy to conjure up using ranks of red geraniums on a whitewashed wall.

fresh ways with geraniums

With a flowering season that stretches for months, happily tolerant of being allowed to dry out and with a vast range of varieties to choose from, the geranium is deservedly the king of container plants.

Geraniums epitomise the atmosphere of summer holidays in Italy and Greece with hot sun and blue skies. Even in a cooler climate, the ranks of scarlet geraniums in the stunning courtyard (above right) create the illusion of sunshine on the dullest day.

The simplicity of the planting – 60 identical plants in plastic pots – works perfectly against the plain white wall. Because it reflects the sun that they love, white is the perfect background for geraniums; they never stand out as well against red brick.

Bright red geraniums are the choice to make if you want a Mediterranean look, but in the softer light of a northern summer, quieter tones can be equally attractive. Although you will often see geraniums mixed with other summer bedding flowers, their strong colours mean that they often look most splendid on their own.

The softer arrangement (left) is a reminder that hanging baskets do not always have to be attached to a wall. The silver bucket and chain makes an unexpected but harmonious contrast to the pale bark of the Worcester Pearmain apple tree, and the pastel flowers blend softly into the summer foliage.

If you want to mix geraniums with other plants, stay with shades of a single colour, for instance, by mixing a mauve flowered geranium with some purple verbena. Or you could try a red geranium with mimulus and red lobelia for a truly dramatic effect.

GROWING TIPS

Geraniums thrive in direct sun and you need to choose any planting partners with care: trailing lobelia, for example, needs regular watering and will suffer in the dry conditions that geraniums love. Deadhead all geraniums regularly and pull off any dead leaves.

Geraniums are not really hardy plants, but they can be overwintered outdoors in a sheltered city garden. Here they will harden off and flower even better the next year.

KEY FACTS

Geraniums (*Pelargoniums*) are strongly formed plants, some more upright than others, which bloom with double or single flowers.

• **Zonal pelargoniums** are bushy and upright, with horseshoe-shaped markings on the leaves and single and double flowers.

• **Regal pelargoniums** have enormous flowers, with or without petal markings, and are usually single. They grow to 46cm (18in) and are suited to large containers.

• **Ivy-leaved pelargoniums** have single or double flowers. This trailing form is ideal for hanging baskets and for edging containers.

• **Scented-leaved pelargoniums** are a more shrubby form. Typically grown for their aromatic leaves, which vary in size and shape, they usually have small, single pale pink flowers.

• **Angel pelargoniums**, sometimes known as 'Tip-Top', are dense plants with delicate two-tone flowers.

▶ **Velvety purple petunias** accent the paler tones of a 'Felicia' musk rose, blush pink nicotianas and their ornate pinky terracotta pot. The enchanting miniature version without the rose, planted in a seed pan, reinforces the theme.

EXTENDING THE SEASON

early summer

midsummer

late summer

early summer

midsummer

late summer

• **Early summer** A pot of stocks (*Matthiola*) in soft purples and pinks will give fragrance from late spring into summer. Team them with a small pot of white freesias.

• **Midsummer** Plant the main arrangement on the right.

• **Late summer** Remove the nicotianas and the rose as they fade and replace them with a white gardenia – a deliciously scented evergreen shrub. Repeat the colour theme with a small pot of pink and white dianthus.

the heady scent of summer blooms

The sweet-smelling perfume of roses and other fragrant flowers wafting gently on a summer breeze is a delight. Reap the pleasure with these glorious container ideas.

Nothing proclaims summer better than the wonderful fragrance of flowers. Container gardeners do not have to miss out on the delightful scent of roses: while patio varieties are the obvious choice for growing in pots (see pages 172-173), the more blowzy and heavily scented border varieties will do just as well if you take care to meet their needs. All shrub roses like to put out deep roots, so make sure that your container is at least 60cm (2ft) tall and that it is filled with a good rich compost.

For a sweet scent, choose any of the hybrid musk roses, all of which are renowned for their long, graceful growth and delicate colours. 'Felicia' – the centrepiece in the main arrangement (left) – is one of the finest examples. It is a compact, bushy grower with silvery pink flowers, which bloom profusely in early summer and intermittently until autumn, and contrasting dark, shiny leaves.

Purple *Petunia* 'Priscilla' and pale pink scented tobacco plants (*Nicotiana* Domino Series) surround the base of the rose and fill a smaller separate pot. These annuals will provide colour and scent throughout summer, when the rose is at its best. Lift them out when flowering has finished and move the main pot to a less prominent spot within the garden until the rose is ready to bloom again next summer. Prune the rose carefully in winter by taking off half the previous season's growth to retain its bushy shape.

INDULGE YOUR SENSES

Make the most of a secluded corner by surrounding a seat with scented plants to create a pleasant retreat for a balmy afternoon, when the flowers' perfume will be most distinct.

The alternative arrangement (right) teams a long tom of 'Journey's End' lilies with a shallow bowl filled with other fragrant plants. Three varieties of alpine pinks, or *Dianthus* – 'Brilliant Star' (white), 'India Star' (ruby red) and 'Pixie Star' (lavender pink) – blend their sweet scent with the aroma of variegated 'Silver Posie' thyme.

▲ **Clashing reds and pinks** make a hot summer display. A striking red seat picks out the common colour of the ruby-veined, pink-speckled 'Journey's End' lilies and the mixed alpine pinks.

ringing the changes

Reflect the cycle of the seasons in a single container by choosing just one kind of hardy shrub or evergreen as a permanent backbone for your pot, and planting colourful variations around it throughout the year.

Simply by planning ahead you can keep a single container looking its colourful best all year long. With a permanent plant as the basis of your scheme, a succession of seasonal variations will add fresh interest as the months go by.

Choosing the right pot is important if you want an arrangement to last all year. It must be frost-proof and should provide plenty of space for the roots of the permanent plant to spread.

START IN SUMMER

French lavender (*Lavandula stoechas*) is the backbone of the main arrangement on the right and will remain in the pot all year round. Its dense flowerheads are a deep purple, with rosy purple bracts perching like butterflies at their tips. Surround the fragrant stems with pretty blooms in toning colours by adding a miniature pink rose in front of the lavender and purple violas around the edge.

As the seasons change, change the planting (top right). Vary the colours of the seasonal plants to complement the lavender as it shifts from its regal purple when in bloom to the silvery foliage later in the year.

Include a slow-release fertiliser when you first plant up the container and add a little fresh compost each time you change the plants.

◀ **Focus on the front of the pot,** and away from the pruned lavender, by planting low-growing crocus and foliage. Nestle a few pine cones in the display for a wintry effect.

- **Summer** Plant pink roses in the centre of the pot and purple violas at the front.
- **Autumn** Replace the roses and violas with rosy pink and white ornamental cabbages.
- **Winter** Prune the lavender, remove the cabbages and add silvery plants to highlight the lavender foliage: pale lilac crocus, silvery *Senecio cineraria* and variegated ivies.
- **Spring** Return to a darker purple as the lavender buds begin to show, by filling the space in front of the shrub with *Iris reticulata*.

summer   autumn

spring   winter

◄ **Pick out the purple** of the French lavender with a frilly collar of matching violas. Miniature pink roses provide substance to the arrangement and echo the rotund shape of the big-bellied pot.

183

▲ **A mixed group** of pink busy lizzies and purple lobelia brings a refreshing cottage garden look to a formal setting. Their relaxed shapes soften the firm outlines of the tiered box ball, bamboos, ferns and acanthus.

fresh ways with busy lizzies

For colour that will glow all summer long, even in the gloomiest basement, no plant is so rewarding – and so foolproof – as a simple busy lizzie.

Busy lizzies (*Impatiens*) are often under-rated by gardeners. They are associated with council planting and garish pub hanging baskets, where they have been chosen because they are so easy to grow. But they make wonderfully good-natured, long-lasting container plants, and have the inestimable benefit that they thrive in shade: a pot of white busy lizzies will create a pool of light in the darkest corner. Just consider grouping and texture as you plant them and you can enjoy their many good qualities.

If you want to arrange busy lizzies in a group, use three different sizes of matching containers and go from pale to bright, drawing the eye to a dramatic climax in the largest pot. In the main picture (above) the pots are stepped up in size like building blocks, with the smallest one planted with the palest pink flowers, the medium pot with lilac and

◀ **Pots of busy lizzies** make bold brush strokes of colour in the shade of a large shrub. By keeping the planting simple, the vibrant combination of pink, lilac and coral works well.

▼ **Lighting can transform** a simple container arrangement of a single variety of busy lizzies into something special. This candleholder is an old Christmas decoration, recycled to add a 'table setting' feel to an outside display.

◀ **For interesting combinations** look outside the usual container plants. Here a border perennial, *Alchemilla mollis*, rubs shoulders with elegant lilies and modest busy lizzies to make a display that will bloom in shade.

KEY FACTS

Impatiens are sold mostly as annual bedding plants, although there is a shrubby form known as *Impatiens* 'New Guinea' (above).
• The **'Super Elfin' Series** of *Impatiens walleriana* are low growing, but can also be used as trailers. The Tempo, Swirl and Accent Series all derive from this species and the colours range from pastels to shades of pink, orange and violet.

• **New Guinea** impatiens have larger leaves, with mainly single flowers but there is a double form known as 'Double Impatiens'. Colours include rose, salmon, lavender, white and many bi-colours; 'Spectra' also has variegated leaves.
• **Dwarf cultivars,** such as *Impatiens balsamina* 'Tom Thumb' grow to just 30cm (12in), with big double flowers in white, pink, scarlet and violet.

the largest pot with the strongest colour – an orangey red – underplanted with trailing *Sutera* (*Bacopa*) 'Snowflake'.

A RING OF COLOUR

Another way of using busy lizzies is to make them the frame for a focal point, such as a group of lilies. A good starting point is to find a container that catches your eye in the garden centre and to decide where you will put it. You can then wheel it around the centre while you select the plants that will suit the pot and the position.

The arrangement at the top shows the very dark green glaze of the pot mirrored in three shades and textures of foliage. It starts with four pink-centred white-flowered *Impatiens* 'New Guinea', which have deep green leaves to pick up the green of the pot. These alternate with four *Alchemilla mollis*, whose velvety foliage helps to soften the stiffer leaves of the busy lizzies. Together they make a wonderful setting for the dramatic centrepiece of 'Casa Blanca' lilies, whose spiky leaves add yet another variation of foliage.

GROWING TIPS

Plant busy lizzies in well-drained multipurpose compost in spring after the risk of frost has passed. Pack lots of plants into the container as they will flower best when pot bound.

Busy lizzies prefer dappled sunshine to full sun and will flower reliably in shade. Pinch out the tips of the young plants to encourage them to bush up. Water them regularly and give them a weekly liquid feed. Deadhead busy lizzies frequently and they will continue to flower into autumn.

▶ **A clump of purple bearded irises** flourish in a former fisherman's bucket. In front are the 'Storm' variety of petunias, bred to retain their flowers in rain and wind. A potted cordyline and a small bay tree also grow happily at this sheltered end of the terrace.

▼ **Silvery sea kale** is grown for the kitchen in a raised bed, mulched with cockleshells, "after we'd eaten the cockles" says Susan. Assorted pots of sedums and sempervivums add their toning foliage colours.

▶ **Susan keeps her containers** on the terrace beside the house, as the building offers some protection from the wind. Nearest the sea are tubs of tough agaves, *Euphorbia milii* (crown of thorns) and other succulents, while more delicate plants such as lavender and geraniums snuggle in the centre.

in the teeth of a sea breeze

For more than 20 years, Susan Campbell grew only fruit and vegetables in her seaside garden in Hampshire, plundering the Solent coast for seaweed to use as a mulch. Already the author of a number of cookbooks, she became an authority on the English kitchen garden. But when her sons grew up and there was less need for a bumper harvest, she turned her creative energy into "making the place look a bit nicer. One of the things I hate is lazy people with country cottages who have nothing but grass. A cottage needs setting off with flowers and shrubs."

Her garden sits on the very edge of the beach, only prevented from actually slipping into the sea by a stretch of rocky sea defences she has built, so the first need was for a shelter belt. Along the shoreline ▶

187

◄ **A houseleek** has spread in a low mound to fill this shallow pie dish, with its pretty fluted edge.

◄ **Seed trays and cuttings** keep the garden supplied with new plants. They start out in the greenhouse and are moved onto the terrace when they are robust enough to survive.

◄ **The fleshy leaves** of the spiky agaves and the maroon *Aeonium arboreum* protects them from the drying effect of the salt breezes. A pretty pottery mulch helps to cut down moisture loss from the compost.

Susan has planted a striking row of foamy pink tamarisk, trained as standards, rising out of clipped rounded bushes of grey *Atriplex halimus*. "The theme is the sea rolling in" she explains. "The halimus is the waves and the tamarisk is the foam."

Her container garden stands on a sheltered terrace by the kitchen door and grew slowly. "It started with herbs in pots, put out there for the kitchen. Because I had a dog, I had to raise them up to stop him peeing on them and I began to realise I could make sorts of pyramids using bits of tree trunk. We had had to cut down a tree so there were plenty of thick slices available."

At the windy end of the terrace, nearest the sea, are tubs of succulents including the giant maroon *Aeonium arboreum* 'Arnold Schwarzkopff' and an impressive agave, which are taken into the greenhouse in winter.

" **The containers get changed around every so often** because something is in flower and something else has stopped and you want to see the thing that is in flower."

◄ **A wooden jetty** stretches over Susan's craggy sea defences. In between the rocks she has planted pockets of seaside plants such as thrift and yellow-horned poppies.

"This relay race begins, bringing things on in the greenhouse and putting them out as soon as they are ready and the weather isn't too awful."

◄ **Plants and pottery are interwoven.** A pink-patterned fragment **(1)** is teamed with a red-edged houseleek and a twiggy limonium. Broken shards **(2)** are softened by an alpine pink.

▲ **Old sinks are recycled** into rock gardens. Among the plants are tiny treasures, from seashells to fragments of china, brought back from Susan's frequent beachcombing expeditions.

"The agave came from Ecuador – I found it when I was on holiday – and it keeps on having babies. Carrying it is the big problem."

In the centre of the terrace are slightly more tender plants such as geraniums, heliotrope, lavender, trailing blue lobelia, petunias and stocky alliums. Tubs of alpine strawberries and bulbs, including irises and the gladioli-like *Schizanthus*, or 'poor man's orchid', are placed at the innermost end, sheltered from the south-west wind off the sea.

In time, the container display on Susan's terrace has grown more and more elaborate. "I got a greenhouse for my 60th birthday and from that moment on realised what an asset they are." It enables her to raise more young plants and fill even more containers. "All the geraniums are grown from seeds or cuttings. I just experiment and see what likes it out there, rather than buying plants."

Among the tiers of containers on Susan's terrace are two round raised beds planted with silvery sea kale, and surrounded by a pattern of shells and stones, one representing the moon, the other a buoy. And by the backdoor is a collection of old sinks and troughs filled with the bounty of many beachcombing walks – shards of pottery,

shells, animal skulls and bones. These are all interwoven with common shoreline plants, such as biting stonecrop and thrift, as well as miniature alpines and tiny conifers. When her grandson comes to visit Susan tells him stories weaving in all the different objects.

"The containers get changed around every so often, because something is in flower and something else has stopped and you want to see the thing that is in flower. Or one plant is clashing with another, or has grown too big, or died. So you keep moving them: that's very important. I'm not consciously a container gardener – I just think I'll try something."

◄ **A medley of mints** makes a pretty display. Mints spread fast on runners, so plant them singly in separate pots to prevent them from swamping your other herbs.

bundles of herbs for fragrance and flavour

Herbs enhance so many dishes: grow your own favourites and keep them fresh to hand close to the kitchen.

Mixed herbs look pretty and provide delicious fresh additions to salads, soups and all kinds of other dishes. Keeping a pot in a sunny spot outside the kitchen door makes it easy to snip a sprig of sage or a handful of fresh basil for your cooking when you need it – in fact, using herbs is the best way to keep the plants bushy and compact.

A pot of herbs also makes an attractive and aromatic feature on the patio, so choose varieties that will give a mixture of colour, scent, shape and flavour. A herb pot, like the one used in the main arrangement here will hold a variety of herbs, and is similar to a strawberry pot, but with cups sticking out from the sides to support the herbs.

A CULINARY TOWER

Choose the herbs you use most of and position floppy or trailing species in the side holes and bushy plants in the top. The large terracotta pot used in the arrangement (right) has chives and the silvery curry plant in the top. The holes in the side contain catnip, coriander, variegated lemon balm, lemon thyme, common and golden marjoram, oregano, peppermint, variegated pineapple sage and white horehound.

A small jar over-spilling with a single pretty herb – in this case thyme – makes a charming accompaniment to the main arrangement. This would also be a good way of growing rampant mints.

OUTSIDE THE KITCHEN DOOR

Growing herbs in a hanging basket is another good way to keep them handy for the house. Dill, basil, prostrate varieties of rosemary and thyme all work well in culinary hanging baskets, where they tumble over the edges.

You can plant more densely in containers than in the ground. The basket in the alternative planting (top right) is brimming with herbs, including bergamot, camomile (with its white, daisy-like flowers), chives, feverfew, variegated lemon balm and lemon thyme, mints, oregano, parsley, sages and other thymes.

When leafy herbs die down in autumn, you may want to replace them with more wintry flavours, such as rosemary and sage.

How to plant a successful herb pot – see pages 230-231

▶ **For the freshest possible flavour,** hang a herb basket where you can pick a few leaves as you cook. Remember to keep the basket well-watered, especially if it is in a sheltered spot, out of the rain.

GREAT HERBS FOR CONTAINERS

- **Basil** cinnamon; lemon; lettuce leaved; liquorice; Minette; Red Rubin; sweet; Thai
- **Chives** common; garlic
- **Lemon balm** common (*Melissa*); golden (*M. officinalis* 'All Gold'); variegated (*M. officinalis* 'Aurea')
- **Oregano** compact (*Origanum vulgare* 'Compactum'); golden (*O. vulgare* 'Aureum'); variegated (*O. vulgare* 'Variegatum')
- **Parsley** Curlina; moss curled; plain leaved
- **Sage** common; golden (*Salvia officinalis* 'Icterina'); purple (*S. officinalis* 'Purpurascens'); tricoloured (*S. officinalis* 'Tricolor')
- **Thyme (dwarf and creeping forms)** 'Bertram Anderson' (lemon scented, golden); 'Doone Valley' (gold variegated); wild (*Thymus serpyllum*); woolly (*Thymus pseudolanuginosus*); **(bushy forms)** garden (*Thymus* 'Porlock')

◀ **The keen cook** would use every one of the 13 herbs in this arrangement. If you have just a few favourites, plant a smaller herb pot, with fewer holes, or add a splash of colour with some edible flowers (see page 194)

191

◄ **The colours of Mediterranean cooking** provided by the aubergine, peppers and tomatoes are enriched by a gold-rimmed pot with a Greek feel to its decoration.

Choose your plants and containers wisely and you will be surprised how easy it is to raise a crop of summer vegetables in pots.

All vegetables need a good, general-purpose compost with plenty of nutrients if they are to produce a tempting harvest. Most also need room in the pot for deep roots or plenty of space to spread sideways.

ROOTS AND SHOOTS

The main arrangement on the right contains root vegetables – 'Red Ace' beetroots and maincrop 'Senior' carrots, under-planted with beans. To give them a good root run they are planted in a deep half-barrel.

Their harvest may be buried, but the beetroots and carrots give foliage interest as they grow. The crimson-tinted broad leaves of the beetroots mingle with the feathery green ones of the carrots behind the abundant and dominant bean foliage.

The beans chosen for this collection, dwarf runner bean 'Flamenco', hang down to soften the sides of the barrel.

an allotment
in a pot

Harvest a healthy crop of delicious vegetables by planting a mixture of family favourites that would grace any patio.

▼ **Enjoy a leafy abundance** while you wait for your crop to ripen. You can keep picking the beans until it's time to dig out the root vegetables.

▲ **Decorative and delicious,** beans bring pleasure with their delicate flowers and their crisp fresh flavour.

In early summer, orange and white flowers dot the foliage before the beans appear.

The beans can be picked over a period of several weeks. By the time they are over, in early autumn, and it is time to dismantle the pot, the carrots and beetroots will be ready to harvest.

Sow your seeds straight into the container in early spring or raise them in individual pots and put the arrangement together once they are established. The beans should be started off under glass, and planted out after the first frost.

THE TASTE OF SUMMER

If a Mediterranean flavour is more to your taste, and you have a sunny spot to site a container, you could grow the aubergine, peppers and tomatoes in the alternative arrangement on the left.

Trailing 'Tumbler' cherry tomatoes spill over the side of the golden pot, heavy with their fruit, while the 'Fruit 'n' Spice' dwarf pepper stands upright behind them.

With this variety, ripe red and yellow peppers grow on the same plant and add a slight chilli flavour and spicy kick to any dish. To complete the ratatouille mix, a purple and white aubergine, 'Mr Stripey', squeezes into the pot with its plump crop.

snip a few leaves for a salad

1

2

3

From a handful of seeds you can grow all kinds of different salad leaves to cut and cut again all summer long and put freshness on your plate.

Salad leaves are a pretty and practical alternative to bedding plants for a summer window box or free-standing trough. Loose-leaf varieties of lettuce with interesting or coloured leaves, either grown alone or mixed with other salad leaves, allow you to pick a portion at a time without ruining the main display.

To make the planting even more interesting, try adding plants with edible flowers, such as marigolds (*Calendula officinalis*) – particularly the double forms such as 'Fiesta Gitana' – nasturtiums or violas. For the best and quickest results, use a rich compost and feed the plants up to twice a week when they are in full growth.

In a large tub, even low-growing leaves will make an impact. The main collection

here (below) is packed into a plastic trough which looks pleasingly like an old lead planter.

The seedlings were grown in small pots and planted out in the

tub when they were still small, positioned for the best display of foliage colour and texture. You can pack the lettuces in tightly and then pick off single leaves as you need them.

One sowing should last throughout summer, provided the leaves are

▲ **Brighten your salads** with a few small flowers or edible petals. *Viola cornuta* (**1**) and marigolds (**2**) taste as good as they look. Delicate blue borage, *Borago officinalis* (**3**), also has a special affinity with Pimms.

picked regularly to keep the plants bushy – encouraging you to eat your greens.

SALAD ON THE SILL

If you want to bring your salad collection closer to your kitchen scissors, grow it in a window box, like the display on the right.

It is planted with the same mixture of leaves as the main arrangement, but 'Peach Schnapps', a new variety of nasturtium with two-tone flowers, has been added to trail over the front and sides, softening the edge of the box.

A wrought-iron window-box holder was fixed to the outside wall of the house so that the seedlings could be raised separately. When the plants were looking good and ready to enjoy, the box was dropped into position in the bracket.

◄ **A trough of fresh salad leaves** fits into any sunny spot. This one holds, from left to right, 'Mira', a red-blushed butterhead lettuce, 'Frisby', a frilly green variety, pale crinkly endive and the smaller leaves of lamb's lettuce and land cress.

▲ **An edible display in a window box** brings your salad within reach. Plant taller lettuces at the back, small cut and come again leaves in the middle and a pretty nasturtium – which can also be added to the salad – at the front.

OTHER DELICIOUS SALAD LEAVES

- **Summer lettuces** include red-leaved 'Redina' and radicchio 'Palla Rossa', frilly red or green-leaved Lollo and green 'Nevada', which is especially crispy.
- **Small varieties** of lettuce are the best choice for a modest container. Little Gem, a small Cos, and Tom Thumb, a small butterhead lettuce, both grow easily from seed.
- **Mixed salad leaves,** which combine different flavours, texture and colour, are sold under their own names by many seed companies. They produce leaves but no heart so it is easy to keep snipping a few as and when you need them.

soft fruits for a fresh summer pudding

▲ **Gooseberries, strawberries and redcurrants** look lovely and taste intensely sweet picked from your own plants.

Indulge your love of summer flavours by planting containers full of sweet berries and fruit, and pick the freshest of the bunch for luscious desserts.

You can enjoy the seasonal flavour of summer fruits picked fresh and juicy from your own bushes by choosing those that thrive in containers.

Soft-fruit bushes should be planted singly in large pots and grouped together for display. However, lowbush blueberries (bilberries) and strawberries can be planted at the base of standard 'lollipop' fruit bushes to cover the bare compost and hang down over the side of the pot.

For the best results, feed your plants every two weeks in spring and summer, and always keep the compost wet.

A SWEET COLLECTION

The larger pot in the main arrangement (far right) contains a standard gooseberry, 'Rolanda', underplanted with 'Elsanta' strawberries. It was planted in John Innes No.3 compost and will live quite happily in

its 60cm (2ft) pot for two or three years, but should then be transplanted to a 80cm (2ft 8in) container.

The complementary terracotta pot holds redcurrant, 'Redstart', which will produce some fruit in its first year and a substantial crop the next. It will thrive for three years in this pot, then need a larger one.

The strawberries will produce decorative runners after fruiting that will hang over the side of the pot to give late summer interest. It also has pretty autumn foliage, but trim off any leaves and runners before they rot. New leaves will start to grow the following spring.

Both the gooseberry and the redcurrant are late-maturing varieties, and in a normal year will ripen in July, after the strawberries.

EASY-GOING BERRIES

Blueberries are ideal candidates for containers as they do not make a strong root

system and need acid soil. The 'Bluecrop' variety (above) will live happily for many years in ericaceous compost. An extra pleasure of growing this blueberry in a container where you can see it is its brilliant yellow autumn foliage.

▲ **An intense blue glaze** that will accentuate the colour of the ripe berries makes this terracotta pot the ideal container for an established blueberry bush.

Strawberries make eye-catching fillers for large, solid-sided hanging baskets, the sort that dry out slowly. The height keeps the fruit off the ground where it won't pick up soil, and also makes it delightfully easy to spot any ripe berries.

▲ **Strawberries need sunshine** and a good circulation of fresh air for best results. Hanging the container from a bracket makes it easy to provide them with both.

◄ **Soft-fruit bushes** need plenty of room to grow. The gooseberry shares its pot with a strawberry that trails prettily over the edge. The redcurrant gets a pot of its own. Both pots were given a protective mulch of gravel.

197

fresh ways with petunias

With their slightly unkempt cottage garden look, petunias add a cheerful note to summer schemes and mingle easily with a variety of other plants.

▲ **A dramatic setting** shows off the brilliant trailing petunia 'Surfinia Pink Vein'. Here the striped *Yucca flaccida* 'Golden Sword' is centre stage, framed by petunias and the delicate flowers of *Nemesia* 'Confetti'. Orange gerberas, placed either side like spotlights, draw the eye to the display.

Plain or striped, veined or frilly, upright or trailing, single or double, the trumpet-shaped flowers of petunias will fill a pot or hanging basket with a mass of dependable colour from midsummer to the first winter frosts.

The original colours of petunias were strong and dominant – white, cream, pink, red, mauve and blue. But some of the newest strains have single flowers in gentle pastel shades that suit more restrained arrangements.

In the simple grouping on the right, the most vibrant element is the white and lime-green stripes of the half-barrel. The colours of the plants are intentionally and subtly low-key, although when the hosta flowers, its lilac-blue spire will add welcome height to the display.

After the petunias have died down, the hosta could be underplanted with yellow winter pansies, replaced the following spring with primroses to keep the creamy colour scheme going.

GROWING TIPS

Petunias will flower in the first year from seed, but for containers it is simpler to buy young plants. Plant them in multipurpose compost and give them plenty of drainage.

They can stand full sun and benefit from a liquid feed every two weeks once they start flowering. Keep dead-heading to encourage more flowers.

KEY FACTS

Most of today's petunias are derived from F1 hybrids:

• **The Multiflora group** grows to around 30cm (12in), is vigorous, large flowered and tolerant of poor weather. 'Delight', 'Carpet' and 'Duo' are semi-double, while 'Mirage' has the largest flowers. The Surfinia Series flowers extra vigorously.

• **The Grandiflora group,** including the 'Cloud', 'Pirouette' and 'Super Cascade' Series, has the largest flowers, but is not as bushy as the Multifloras and is less resilient to wet weather.

• **The Milliflora group** includes 'Million Bells' and 'Carillion', which produce masses of small flowers and are especially suitable for hanging baskets.

In a shady spot, the eye is drawn by the vertical stripes of the barrel, echoed in the stripy leaves of the hosta. The muted flowers of Petunia 'Cascade Yellow Eye', a new variety, add a more restful note.

add warmth with colour in autumn

► **Chrysanthemum plants** are best bought in flower or with fat, coloured buds, just ready to burst. Immature green buds may fail to open.

Chrysanthemums are available all year round, but they are at their best in autumn, when the pot-grown dwarf plants make a glorious container display for six to eight weeks. After flowering they are best discarded, but if you can plant them out in a garden border, they will grow taller and may flower again the following autumn.

In the main arrangement on the far right, a collection of pink, purple and deep red chrysanthemums with daisy-like flowerheads throngs the edge of a large pale stone container. They are interspersed with a few hardy plumbago plants (*Ceratostigma plumbaginoides*), shrubby perennials that bear clusters of tiny bright blue flowers in late summer and whose leaves turn an attractive red in autumn.

In the centre of the large pot stands a smaller pot, planted with *Heuchera* 'Chocolate Ruffles'. The deep purply red foliage of this evergreen makes a striking focal point and emphasises the rich and luxurious colour scheme. After the chrysanthemums finish flowering, you could lift them out and replace them with an alternative such as deep pink cyclamen, without disturbing the heuchera (see box below, far right).

WARM COLOUR, SWEET SCENT

For a glowing alternative to the burnished purples of the main display, choose burnt oranges, yellows and deep bronzes (right). Here, double daisy-shaped chrysanthemums massed in a glazed pot punctuate the season with fiery colour. Perfume is always a welcome addition to any planting and a new variety of wallflower (*Erysimum* Aida Series) planted with them has strongly scented flowers in autumn and again in spring. Remove the seed heads as they form to prolong the flowering.

Take your cues from the trees and fill your autumn containers with rich shades of russet and bronze. As the temperature starts to fall, these fiery colours will add a glow to any garden.

▼ **A deep mustard glazed pot** echoes the rich bronzes of autumn flowers and leaves. Stand this display where it will pick up the colours of a tree or add interest to a dull spot.

◄ Stacking pots adds height to an arrangement of short plants and allows you to mix species that need different composts. Choose pots from the same family and put an upside-down flowerpot in the lower container to support the inner one.

CHRYSANTHEMUM LOOKALIKES

The chrysanthemum name encompasses a wide range of different flowers from top-heavy pompoms to dainty daisy-like blooms. If you want alternative summer daisy style flowers for this display, try one of these species: *Argyranthemum* (Marguerite daisies); *Dendranthema*; *Leucanthemum* or *Leucanthemopsis* (Moon daisies).

EXTENDING THE SEASON

Evergreen heucheras flower in summer. Vary the plantings in the outer pot to complement the heuchera throughout the year.
• **Summer** Fill the larger pot with sweet williams (*Dianthus barbatus*) in reds and pinks.
• **Autumn** Replace the sweet williams, following the planting suggestions in the recipe (left).
• **Winter** Take out the hardy plumbago and chrysanthemums and replace them with white and pink heathers for winter colour.

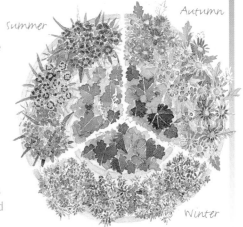

Summer   Autumn

Winter

PRETTY PLANTS FOR A COTTAGE GARDEN

• **Many old favourites** from the cottage garden can be grown in containers, including candytuft, Canterbury bells, dahlias, dianthus, lupins, verbascums, veronica and violas.

• **Group several pots** at different levels, such as the verbascums below to re-create the feel of a border, or mix and match a variety of hardy perennials to achieve a natural effect.

▼ **This exuberant arrangement** of herbaceous plants will provide colour and interest for many months. Even in autumn the last of the flowers and the varied foliage keep the display alive.

the homely mix of a cottage garden

Re-create the casual crush of an old-fashioned border in a pot with a carefully chosen combination of perennials. Mix colours, shapes and textures for a natural effect.

The centuries-old cottage garden arrangement is an informal, textured scheme using plants that have something to offer all year round. Where the owners of the great houses wanted simplicity, and favoured a garden that offered herbs, topiary and a statue, the workers in the cottages chose a procession of bulbs, roses, herbaceous plants and shrubs offering a continual visual treat. And it was exciting: they would throw down a handful of seeds and see what came up. The effect was dense, not sparse.

Nor were they afraid to use different colours: a cottage garden would mix red roses, blue delphiniums, yellow rudbeckias, purple foxgloves and sweet peas in all shades, combining pastels with strong colours all at once. It is the opposite of the modern fashion for using only one or two plants in a single hue, and it still has a strong appeal.

A CONTAINER COTTAGE GARDEN

To achieve the effect in a container, you need to choose perennial plants rather than popular bedding plants, to give the succession of effects and the critical mixture of textures.

The main arrangement on the left is planted with herbaceous perennials including the autumn-flowering *Verbascum* 'Raspberry Ripple', with its pink spikes, the rounded heads of *Sedum* 'Autumn Joy' and the soft colours of a toad lily, *Tricyrtis formosana* 'Stolonifera'. Tucked among them are the bright little flowers of a late pink, *Dianthus* 'Marquis'.

The big rough leaves of a foxglove, *Digitalis purpurea* 'Sutton's Apricot' and the jagged leaves of *Acanthus hungaricus* are the remains of plants that provided flowers earlier in the year. The maroon leaved *Heuchera*, 'Plum Pudding', will not die back completely, but retains its foliage into winter. Even after the sedum has finished flowering, its brown seed heads will look good through winter, so in all, the display will reward your efforts with six to seven months of interest.

ECHOES OF A GOLDEN SEASON

The alternative planting in the small hexagonal wooden tub on the right offers a smaller cottage-style display. In autumn the dominant flower is the black-eyed Susan, *Rudbeckia fulgida* var. *sullivantii* 'Goldsturm', but in summer the display was lit by another yellow flower, *Solidago* 'Goldkind', teamed with blue spikes of sea holly, *Eryngium variifolium*.

The arrangement first began to flower in spring when the purple blooms of bloody cranesbill, *Geranium sanguineum* opened: its matt of dark green leaves continued to provide colour for the flowers that were to come.

▲ **Bright yellow petals** surround the distinctive centres that give *Rudbeckia* (above) its common name of black-eyed Susan. They pick up the golden tones of autumn leaves (above left) for a seasonal display.

▼ **A final burst of harvest gold** from a long-lasting cottage garden collection of black-eyed Susan, geraniums, golden rod and sea holly looks dashing set against the crimson berries of a pyracantha.

bringing
home
the autumn
harvest

Capture the spirit of autumn with a colourful harvest of decorative fruit and vegetables. Choose inedible varieties you won't be tempted to pick, and enjoy this display on misty October and November days.

▲ **A twiggy basket** evokes the spirit of harvest festival when it is filled to overflowing with an autumn bounty of vegetables and fruits, both edible and inedible.

▶ **Heathers and pernettya thrive in acid compost** while the peppers in this arrangement do not. The peppers were sunk into the display while still in their own pots, each filled with the standard compost they prefer.

S hiny scarlet and orange peppers and crinkly purple cabbages make an exotic take on the traditional harvest festival basket in the main arrangement on the right. The pepper used is *Capsicum annuum*, the ornamental pepper. These are, in fact, edible (although not necessarily tasty), but be sure not to confuse this pepper with *Solanum pseudocapsicum* whose fruits are extremely poisonous.

Ornamental peppers vary in colour and shape from the long tapering red hot chilli peppers to the cone-shaped peppers used here, which are white or green when immature and eventually turn scarlet or purple.

GATHERING THE FRUITS

The bare branches of late autumn trees are echoed by a rustic planter – a loosely woven twiggy basket – which adds to the sense of a newly gathered autumn harvest. The basket has been lined with dyed sisal fibre, a longer-lasting and more environmentally friendly choice than moss. Plant the cabbages and peppers close together for maximum impact and to help retain moisture: this is an arrangement that needs to be kept well watered.

In frost-prone areas, keep the basket raised above ground level and place it in a sheltered spot – perhaps near a back door or under a kitchen window. All these plants are annuals and are best discarded after two or three months or as soon as frost strikes.

A SPLASH OF RED

In the alternative arrangement (below left), ornamental peppers add brilliance to a pair of glazed pots filled with the perennial evergreens *Erica gracilis* and *Gaultheria mucronata*.

The pink sheen of the gaultheria berries, the glossy peppers and the oily blue-green glaze on the pots all work together to give a superbly rich effect. You can leave the peppers in their individual pots and sink them into the compost: the rims will be completely

hidden. Once the peppers fade, they can be removed, leaving small empty pots in which you can plant winter pansies or spring bulbs to keep the arrangement going for as long as the heather looks good.

The heather, *Erica gracilis*, or 'Cape Heath', is a compact bushy plant with tiny urn-shaped flowers that appear in autumn and continue through to spring. *Gaultheria mucronata* needs to be planted in groups to ensure cross-pollination, if it is to produce its masses of white, pink, red or mulberry-purple berries.

▼ **A visual autumn feast** can be as bright as any summer collection. For the best display choose pepper plants with fully formed fruits; they will last for between four and six weeks, or until the first frost.

late bulbs add an oriental touch

▲ **Luminous white blooms** and soft grassy seed heads add light and texture to a subtle autumn display.

Falling leaves allow a dappled light to filter through newly bare branches, encouraging autumn bulbs and corms to sprout and flower.

The term 'bulb' includes corms, rhizomes and tubers – all of which store food beneath the ground during periods of drought and dormancy (see box, far right). They are mostly associated with spring, but the autumn-flowering plants in the main arrangement on the facing page grow from corms.

◀ **A delicate foil** of tall grasses and feathery ferns suits flowering plants with slender stems, such as the pale anemones and cyclamens featured here.

The poppy-like white anemone, strappy liriope and black ophiopogon originate from China and Japan. They have been planted in a wide, shallow bowl to create an appropriately oriental effect.

All these plants grow best in a rich, slightly acid soil. This needs to be kept moist, so in a rare dry autumn you will probably have to water the pot regularly as moisture will evaporate fast from this large surface area.

Anemone 'Honorine Jobert', planted in the centre of the bowl, is a beautiful hardy perennial with single white flowers, tinged with pink on the underside and with golden-yellow stamens.

Unlike daffodils and other spring bulbs, which store energy from their dying foliage, anemones need to be cut right down to ground level after flowering.

However, because this anemone is surrounded by a ring of evergreen perennials – both members of the lily family – any gap left in the arrangement will be well disguised. *Liriope muscari* 'Variegata' has narrow, glossy dark green and yellow variegated leaves with dense spikes of bright violet-mauve long-lasting flowers; *Ophiopogon planiscapus* 'Nigrescens' has dramatic black grass-like leaves. In late summer this plant produces spires of lilac flowers which are followed by round fleshy black fruits.

This arrangement is best planted in early summer to allow plants to establish – most hate being repotted when close to, or in, flower.

POTS IN DAPPLED LIGHT

In an alternative planting on the left a group of matching pots in various sizes brings together a diverse collection.

Many grasses are at their best in autumn when their fluffy heads sway in the breeze – although they can get tatty if they are exposed to strong winds. The elegant waving grass, *Pennisetum alopecuroides* 'Hameln', with its soft plume-like flowerheads in the golden yellow of wheat, likes full sun, as does the white *Cyclamen*

persicum which is in the smallest pot, so these occupy the foreground where there is most light.

Behind them, the graceful white anemone, 'Honorine Jobert', makes an ideal container companion for *Blechnum spicant* (hard fern). Both are happy growing in the dappled shade at the edge of a summerhouse or bower.

BURIED STORES OF ENERGY

- **Bulbs,** which plants like daffodils grow from, are made up of fleshy leaf bases.
- **Corms,** from plants such as cyclamen, are swollen stems with buds at the top.
- **Rhizomes** are fat stems that creep horizontally, such as those of irises.
- **Tubers** are thickened roots, found in plants like dahlias.

◄ **Subdued tones** work best with this delicate oriental-looking collection. The bright orange of new terracotta would be too harsh, so paint on a very thin coat of diluted white emulsion, using a teaspoon of paint to a mug of water.

▶ **"The bigger the better"** is Liz and Richard's motto for pots. Feeding and watering is easier and "they look so much better". Their half-barrel massed with bright yellow Jamaica primroses (*Argyranthemum*) is a good example: just four plants in the pot produce up to 400 blooms.

▼ **Agapanthus heads soar** above their terracotta pots. The plants are from the Isles of Scilly and the Yorkshire sun is sometimes not hot enough for them to flower their best, but they overwinter in the warmth of the greenhouse.

▶ **A new raised bed** swallowed up 12 tons of coarse road chippings that were scraped off the drive. The bed has a wild appeal, with tall plants, such as alliums, eryngiums and *Zauschneria* 'Dublin', that rustle and sway in a gentle breeze.

a **plant lover's** plot in **paradise**

The winds may be brisk in Yorkshire, but in Liz and Richard Tite's garden there is always something to cheer the heart. "We're plant people," they proudly confess, and since they left their jobs as horticultural advisers have concluded that they are also "designed to be retired." Their garden is a joint effort, although "Liz trained at Kew so she thinks she's a bit superior," Richard sneaks in with a smile. They admit they are "plantaholics before designers", but that it is Liz who has the eye for style and puts pots together. "I think, in general, a mass of one type of plant is ▶

209

◄ **Pots of single fuchsias** edge a deep border at the side of the house. The lilies in the border are grown in pots and sunk into the ground (inset) for summer then overwintered behind the garage.

▼ **A concrete urn,** tucked in a border behind the pond, is only visible late in the year when some plants have died back. When a pot is far away, Richard asserts it should be "huge, sculptural and probably empty".

▶ **Mixing textures adds interest.** Liz grouped these pots for "the contrasts of the spiky agave (inset), the comfy rosettes of the echeveria in the shallow urn and the feathery leaves of the daisies".

better than a mixed display," she muses, but admits that with 200 containers she has the luxury of combining plants on a large scale.

Their largest pots hold 300 litres and, even though many are permanently planted, Liz and Richard "couldn't afford to buy all those bags of compost." Instead, they make their own, using mushroom compost and a good loam. "It's like cooking by instinct" Richard demonstrates, "when you get your hands in, you know when the texture feels right."

Each year they push 400 slow-release fertiliser pellets into their pots when the summer planting is complete. These last for six weeks, after which they feed needy plants weekly and water everything every third day "with a can, so we can control the quantities". It is a successful regime: "the proof of the pudding is in the plants," Richard beams.

Their garden has a sandy, free-draining soil, and in very dry summers, such as 1995 and 1996, when many local reservoirs

ran dry, the pots were the stars. Winters are also a problem and although their part of Yorkshire is not as exposed as the open moors, they still face spells cold enough to freeze roots in pots.

Tender plants are moved to the shelter of the greenhouse, but they try to avoid wrapping anything that stays out – "the garden still has to look nice," they point out. A wonderfully sculptural agave (above) will not withstand the cold and Liz and Richard take it into the house for

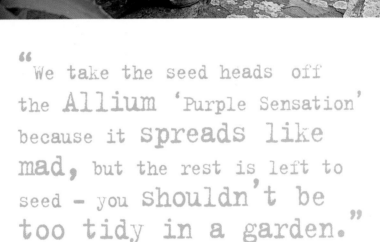

> " We take the seed heads off the Allium 'Purple Sensation' because it spreads like mad, but the rest is left to seed - you shouldn't be too tidy in a garden."

winter. It is fiendishly spiky and they carry it up to the attic at arm's length on a tray. However, it is getting too big to handle, so they have propagated an offset in case they lose the parent plant.

Many of their pots have been made by their friend Roly, at the village pottery – the only British pottery still digging its own clay. He works alone, so his pots are limited by the weight he can lift and in height to the length of his arm. For a year, Liz and Richard ran 'Terracotta Gardening' courses with him, showing how to make and then plant a pot.

As they wander round the garden pots and plants spark stories. For example, near the greenhouse is a cluster of icy blue *Agapanthus* 'Phantom'. "We bought them at a show," Liz recalls, "and the man selling them quizzed us to see whether we would be suitable 'parents' before he let us have them."

At the front of the house is a memento from Richard's first job, in Regent's Park: a geranium, 'Harry Hieover', grown from a cutting he took in 1959. And to the left of the bench and table overlooking the lawn in the walled garden is a very special pot of fuchsias.

Fuchsias dot the garden, despite both Liz and Richard admitting they are not their favourite plants. However, Richard's father bred them, "so it seems important to keep some". This one, though, is one of their favourites, and Richard thinks one of his father's best. It is *Fuchsia* 'Paula Jane' and deserves its special place in the garden because it was named after Richard's eldest daughter.

▲ **Before the winter gales,** Liz and Richard tie up the cordyline (top) to protect its leaves. The pot store (centre) is cleared for overwintering lilies, and bowls of spring bulbs wait in the wings (above).

fresh ways with winter pansies

Simple and sweet, with their vibrant colours and upturned faces, pansies brighten even the dreariest winter days. Despite their small size, they are endlessly versatile.

▶ **Simple pansies get a formal style makeover** when they are joined by the glossy black grass, *Ophiopogon planiscapus* 'Nigrescens' in a sharp-edged galvanised box.

Pots of winter pansies will flower from autumn right through winter and produce a second burst of flowers in March. They thrive in the warmth of big cities and in the south of Britain. Farther north they benefit from being close to a house wall radiating heat.

Pansies are part of the viola family, which includes pansies, violas, violets and violettas, in decreasing size. Pansies have a sweet scent, so put the container where you can catch the fragrance. Violas are also fragrant, and many new varieties will also flower from mid February.

Viola flowers are smaller and less flamboyant than those of a winter pansy, and there is not the same colour range, although some have blotches at the centre of the flower. However, they are tougher and more compact.

One of the best ways to display winter pansies is in a theatre, like the one on the right, traditionally used to house collections of auricula flowers. The theatre not only gives the plants protection from winter weather, it also allows you to make a big display with relatively few plants. The low stature of winter pansies also makes them a pretty foil for larger foliage plants, such as grasses and heathers.

GROWING TIPS

Although they will endure some shade, for best results stand pots where they will catch all the available sun that winter days can offer. Use a good multipurpose compost with a generous layer of drainage to allow heavy winter rain to run through quickly before it can chill the roots, and add a handful of Perlite to soak up excess moisture. As a

◀ **Small plants make a big impact** when grouped together. A wooden 'auricula theatre' houses a charming display of winter pansies and violas. Rearrange the display when you feel like a new look, moving pots, or adding fresh plants or souvenirs from a winter walk.

▼ **Echo the colour of your pansies** in their pot so it does not dominate the display. Here, twirls of *Carex rubra* tone with crimson winter pansies in a warm terracotta jar. A touch of frost will only enhance this wispy arrangement.

KEY FACTS

- **Hardy and vigorous,** winter pansies (*Viola* x *wittrockiana*) are large-flowered hybrid pansies, which provide rich, deep colour for winter containers. There are a number of colour series, but most have markings or 'faces' at the centre of each flower and some have a thin rim of a different colour at the outer edge of the petals.
- **Bingo, Delta, Fama and Imperial Series** all have large blooms in a range of colours, with and without central blotches.
- **The Universal Series** is an intermediate size with a broad range of single colours, often with a central blotch.
- **The Ultima Series,** such as 'Regal' and 'Joker', have medium-sized flowers in a range of colours.

final aid to drainage, raise the pot on feet or place a few pieces of broken pot or stones underneath it.

If possible, buy more pansies than you need and keep the surplus to one side, ready to replace any that fail to perform. Discard winter pansies at the end of their flowering season – you will get better results with fresh plants the following year. Use fresh compost for your summer pansy display, or you might encourage an outbreak of debilitating 'pansy sickness'.

213

foliage
fairy and
lights

As the nights draw in add a twinkle to your container arrangements with lighting to welcome you home on dark evenings or bring your garden back to life in the gloomy depths of winter.

▼ **On a dusky evening** white petals and silvery leaves reflect the glow from a cluster of garden lights. Stand your pot on a base of crushed glass that will add to the overall sparkling effect.

▲ **Illuminate your garden** with night-lights in wind-proof holders, a cluster of fairy-light bulbs shining up through a shrub from its base or, on a still evening, a candle.

Between the rich hues of autumn and the fresh greens of spring, winter can be a drab time in the garden. But a container filled with white flowers and silver or variegated foliage will brighten even the gloomiest day.

In the main arrangement on the far left a ring of white primulas shines like spotlights around the edge of a wide shallow bowl. A thick layer of wispy sisal fibre fills the space between each primula to insulate the roots against frost and freezing winter winds.

Behind the primulas alternating evergreens form an inner circle. The velvety grey-green foliage of *Ballota pseudodictamnus* and the steel-coloured leaves of *Convolvulus cneorum* pick out the metallic tones of the shiny metal butterfly shaped plant markers that seem to hover above the pot.

At the centre of the display is a metal topiary ball frame stuffed with white outdoor lights. Keep the transformer inside the house and let the lights shine in the garden.

Primulas from the *Polyanthus* Group (see pages 152-153) start flowering in autumn. As they fade in spring, replace them with pale brachyscome, petunias or verbena, to complement the ballota and convolvulus when their pinky white flowers emerge in summer.

TWINKLING IN A TREE

Hanging baskets are usually associated with spring and summer, but they make great containers for trailing ivy in winter. An alternative way of incorporating lights into your containers (above left) is to hang night-lights in miniature lanterns from a basket in a tree.

Fill the centre of the basket with white primulas then surround them with silver and cream variegated ivies. Twine the ivy around the base of the basket and up the chains to disguise the frame for a natural effect.

Even without the lights, these simple plants would brighten a dark corner, but the addition of a few twinkling tree decorations completes the display.

EXTENDING THE SEASON

Enjoy the lights in the run-up to Christmas, but if you feel superstitious, remove them on Twelfth Night and plant a small white-berried shrub, such as a gaultheria, in their place.

before Christmas

after Twelfth Night

▲ **Glass icicles and mirrors** reflect the light from candle lanterns, hung from a basket with invisible fishing line. Position the lights so there is no danger of them setting fire to the plants in your display.

For more creative lighting ideas in the garden, see pages 78-79

▶ **Group plants by height** for a successful display. Work from the tallest plant, the holly, at the back to the low-growing cyclamen at the front. To fill a gap left by bare trunks, raise a pot planted with a low shrub, such as the viburnum, by standing it on another, upturned container.

▶ **Use accessories** to balance the glaze of pots. Hang tiny garden tools from branches, mulch with nuts, or use tree or shrub prunings as stakes.

choose shrubs for winter colour

On the darkest of days evergreens add interest to the garden. Team them with early bulbs for a display to carry you through to spring.

▼ **Glazed pots may crack** in wet and freezing weather, so stand them on pot feet to let water drain freely away. Raising pots off the ground will also prevent your patio surface from being water stained and protect the plants from ground frost.

Bare branches make dramatic silhouettes against frosty skies, but particularly in very small gardens, leafless twigs can look rather bleak. However, many evergreen trees and shrubs will thrive in containers if placed in a sheltered position away from strong winter winds.

In the main arrangement on the left, two standard trees, a variegated holly (*Ilex aquifolium* 'Aureomarginata') and an olive (*Olea europaea* 'Frantoio'), stand neatly together. To the left of them, a slender *Ceanothus griseus* 'Silver Surprise', or Californian Lilac, adds colour with its creamy white variegated leaves.

To the right, as a contrast in shape, is a *Viburnum davidii*. This compact shrub has large oval, veined leaves and delicate white spring flowers followed by metallic blue fruits in winter. A small pot of cyclamen adds a blast of bright colour at the front to emphasise the red berries of the holly.

As an alternative to the group on the left choose just one evergreen as a background for a collection of winter-flowering bulbs (right). The grey bark and silvery green leaves of the olive work well as a foil for white hyacinths and *Narcissus* 'Paper White'. Give the bulbs support by pushing short prunings from the deep red branches of a cornus into the pot.

decorating with pots for Christmas

When it is too cold to venture into the garden, turn your attention to the house and plant festive container arrangements to decorate a conservatory or to give visitors a cheery welcome.

◄ **Silvered rims** pick up the glint of the fine tinsel draped through the branches of these matching spruces. The trees will sparkle on frosty mornings, but the warm terracotta of the pots ensures that the overall feel is not too cold.

Rich, deep colours are the traditional choice for decorating at Christmas time. Scarlet poinsettias, *Euphorbia pulcherrima*, have become as much a part of the festive season as the Norway spruce. But the apricot and cream tones of the marble poinsettia used in the main arrangement on the right, and the soft pink of the smaller one in front of it, bring a new twist to the tradition. These subtle shades set the tone for a soft-coloured indoor display for a bright window or conservatory.

At the centre of the display stands an *Amaryllis* 'Apple Blossom' flanked by two coppery square pots of *Phalaenopsis* orchids. Each amaryllis bulb produces one or two thick stems with huge, sweet-smelling blooms, but the flowerheads can be rather top heavy and may appreciate the support of metal flower markers or long twigs, which look more attractive than the usual bamboo canes.

Phalaenopsis orchids, which are also known as moth orchids, are perfect for this collection as they tolerate shade and are quite happy with good indirect light, which also suits the amaryllis and poinsettia. Their heads nod on slender stems and fill the centre of the arrangement.

SEASONS GREETINGS

Bringing seasonal cheer to your home does not have to be restricted to the indoors. In the alternative grouping on the left, two blue spruce Christmas trees stand on stone steps leading up to a front door. Their thick foliage provides an aromatic invitation, drawing guests into the house.

Thick bows of dyed garden raffia add a further festive touch to the green and silver colour scheme, and break the hard lines of the tapered pots.

ADD A TOUCH OF FESTIVE PAINT

A metallic varnish was rubbed onto the square terracotta pots featured here, to give a warm copper glow that enhances the pink tones of the blooms. A scattering of shimmering wooden apples and hazelnuts completes the display.

◄ **Tall stems of the amaryllis** bring height to this arrangement, with the pale pinky white trumpet-shaped flowerheads drawing the eye to the top of the collection.

turning the corner from winter to spring

▲ **Early flowering bulbs,** such as crocus and *Iris reticulata*, glow with warmth on a chilly day.

◄ **The wineglass-shaped flowers** of *Crocus vernus* open wide in even the weakest rays of winter sun to reveal bright orange stamens. Packed tightly in a pot, they make a vibrant pool of colour.

If you can have only one container plan to keep it blooming with a succession of flowers that will take you from the chills of winter to the bright days of spring.

▶ **A frilly collar of winter aconites** sets off the robust blooms of the daffodil, 'Rijnveld's Early Sensation' and softens the lines of the square pot. The display makes a bright contrast to the earlier crocus.

▼ **Last in the pot** are the 'Angélique' tulips. The buds will not open until early May, so there is no danger of them needing to go into the container while the daffodils are still looking splendid.

Continuous planting is an effective way of making an impact with spring bulbs. They often look most dramatic when a single variety is planted densely in the container to create a block of colour. Plant in autumn (see below), choosing your plants carefully, so that as one pot of flowers starts to fade, the next will be ready to bloom. And consider the effect of colour: do you want a continuous theme or to increase the intensity of the display into spring before softening the palette as summer approaches?

The starting point for this display (left) is a crocus with larger than normal blooms: *Crocus vernus* 'Blue'. For a complete contrast, this was followed by the earliest trumpet daffodil to flower, *Narcissus* 'Rijnveld's Early Sensation' (top right). This short daffodil grows to only 30cm (12in) and stands up well in winter winds. The third flowers to go into the container are a soft pink tulip called 'Angélique' (centre right), chosen because it is one of the last tulips to flower. It is a type of tulip often called peony-flowered because of its huge double blooms.

PREPARE AHEAD FOR SUCCESS

Plant the crocus bulbs in your chosen container in September. All bulbs need the largest pot you can manage for maximum protection against frost. Even hardy bulbs can suffer in a small pot because they get frost from all directions – top, bottom and sideways.

The best compost for bulbs is John Innes No.1, with an added handful each of multipurpose compost and grit. Plant bulbs no more than an inch apart

or even touching; any gaps will look unsightly in a container display. Plant the daffodils at the same time as the crocus in another pot, or in several if that is more convenient. It doesn't matter if these pots look a little shabby, because the flowers will be moved into your chosen pot for the display. You can plant the tulip bulbs as late as November, again in spare containers.

Put all the pots in a sheltered place to grow, ready to be brought forward one at a time. Deadhead after flowering, then lift the plants to make room for the next ones. The old bulbs can be moved into your borders, or into other pots to die off and be stored until next year.

PLANT WINTER FLOWERS FOR AN EARLY START

You can experiment with other bulbs in succession. Winter aconites and muscari are good early choices, followed by hyacinths, or different varieties of daffodils and tulips.
• **For an earlier start** than the crocus, combine snowdrops and *Iris reticulata*. The variety 'George' (right) has velvety purple petals and is well-suited to growing in pots.
• **Buy snowdrops that are already sprouting,** or 'in the green'. *Galanthus caucasicus* and *G. elwesii* will flower the first year they are planted, but most varieties, including the common snowdrop, *G. nivalis* will not.

practicalities

a good start for your containers

Successful container gardening depends to a large extent on the planning and work put in at the beginning. There's more to a great display than just putting a plant in a pot and hoping for the best.

Selecting the right pot

Think about the pot and plants you want for your display at the same time, bearing in mind where you plan to put it and what else is growing nearby. If you are shopping for the pot and plants together it can be helpful to choose the pot first and wheel it round with you as you select the plants.

It is essential to choose a pot that is the right size for the plant or plants you intend to put in it. A container that is too small will soon become full of roots; it will be difficult to feed and water adequately and the plants will suffer. Conversely, a young plant in an over-large pot can also struggle, because the compost will remain wet for long periods.

If you want to keep the plant for several years – for example, a camellia or large shrub – and are starting with a young specimen, it is better to pot it on when necessary into successively larger containers, than to start it off in an over-large tub. ❶ Each time you repot a plant, increase the diameter of the container by about 10cm (4in).

Choosing your plants wisely

Do not select the tallest specimen, or the one with most flowers when you are buying plants. Instead, opt for one that is bushy and bursting with health. Whether you are planting a large tree or a tiny alpine, follow the same basic rules to choosing well.

First look under the pot. ❶ An established plant will fill its pot with roots and some may be visible through the drainage holes. ❷ If a plant resists when you lift it, it may have rooted into the bed it is standing on. This indicates that the plant has been in the same pot (and untouched in the garden centre) for some time and is quite likely to be pot-bound.

Pulling the roots out of the bed will damage them, and you will almost certainly find it difficult to remove the pot for planting when you get home.

Other signs of neglect are moss and weeds on the top of the pot ❸, a straggly habit, obvious signs of pests or disease, poor leaf colour and dry compost.

On the other hand, avoid newly potted plants which have been put on sale before they have had a chance to re-establish themselves. If the compost looks fluffy and new ❹, or if the plant seems loose when tugged gently ❺, you may have difficulty replanting it without damaging the roots.

When you get a new plant home, give it a good soaking even if the compost appears moist. If it is at all dry, it is best to water and then wait a day before planting to allow it to recover. After planting, water your arrangement in well, then wait until the compost is starting to dry out before watering it again.

HOW TO PICK A HEALTHY PLANT

It is clear which of the two *Ajuga reptans* below ❶ is healthy, and which is suffering from neglect. But two simple checks will eliminate less obvious problem plants.

• **Check under the pot** ❷ for weeds and signs of infestation, such as the slug here.

• **Lift the leaves** and look for evidence of damage and disease. The sick plant ❸ is thin and its leaves have been nibbled, while the healthier plant ❹ bursts with new growth.

Letting the water drain away freely

Good drainage is essential to prevent waterlogging, which will eventually kill plants, so make sure every pot has plenty of holes in the base. Make more with a drill ❶ if necessary, using a masonry bit at a slow speed for terracotta. You may need to punch out holes where marked on plastic pots ❷.

Water will escape more freely through several small evenly spaced holes ❸ than one large hole. Your pot will also need a good layer of drainage material in the base to prevent the holes from getting blocked.

Coarse gravel, or broken crocks are the traditional choice for drainage, but crumbled polystyrene plant trays ❹ are a lightweight and inexpensive option.

Whatever you use, fill the container to a tenth of its total height.

However well water drains through the compost, it will not be able to run free if the pot is standing on the ground. Raise the pot by standing it on bricks or similar flat objects, taking care not to cover up the drainage holes. Or ❺ add a professional finishing touch with ornamental pot feet.

If you prefer to stand your containers in saucers, you will need to keep a careful eye on them. The saucers will retain surplus water, which can cause the roots to freeze in winter. The benefit of saucers is that you can leave plants standing in a little water when going away for a few days to make

sure that they have enough moisture. Saucers also prevent freshly watered pots on balconies dripping onto neighbours living below.

Some plants, particularly herbs, succulents ❻, alpines and Mediterranean species require perfect drainage. Grey-leaved plants, such as *Artemesia* 'Powis Castle', *Brachyglottis* 'Sunshine' and *Perovskia* 'Blue Spire' are good examples of such plants.

If you are growing plants like these, you can improve the drainage of proprietary composts by adding fine grit ❼ or sharp sand ❽. You will usually need about 10 per cent by volume. If it is important to minimise the weight – for example, if your pots are on a balcony – add perlite ❾ or horticultural vermiculite instead.

plant food and toppings

Picking the best growing medium

There are two basic kinds of compost: those containing soil and those that are soil free and are based on peat. If you are concerned about the environmental effects of cutting peat, choose a soil-free compost made with a peat substitute. These are usually based on coir, and may need extra fertilisers and more frequent watering.

Proprietory 'container' or 'multipurpose' composts are generally soil-free with a slow-release feed, wetting agent and sometimes with water-retaining gel added.

All soil-free composts contain additives, such as lime to reduce their acidity, sharp sand to improve drainage, and a fast-acting fertiliser. They are excellent for a summer display, but tend to tire quickly, so are less suitable for permanent plantings. Lighter than soil-based composts, they are a good choice for balconies and roof gardens.

Composts containing soil are a mixture of loam, peat and sharp sand, and are largely based on the 'John Innes' formula. They contain varying amounts of fertiliser, depending on what they are to be used for.

John Innes No.1 contains very little fertiliser, making it suitable for young plants, which do not grow well in high levels of plant food. John Innes No.2 has twice as much fertiliser as No.1. It can be used for fast-growing young plants and for slow-growing plants which will be over-stimulated by too much fertiliser.

For large or mature specimens use John Innes No.3. This contains three times as much plant food as No.1 and will sustain plants in the same container for several years.

If you want to grow thriving acid-loving plants, such as rhododendrons, you will need an acid compost. These composts are lime free and are usually labelled 'ericaceous'. They also have plant foods added.

Dressing the pot

Some arrangements are so dense that the surface of the compost is hidden. However, if the compost is exposed, it is vulnerable to invasion by weeds, and moisture will evaporate from it in hot weather, making frequent watering essential.

The answer is to cover the compost with a layer of mulch (see the examples on the right), which will help to reduce these problems.

Bark chippings and cocoa shells sold for mulching garden borders are also suitable for containers. Heavy mulches, such as pebbles, have the extra benefit of adding weight to plastic pots, which might otherwise blow over. The extra weight can also help to deter doorstep thieves.

Use a mulch to add an original decorative touch of your own to a container display. Think about the container and the plants you are using and choose a mulch that will set them off to perfection.

▶ **Use natural mulches** to give your pots a theme. A little moss from the garden, or a few pine cones or conkers gathered on a walk, all work well with woodland plants and shrubs. Shells, which can be bought in many shops and should never be picked up off the beach, instantly evoke the sea.

▶ **Standard trees,** if not underplanted, and fountain-like plants, such as agaves (below), leave a lot of exposed compost on the top of the pot. Make the most of the space by adding decorative and imaginative arrangements of differently coloured pebbles or mixed mulches.

◄ **Water the compost** before you begin to add your plants. When planting is complete, water again and add a layer of mulch on top to lock in the moisture.

▶ **Stones and gravel** are a traditional choice that can easily be given a stylish twist. Use a honey-coloured gravel with terracotta or white chippings to highlight a pot. Mix materials, such as slate and gravel for a natural 'scree' effect, or pile on smoothly rounded pebbles.

▶ **A coloured mulch** adds flair to a contemporary arrangement. Recycled glass chippings twinkle in the light, while coloured gravel, such as ice white, or coal black have a more subtle effect. Match the colour of the flowers, pot or surroundings for a professional finishing touch.

the foolproof way to plant a pot

Follow these simple guidelines and your containers should flourish from the day you plant them. By taking care early on, you will reap the benefits throughout the life of the display.

How to plant a mixed container

The first step when planting a container is to put a layer of drainage material in the base. This allows water to drain away but stops the compost slipping out of the pot. Fill the pot to a tenth of its height with crushed brick, coarse gravel, small stones, smashed terracotta or broken polystyrene trays.

Next, add compost ❶ until the container is about two-thirds full. Push down with your fingers ❷ to firm it very gently. Do not ram it down hard; air is needed for a healthy root system, and compressing the compost makes it hard for plants to root into. Begin to introduce the plants ❸, starting with the largest. Do not dig a hole: instead, draw the compost back with a trowel ❹, pop your plant in the space created, then let the compost fall back around it.

Ease plants out of their pots or trays ❺, and unless the label says otherwise, plant them at the depth they were in their original pots. Add compost as you go so that smaller specimens are at the right level. Leave at least 2.5cm (1in) between the surface of the compost and the rim of the pot.

Once your plants are in position, fill around the roots with compost ❻, firming gently to get rid of any large air pockets. Then water well ❼ and top up the compost if it has settled. Now is the time to tuck a discreet plant label at the back of the pot.

Finally, position the pot. It is best to raise it off the ground on pot feet ❽ to prevent the drainage holes from becoming clogged.

Plant containers with care and watch the results bloom

How to plant a tree or large shrub for lasting pleasure

When planting a tree or large shrub, use the most substantial container you can find: remember, the tree will be in it for some time. And if the pot is ceramic or terracotta, make sure it is frost-proof.

It is sensible to place the container in its final position before you start: when you have finished it will be too heavy to move. Stand it on bricks or pot feet to raise the base well above the ground, taking care not to block the drainage holes.

WEIGH DOWN THE POT

Start with a layer of drainage material. For tall plants, use something heavy, such as pieces of broken terracotta ❶ for additional stability. Then partially fill the pot ❷ with John Innes No.3 compost or, in the case of a very large container, a crumbly mixture of good-quality loam, sharp sand and peat substitute.

Place the tree on the compost to gauge the depth. When the container is filled to within 5cm (2in) of the rim, the plant should be at the same depth as it was in its original pot.

Be careful when planting dwarf fruit trees not to cover the graft between the rootstock and the main trunk with compost. If you do, the main trunk may start to put out roots, and you will lose the dwarfing effect of the rootstock.

When you are sure that the tree is in the correct position, ease it gently out of its pot ❸. If you are planting an acer, like this one, do not tug it by the trunk, as this will stress it. Other species of trees and shrubs are more robust.

Fill in with compost around the tree, firming gently around the rootball. If you are planting a bare rooted tree, carefully work the compost around all the roots so that there are no large air pockets.

Finish off with a gravel mulch ❹ or plant spring or summer bedding or heathers around the trunk for a temporary show.

Water thoroughly until liquid runs through the holes in the bottom of the pot ❺. You will not need to water a newly planted tree again for at least a fortnight if planted in this way.

how to plant a variety of pots

Different containers need different techniques. Whether you want to plant a tower of herbs, a window box, a flower pouch or a bowl of spring bulbs, follow these tips for success.

Fill a tower with a fragrant collection of herbs

Herb or strawberry pots – tall pots with holes around the sides – are ideal for growing a selection of herbs or a tower of strawberries in a small space. Strawberry pots merely have holes in the sides so that the plants' runners can trail, whereas herb pots have protruding cups to give support to the plants growing there.

There is a danger with these kinds of tall pots that the plants at the top will become waterlogged and the ones at the bottom dry out. To make sure that water spreads evenly through the pot, include a central core of grit when you plant.

Position a pipe ❶ in the centre of the pot. An offcut of plastic plumbing pipe or the cardboard tube from a roll of kitchen towel will do. Hold the pipe steady then fill around it with compost as far as the first holes.

Then start to introduce the plants. Always plant trailing varieties in the side holes and bushier herbs in the top. Push them through the holes from the inside ❷, and firm the compost around the plants as you go. Work your way up the pot until you reach the top.

Before you can plant in the space at the top of the pot, fill the pipe with grit ❸

to the level of the compost in the pot. Gently ease the pipe out ❹, leaving the core of grit behind, then put the plants in the top.

PLANTING WINDOW BOXES

A window box will dress the outside of a house and can be fragrant, formal or a flowering mass (see pages 32-33). Plant one just as you would any pot, but think carefully about what plants to use.

Choose compact, bushy varieties that will not block your view when mature, and will not prevent the window from opening. Place tall plants at the back, followed by a row of lower-growing ones if there is room. Then fill the front row with prostrate or trailing plants, which will hang prettily over the edge of the box.

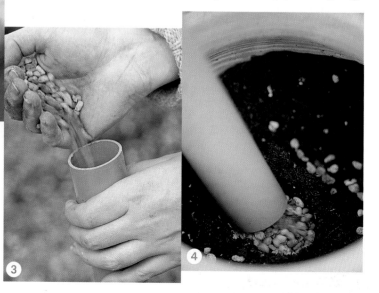

Planting bulbs

The one rule for planting bulbs in containers is to ignore the traditional rules about spacing them out. In the ground, bulbs need room to spread and increase, but in a container, where they will live for one season only, planting for a densely packed display is the most important consideration.

Plant bulbs as close together as you dare – it doesn't even matter if they touch. And if you have a deep container, plant more

than one layer, so that the lower bulbs will come through later and extend the life of the arrangement.

▶ Rich, glossy hyacinth bulbs are treated with a chemical which can irritate the skin. Always wear protective plastic gloves when you handle them.

Fill a bowl with bulbs and enjoy a glorious display – see pages 156-157

Hang a colourful flowering pouch

Flower pouches are slim vertical grow bags, around 50cm long and 20cm wide (20x8in). The best plants for them are bushy species, such as busy lizzies, pansies and petunias, which will spread to hide the bag.

For the best results use plug plants, which are small and easy to push into the pouch, and avoid mixing varieties, so that the plants grow and mature at the same rate. Single colours or very simple colour schemes also tend to look best.

Fill the pouch with potting compost ❶, mixed with water-retaining gel granules and slow-release fertiliser tablets. Then push your plants in through the perforations on the face of the bag ❷. Hang the bag in an inconspicuous spot while the plants mature then move it to cheer up a bare wall or fence ❸ when the flowers bloom.

231

plant a hanging basket or flower ball

A globe of solid colour or a shaggy mass of blooms swinging by a door or window will brighten any outlook. Follow these simple steps for guaranteed success with hanging baskets and flower balls.

Plant a basket full of trailing plants and foliage

There are many different styles of wire hanging baskets and liners available. If your aim is to grow a mass of trailing plants you can use a plain basket and utilitarian liner ❶, because they will be hidden when the plants are mature. If the basket will show, choose a more decorative one and line it with moss, if you have plenty around the edges of your lawn, or dyed coir, a moss substitute that will remain green for longer than the real thing.

Cover the basket base and about the first 5cm (2in) of the sides with a layer of moss or moss substitute ❷. Put an old saucer in the bottom ❸ to prevent water from running straight out through the moss, then add a layer of compost up to the height you want your first plants. If you are using a cardboard liner, cut out holes where you want the plants before you add the compost.

Introduce your first ring of plants pushing them between the wires from the inside of the basket out. Wrap the plants in stiff paper ❹ to protect them as you work. Use young specimens for the sides: they will be easier to push through than mature plants and will establish quickly, hanging down to create a pretty trailing effect.

Continue adding moss, compost and plants and work your way up the sides of the basket. Hanging baskets look best when packed with plants, so the demands on the compost are great. Include some water-retaining gel, or 'swelly gelly' (see page 237) and slow-release plant food (see page 238) now to make the maintenance of your basket easier throughout the season.

Finally plant the top with taller, more erect species in the middle and trailing ones around the edge to hide the rim.

Sandwich two hanging baskets together and make a blooming flower ball

The easiest way to create a flower ball is to choose plants that are naturally bushy, such as busy lizzies (*Impatiens*) or fibrous-rooted begonias (*Begonia semperflorens*). Plant them in a single hanging basket and as they grow, they will merge together to make a dense ball shape.

If you want to choose from a wider variety of plants, you can also make a flower ball by planting the sides and bases of two separate wire hanging baskets and then joining them together to make a sphere.

Follow the instructions on the left for planting a single wire hanging basket, building up a lining of moss, or moss substitute, compost and layers of small plants ①. This basket will be the lower half of the ball, so position your first plants as close to the bottom of the basket as you can, to avoid having a bald patch on the underside. Leave the top of the basket unplanted ②, but make sure that it is filled to the brim with compost.

COMPLETE THE BALL

Next plant a second basket to make the top of the ball. Begin by removing the chains and putting a small upturned plastic flower pot ③ in the bottom of the empty basket. When the flower ball is complete, this will be at the very top, and will provide you with a handy watering point.

Working around the pot ④, plant the basket up as before. Again finish off by firming down the compost. Water both baskets well, and if this causes the compost to settle, top it up so that it is level with the rim.

Place a thin sheet of wood or an old plate on top of the upper basket ⑤ to support the compost. Turn the basket over and place it on top of the lower basket. Gently withdraw the wood or plate and ⑥ secure the two baskets together with lengths of garden wire. Hang the flower ball ⑦ by the chains of the lower basket, taking care not to squash the plants in the upper basket as you do so.

Be patient while your small plants grow and turn into a globe of glorious colour

plant props and supports

Many popular pot plants need some sort of underpinning when they are in full growth. Bushy species soon hide their props, but you can make a virtue of necessity with ornamental solutions.

Keeping tall and lanky plants upright

Naturally bushy plants will keep themselves upright and prostrate and trailing species look best when allowed to hang down over the side of a pot. However, there are many plants, particularly herbaceous perennials, that may topple over when fully grown.

The best time to put in supports is at the beginning of the growing season. That way they will be hidden as the plants mature.

The simplest way to support top-heavy, floppy plants, such as the lupins in the pot on the left, is to insert a ring of canes just inside the rim of the pot ❶. Twist garden twine or raffia around and between the canes ❷ to stop the stems bending over.

You can make a simple but attractive support for perennials that die down in winter by sinking a ring of fat bamboo canes ❸ into

the pot and tying strands of twine around them. A frill of evergreen *Gaultheria* makes a year-round display until the grass at the centre of the arrangement spurts out like a fountain in summer.

HELP FOR CLIMBERS

Climbers in tubs need good support from the outset. This can be a trellis fastened to a wall adjacent to the pot or, for a free-standing feature, some kind of obelisk or wigwam (see right).

Very tall vegetables, such as tomatoes or runner beans, often need supporting. Those grown as cordons, on

a single stem with all side shoots removed, each need a single, strong cane. In a trough or grow bag the uprights should be tied firmly to another cane, placed horizontally near the top, for stability. Various ingenious grow bag plant supports are also available in nurseries and by post.

It is important to take care that the plant ties you use are always soft, and are loose enough not to cut into stems and branches as the plants grow. Pipe cleaners, raffia, soft string and self-fastening cable ties are all ideal for the job.

The slender stems of a nodding lupin may bow under the weight of its flowers without support

Making a cane wigwam support

Climbing plants in pots, such as clematis, morning glory, sweet peas and runner beans all need support. Without something to cling to, their long stalks will flop down in a heap onto the top of the container.

Metal and woven wicker obelisks are both available in garden centres, but plants also look pretty scrambling up a homemade wigwam.

To make your own wigwam you will need six long twigs, lengths of bamboo or canes. ❶ Pull them together about 25cm (10in) from the top and bind them with garden wire or twine. ❷ Splay the canes out so the bottoms are spaced evenly around the edge of the pot, and sink them firmly into the compost. Loop garden wire around each cane about 20cm (8in) from the bottom, to make a ring that will steady the feature.

Add further rings of wire up the wigwam if necessary to support the climbers as they grow.

Some plants spread out of control, or flop over under their own weight as they grow. The pot of twisted sedums (*Sedum alboroseum* 'Frosty Morn') below ❶ has a certain unkempt appeal, but would look out of place in a formal setting.

For mature plants like these, it is a good idea to buy proprietary supports. These are often dark green and less visible than canes and twine.

A pair of stakes and a length of wire looped between them ❷ is all it takes to make the plants vertical again. But this leaves the arrangement with a gap at the base of the plants ❸.

Planting smaller flowering species, such as these 'Monte Cassino' asters ❹ will fill the gap underneath the sedums. Or you could complete the display by adding a decorative mulch.

cool water for thirsty plants

Pots and other containers hold a comparatively small amount of compost, which dries out fast, particularly when plants are growing and taking up a lot of water. The compost in containers is also usually warmer than soil at ground level, which encourages drying out in hot weather. Fortunately, there are several simple ways to make watering easier and less time-consuming.

Water-retaining gels

The absorption properties of compost can be improved by adding water-retaining gels. These gels, or 'swelly gelly', look like sugar crystals ❶ when dry, but are capable of absorbing many times their own volume of water, and when fully wet they resemble cooked tapioca. The water-laden granules, or gel, gradually give off moisture into the surrounding compost as it dries out. And each time you water the container, the gel absorbs more water than the compost, thus retaining moisture in the pot for longer.

Many packet instructions advise you to rehydrate the crystals first, then mix the sticky wet gel into the compost. But this is a messy job and it can be difficult to be sure that the 'swelly gelly' is evenly distributed.

It is easier to mix dry granules into the compost and then add the water, but remember that the mixture will swell once it is watered, so you can easily over-fill the container. Err on the side of caution, then top up the pot with more compost if necessary.

Give plants a morning drink of water to stop them drying out in the heat of the midday sun

Self-watering pots

A self-watering hanging basket, pot or trough ❷ works because it has a false bottom, beneath which is a reservoir to hold water. The compost is kept moist by drawing water up into the pot when it is needed through a matting pad and wick. More sophisticated containers also have a tube for refilling the reservoir and overflow holes to allow excess water to drain away.

Self-watering containers can reduce the need to water pots daily, but are still only as good as the person looking after them. It is easy for plants to become over-wet in rainy weather or, conversely, be forgotten and allowed to dry out. However, they can be very useful if you know you don't have time for watering every day.

▶ **Make a feature** of weather-beaten watering cans, and keep them handy for when plants need a drink, by incorporating them in your displays.

Automatic watering

If you have a lot of pots or are often away from home, an automatic watering system could make the difference between coming home to a lot of dead plants or a beautiful garden. ③ In the most efficient systems, water from the mains runs through narrow pipes to adjustable drippers feeding pots that require regular watering. The system can be operated by turning on a tap for the required length of time or, even better, by means of an automatic timer.

The chief drawback is that whereas in a garden you can hide tubing under the soil, it is less easy to disguise it as it runs between pots. On a wall, you can camouflage the tubing by painting it to match the background or by running it along the mortar joints. Be aware that with a timer system your pots will be watered whether or not it has rained, so there is a risk of over-watering.

The most expensive systems can be programmed to set length of watering time, number of times a day required, and even the days of the week on which you want watering to take place. This means that if your plants are on a balcony you can water them at a time when any drips will not disturb people beneath. Variable systems are also useful early and late in the season and during wet weather, when your containers will not need as much water.

In-line feeders can also be hooked up to add a weak dose of fertiliser to the water each time it comes on, making both feeding and watering worry free.

Give pots a soaking in the morning, before the sun gets too harsh, or early in the evening. At midday the water may evaporate before it can reach the roots or cause the leaves to scorch.

237

keeping the container looking good

Growing plants in pots is easy and rewarding. With food, drink and a snug container, your displays will be sure to flourish from season to season.

Choosing your container, plants and compost with care, and watering your pots regularly are all essential for a fabulous display. But a little extra attention will extend the life of arrangements that are intended to last for one season only, and is essential if you are to keep permanent plantings looking their best for many years.

Feeding your plants

All plants need a regular source of food if they are to reach their full potential. There are many kinds of fertilisers available: specific formulations suitable for flowers, trees and shrubs, or fruit and vegetables, but also good general-purpose varieties. Always follow the manufacturer's recommendations – overdosing can be toxic, while underfeeding will not allow plants to reach their full potential.

Liquid and soluble powder fertilisers are fast acting and quickly absorbed by plants, but must be applied regularly because their effects are short-lived. Use them during the growing season and reduce the application gradually once the plants have passed their peak. You don't need

to feed plants in winter even if they still look good, because they are not in active growth.

Foliar feeds are liquid fertilisers in a highly diluted form capable of being absorbed through a plant's leaves; these are useful to boost performance for a special occasion, or as a pick-me-up.

Fertilisers also come in powder and capsule forms. They can be fast acting or release their nutrients gradually over a period of up to 12 months, according to the temperature and the moisture of the compost.

For container cultivation, it is best to use slow-release fertilisers, since your plants will be in the same compost for at least a season. You can mix slow-release feeds into your compost at planting time. Alternatively ① there are special hanging basket slow-release feeds in 'tea bag' form, designed to be included when you plant.

If your containers are permanently planted, push in fertiliser pellets ②, or sprinkle on a top-dressing of granules ③ in spring. Dense displays, such as hanging baskets, may need additional liquid feeds when they are flowering.

Spraying

To protect your plants, you may need to spray them with chemicals against certain pests and diseases (see pages 244-247). Spraying as a preventive measure is no longer necessary, as most modern cultivars are more disease-resistant than traditional varieties. But if fungal diseases, such as blackspot, rust and scab, were a problem in permanent container displays one year, it may be wise to spray plants early in the following season before signs of similar damage appear.

For controlling bugs and blights on plants in containers, an instant trigger spray of the right insecticide or general fungicide may be all you need. However, you may prefer to use a pressure sprayer ❶ if you have a large number of plants, in a conservatory for example, or if you have many awkward-to-reach hanging baskets.

Some chemicals are available as a puffer dust, but this looks unsightly where it accumulates around a pot.

Deadheading

Cutting off spent flowers ❷ has several purposes. It tidies up the plants, removes dead material which can become infected with fungal diseases, prevents the plant putting unnecessary effort into seed production when what is required is flowers and strong growth, and encourages new shoots to grow.

It is possible to deadhead many plants – busy lizzies and petunias, for example – by snapping off the spent blooms with your fingernails, but sharp scissors or secateurs deal more cleanly with geraniums and patio roses. Always make your cut just above a leaf joint to prevent stems from dying-back.

The traditional advice for roses was to deadhead and prune them at the same time, by cutting back to a bud somewhere down the new season's stem. More recent tests suggest that you will have healthier bushes if you leave on as much foliage as possible throughout summer, and just cut off any dead flowerheads.

Envelop plants and pots in cosy layers when the weather turns cold

Wrapping up to keep plants warm in winter

Many patio plants are not fully hardy and may be badly frosted or killed in very cold weather. Insulating the container (see below) will help to keep the roots warm, but the foliage can also be protected. Cover the plant ❶ with a couple of layers of horticultural fleece, or, if this is not available, some old net curtain can be used instead.

As a last resort, you can keep frost at bay by wrapping layers of newspaper lightly around the foliage, but remove it when the temperature starts to rise as plants need to receive all the available light at that time of year. Never use polythene: it will stop the plant from breathing and will cause sweating that can lead to grey mould, or botrytis (see pages 246-247), and rotting.

With a little care many of the traditional 'basket plants', which are grown for their summer flowers, will survive to flower again. *Begonia semperflorens*, fuchsias, bedding geraniums and trailing petunias are all really tender perennials and can be over-wintered in a light place with a minimum temperature of 5°C (40°F).

Most hardy plants need no special winter protection, as long as they are in containers substantial enough to insulate the roots in very cold weather. However, it is drought, not frozen roots, that will kill a plant at this time – when the pot freezes, plants are unable to extract moisture from the compost.

Cold snaps are unlikely to harm plants in heavy terracotta containers, but if prolonged low temperatures are forecast, it is wise to employ some additional protection. The best way to do this is to envelope the pot ❷ in bubble wrap, several layers of cardboard or a piece of old carpet.

keeping things going for another year

Once the season is over, is it possible to keep your container plants – and is it worth it? This guide tells you which flowers to consign to the compost bin, and which will survive to be enjoyed again next year.

Many favourite pot plants – annual lobelia, African and French marigolds (*Tagetes*) and zinnia, for example – will only live for one year and should be discarded once they are past their best. The same applies to hardy annuals, such as candytuft, godetia, larkspur and pot marigold (*Calendula*), often used in pots for instant effect.

Biennials, such as Canterbury bells and forget-me-nots, are sown one year to flower the next, and can be bought ready to plant at the end of their first year. Daisies, stocks, sweet williams and wallflowers – all really short-lived perennials – are also best treated as biennials: enjoy their flowers for a year and then dig them out.

What to do with bulbs when their flowers fade

Bulbs are the mainstay of most spring containers, and a pot of lilies is one of the glories of summer. But once the flowers have finished you are left with unappealing pots of foliage.

Hardy spring bulbs can last for two or three seasons in the same compost before it needs replacing. And all kinds of lilies will flower successfully in the same container for several years if the bulbs are planted in a good humus-rich, soil-based compost. The lilies shouldn't need insulating in cold weather as long as you plant them in good, heavy, frost-proof containers.

Move the pots into an out-of-the-way place and allow the foliage to die down naturally. Cutting leaves off or tying them in knots will stop them from making nutrients for next year's bulbs and will lead to a disappointing display the following spring.

If you have nowhere to relocate the tubs, but feel the dying foliage looks untidy, you can surround the bulbs with bedding or foliage plants as a disguise. Keep the compost almost dry in winter and move the bulbs back into the limelight when the new shoots emerge.

Alternatively, you can carefully lift bulbs and their foliage and plant them out in the garden border. Large-flowered hybrid tulips are not worth growing on, even in the garden, for a second season. They may never flower again, and even if they do the flowers will probably be poor. Discard the bulbs and start again. However, you

Leave it, transplant it or throw it away?

Gaura ① will flower again if you plant it out, but gypsophilia is best thrown away. Lilies ② die back as summer fades, but leave the bulbs in their pot for winter and they will come again. Busy lizzies can be kept in a frost-free place, while the best use for *Alchemilla mollis* is to fill a gap in the border. Hostas ③ die down in autumn, but will re-emerge in spring. Lift dahlia tubers ④ when the foliage has died back, but throw away pot marigolds. Leave rudbeckia and osteospermums in their pot and use them in a new arrangement next year. Patio roses ⑤ will survive if you prune them and the campanula beneath these may also come back next year. Insulate metal containers to prevent the plant's roots from freezing.

can plant botanical 'species' forms of tulip and large-flowered hyacinths in the open ground after their first spring.

Half-hardy bulbous plants, such as dahlias and gladioli should be allowed to die down naturally. Then dig out the tubers, clean and dry them thoroughly and store in vegetable nets or old tights hung in a cool, frost-free, dark place until replanting time. Label the tubers by colour to help you when replanting.

Plants to keep

Many modern half-hardy bedding plants are perennials and can last for longer than just one season in their container. These include bedding geraniums, *Cineraria maritima*, diascia, felicia, fuchsias, helichrysum, lantana, marguerite, osteospermum, scaevola and verbena. If you protect these plants during freezing spells, they should last for several years.

How much protection they need depends on your local climate. In warmer parts of the country and in sheltered gardens, you may only need to drape a temporary layer of light horticultural fleece over the plants. In colder areas, you will probably need to overwinter them in a greenhouse with enough heat to keep the temperature

of the air just above freezing, or indoors on a light windowsill.

Convolvulus, gazania, petunias (including the trailing forms), busy lizzies and New Guinea hybrid impatiens, lotus, mimulus, and perennial nemesia are often discarded at the end of the season as many people prefer to start afresh each spring with new plants and different colours.

However, all these can be overwintered in a well-lit frost-free place. Repot them from late February to early April, and prune them back hard immediately to encourage plenty of healthy new shoots. Alternatively, you can take successful cuttings from most of these plants in early summer. Keep them in a warm, light position over winter and plant them in your arrangements next year.

OUTDOOR TYPES

Hardy perennials, such as bergenia, euphorbia and evergreen heuchera, dwarf shrubs and grasses can stay

USED COMPOST IS PAST ITS BEST

Never reuse compost from your containers for a second year. Its texture will have deteriorated and any fertiliser that remains in it is likely to be too unbalanced to be of any use. Simply tip it on to your flowerbeds or compost heap and start again with fresh compost in clean containers.

outside in their pots all year round. They should be repotted only when they are pot-bound, and this should preferably be done in early spring.

If they are planted in soil-based compost and in substantial pots, these plants will overwinter happily without being moved under shelter. However, in a prolonged cold spell it is wise to protect containers with bubble wrap (see pages 238-239) to prevent the compost from freezing solid around the roots.

You can keep containers of hardy perennials looking good by removing dead growth from time to time. Winter-flowering pansies and violas can be kept in flower virtually constantly for two whole seasons at least if they are dead-headed regularly, sprayed against mildew and pansy aphid, and well fed. Give the plants a good all purpose liquid fertiliser weekly in summer, fortnightly in spring and autumn, and monthly in winter and water them only when the compost is almost dry.

pruning and training for shapely shrubs

Keep plants in trim, and you will be rewarded with a good crop of flowers or fruit every year and a garden full of healthy bushy specimens.

To keep your plants well shaped and healthy, pruning and training are essential. Flowering and fruiting plants will only perform at their best if they are pruned, otherwise they will grow tall and leggy, and produce a poor crop.

As a general rule, shrubs flowering up to the middle of July should be pruned immediately after flowering, and those flowering in late summer and autumn should be pruned in spring. Unlike garden-grown shrubs, which are pruned to encourage healthy new growth, the main aim when pruning container plants is to keep bushes looking good. This is achieved simply by cutting back all the shoots that have flowered to retain the plant's shape. Permanently planted specimens will grow less each year as the roots fill the container, and will need more gentle pruning as they mature.

Pruning evergreens encourages thick, bushy foliage, and plants may need trimming several times during the growing season to keep them tidy. Use secateurs rather than shears to avoid cutting through foliage and leaving untidy ragged edges. Conifers, however, should be pruned as little as possible, since their distinctive look is natural, and most grow neatly and uniformly.

Unlike pruning, training is used mainly to create specific shapes. At its simplest, it merely involves regular clipping, tying in or cutting back, but can involve other, more sophisticated, techniques, such as the use of wires and frames to produce elaborate topiary (see pages 110-111).

Cutting an evergreen cone into a corkscrew

Buying ready-shaped topiary can be expensive, but a simple shape, such as a spiralling corkscrew, is easy to achieve at home. Spring is the best time of year to cut a bush into a topiary shape. The plants are growing so fast then, that any slips with the shears or bare patches will soon be hidden as the bush fills out into a neat shape.

Start by winding a piece of string ❶ around a conical shrub, such as this box. Tie the string at the very tip of the plant and adjust its position as it spirals around the cone until you are happy with the shape. With experience you will be able to shape plants by eye, but for beginners this guide will help.

Cut away foliage ❷ above the string to a point about half way between the lines. Use shears and cut as deep into the plant as you can, leaving the main stem exposed. Thicker branches may need to be cut with secateurs; trim them short so that the blunt ends are hidden within the leaves.

ENCOURAGING BUSHINESS

- **Pinching out** is a very simple technique used mainly with young plants to encourage bushiness through the formation of side shoots.
- **Nip out or cut** the growing tips of the main stems by pinching them between your fingernails or by snipping them with a pair of secateurs.
- **Check the plant as it grows** and, if necessary, pinch out new lateral growths until you achieve the bushy shape you want.

Check all the time ③ as you are cutting that you are not going to remove a 'structural' branch and lose a clump of foliage higher up the tree. Turn the bush regularly and stand back to take a look to make sure the shape is even.

Once you have completed the spiral, finish off ④ by cutting away any new shoots protruding from the remaining foliage and round off the edges. Tidy up the finished topiary ⑤ with a light trim in summer if necessary.

Shaping a spiral with ivy and a frame

A less expensive option than buying an established topiary, and a faster one than training your own box spiral from scratch is to grow a climber, such as ivy, up a frame. Ivy can be slow to get established, but the advantage of this method is that the frame provides the finished shape while you wait. Within a few years you will have a bushy spiral, while a box seedling may take many years to reach the same stage.

Frames come in many materials and styles, including wire, straw, galvanised metal and wicker. This wire spiral ①, twisted around a bamboo cane, fits neatly into a simple terracotta pot to make a formal display.

For the quickest result, buy the longest trailing plants you can, and put at least two in the pot. Twist the stems around the support ② and trim off any growing out of the spiral ③. Check the plant regularly, and to keep the shape ④ tie in new shoots as they develop.

243

look out for
pests in your pots

Your precious plants are a tempting meal to the pests that roam your garden. Look out for signs of unwelcome visitors and keep your flowers for your own enjoyment.

▶ **Snails get everywhere,** as do their relations, slugs. Even height is no deterrent: they are found on balconies and roof gardens as well as at ground level. A daily patrol is the best way to limit the damage they can wreak in your containers.

Surprisingly few pests affect container-grown plants – far fewer than in the open garden. You may notice occasional unsightly bites out of a leaf or petal, but these isolated incidents seldom merit the wholesale use of chemical controls. Only one or two stubborn pests need chemicals to effectively get rid of them.

As a rule, the fewer chemicals you splash around, the more beneficial insects – particularly lacewings and ladybirds, but even wasps and hoverflies – will move in and do the job for you. These mini-predators have voracious appetites for aphids and other insect pests, and with care it is possible to establish a balance between friend and foe.

You can even buy beneficial insect larvae to introduce into the garden, but if you do this, you will need to avoid chemical controls completely. Also, unless you retain a few insect pests as a food source, your population of 'goodies' will eventually die out.

Slugs and snails

Although slugs and snails will attack plants grown in pots, they will not cause as many problems as in the open garden, as they dislike hard surfaces. Putting a gravel mulch on top of a pot, may act as a deterrent, but the best control is to inspect containers regularly and remove any slugs and snails you find. Slug pellets often seem to attract more than they destroy, but a liquid slug control watered over the container will help to deal with severe cases of infestation.

Aphids

The most common pests on container plants are aphids. Although usually referred to as 'greenfly', aphids come in many colours and sizes. They are small sap-sucking insects, and disfigure plants, usually on young shoots, but occasionally elsewhere. The pansy aphid, for example, colonises the stems just above soil level.

Damage caused by aphids tends to be more unsightly than fatal. However, in the case of pansy, lettuce and carrot-willow aphids (which can devastate parsley and other herbs of the same family), you may become aware of the problem only when the plants start to lose condition, by which time it is often too late to do anything about it.

Aphids can spread virus diseases among plants and can also, indirectly, cause the fungal disease sooty mould. The fungus lives on the sticky honeydew the aphids secrete and, if left unattended, clogs up plant pores. The easiest way to deal with this is to wash the affected plant with warm water to which a small amount of washing-up liquid has been added.

Many insecticides control aphids, but one, pirimicarb, is specific to this pest and will therefore not harm natural predators. A solution of soft soap, available in a ready-to-use trigger spray, is a good organic alternative.

▲ **Make friends with predatory insects,** such as ladybirds, by limiting your use of chemicals and they will keep more damaging insects in check for you.

▼ **Destruction can be unexpectedly beautiful,** as the perforations left in this *Canna* leaf by a ravaging slug or snail show.

▲ **Nibbled edges** show where vine weevils have been at work. The adult insects, which eat the leaves, cause little damage to the plant, but are a clue that the more destructive grubs are probably buried in the compost of the pot.

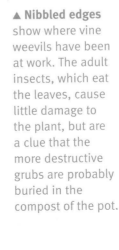

▶ **Aphids secrete sticky honeydew,** which is very attractive to ants. A sudden invasion of ants on a plant, such as this marigold, is often a clear sign of aphid infestation.

Vine weevils

The most serious pest to container gardeners is the grub of the vine weevil. The harmless adult is a medium-sized, black, flightless insect. But the dirty white larvae, which hatch in compost, feed off plants' roots. By the time a plant begins to wilt, it will be too late to save it.

Vine weevil grubs have become more common with the widespread use of soil-free composts, and thrive in waterlogged containers. Avoiding boggy conditions will help, or you could try applying a long-lasting, systemic insecticide called imidacloprid (or Provado) to the roots as a drench. Even if you haven't had vine weevils this is an excellent preventive measure, and also controls a wide range of other pot plant pests.

Animal pests

Larger nuisances can also be a problem in the garden. A cat will be sure to curl up in the middle of your choicest container, and dogs will often pee against pots.

The best way to deter cats is to insert lots of short canes, which will be hidden as the plants grow. To save leaves from the burning effects of dog urine, place a pot in a large outer pot or raise it off the ground.

Squirrels have a nose for bulbs, and can often be caught digging in pots. Putting a layer of chicken wire on the top of the compost may put them off for a while, but a strong-smelling product called Renardine may also help.

good health guide for pots and plants

Massed together, and warmed by heat reflected from paving and walls, plants in pots offer an ideal environment for viruses and fungi to spread, but with care and hygiene, you can keep your container plants disease-free.

▲ **Wash pots thoroughly** if they have been planted before, using clean water and a garden disinfectant. Let them dry before you plant them up.

▶ **Remove wilting leaves** when they lose their colour. Once a leaf turns yellow, it will never go green again, so check plants often and remove any dying leaves in case they may be harbouring any disease.

Prevention of disease begins at potting time, when you must make sure that all your containers are scrupulously clean. New pots should not need any cleaning, but used pots should be washed. Wooden containers will need to be vigorously scrubbed, and treated periodically with a timber preservative that will not harm plants: rotting wood can harbour all kinds of disease spores and undesirable bacteria.

This advice also applies to seed trays, small plant pots and any containers used to raise seedlings. Ideally, containers should be washed as soon as they are emptied so that they are ready for use when needed.

Even accessories such as canes and labels can carry disease and should also be disinfected before they are put into storage.

Cleaning any walls and paving slabs around your pots regularly will remove the dirt and algae that invariably collects. But this does more than just make the patio look better; it will also help to destroy any disease-carrying organisms that may be lurking in cracks and crevices.

Tool cleanliness is also crucial: many diseases are passed from plant to plant on dirty secateurs. When pruning, think of yourself as a surgeon, and wipe the blades of your secateurs with a cloth soaked in disinfectant before moving on to the next plant.

Spotting the signs and symptoms of disease

Bacteria and fungi can also be spread on your fingers, so remember to wash your hands from time to time while working in the garden.

Never reuse old compost. Not only will it contain an imbalance of plant foods by the end of the season, but it may also harbour disease spores and bacteria, which will be carried over to the next planting.

You can usually spread old compost over the garden or on the compost heap. However, certain diseases, such as tomato and potato blight, contaminate the soil so much that it is best to throw away any compost that plants affected with these problems have grown in.

NIP DISEASE IN THE BUD

Always remove dead flowers and leaves, and any other unhealthy plant material as soon as you spot them. Sweep the area around your pots regularly, and never compost anything that you know to be infected.

Like people, plants under stress are more vulnerable to disease than those bursting with vitality. Keep plants well fed to give them the best chance of survival. Fertilisers that are high in phosphates and potash produce strong root systems and tough, disease-resistant growth, while those with high levels of nitrogen can encourage lax, soft growth, which is easily invaded by diseases.

Underwatering also puts plants under stress, making them vulnerable to disease, while plants grown in waterlogged containers will have poor root health and weak, sickly growth.

However careful you are, it is almost impossible to keep plants completely disease-free. The most common problems, such as botrytis, powdery mildew, leaf spots and rust, are caused by fungi, and will spread fast in overcrowded conditions.

Spotty leaves ① that fall earlier than they should are probably infected with leaf spot. If you discover an infection, remove affected leaves and spray with a fungicide to stop it from spreading to new growth.

Rust ② is very difficult to eliminate; only one or two of the fungicides available to the amateur gardener have any effect, so you will need to ask for advice or read all the labels on treatments before buying.

A velvety grey mould ③ on leaves, flowers or fruit is caused by botrytis. The best prevention is to clear away

all dead parts of the plant and not allow water to stand on leaves and soft shoots for long periods in dull weather. Remove affected plants before the problem spreads.

A dusty white coating on leaves ④ is likely to be caused by powdery mildew. This is most common in warm dry weather and weakens the plant.

CURING THE PROBLEM

One of the most effective and wide-ranging fungicides is sulphur, which is also approved for organic use. Some plants, particularly some varieties of gooseberry, are intolerant to it, so check before you spray.

If a particular plant is repeatedly affected, replace it with something more robust. And remember that the best way to avoid problems is to choose disease-resistant varieties.

▶ **Disease is common on roses,** which are very susceptible to black spot, powdery mildew and rust. A regular spray of fungicide on plants you know are vulnerable to disease will help to keep your container displays in peak condition.

start work in the greenhouse in spring

▲ **Old pots** are good enough for the greenhouse. The plants will be moved into stylish containers when they go outside.

The keen container gardener will find even a small greenhouse really useful. Instead of waiting for bedding plants to reach the garden centre, you can get ahead and save money by starting young plants off under glass.

A few packets of seed will give you hundreds of bedding plants at reasonable cost. Sow them in February and early March and you will have young plants ready to be transplanted outside in mid to late May. However, most bedding plants require a germination temperature of 15-17°C (60-62°F),

so you will need to provide heating in the greenhouse, even if you use a heated propagator.

Some bedding plants, including French marigolds, nicotiana and snapdragons, may be sown in an unheated greenhouse later in spring, once the temperature has risen. Use a specific seed compost, and prick out the established seedlings into small

pots, modules or seed trays. Do not sow too early because when the plants are ready to be put outside the weather will still be too cold.

GROWING ON PLUG PLANTS

Most popular bedding plants can be bought as plug plants. These are easier to grow as they can be raised at a lower temperature and in less exacting

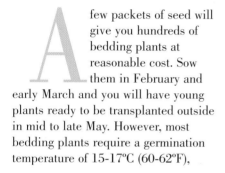

◄ **Seedlings** can be grown on to fill your containers with summer flowers such as ageratum, French marigolds, antirrhinums and petunias.

▼ **For a show of geraniums** that won't break the bank, take late summer cuttings and pot them up in the greenhouse. Next spring they will be ready to fill your containers.

conditions than seedlings. Whenever you buy plug plants from a garden centre or nursery, keep the plants warm and get them home quickly. If buying by mail order, unpack the plants as soon as they arrive and plant them into individual small pots of multipurpose compost. Place them in the best possible light at a temperature of at least 15ºC (60ºF). Keep them damp, but not wet or the plants may rot at the base. Move to bigger pots as they grow.

Harden off the plants by gradually exposing them to cooler temperatures, before finally moving them outside. Do not rush them out too soon (late May is early enough) or you may lose them all in a late frost.

TAKING CUTTINGS

You can increase your stock of many container favourites by raising cuttings in the greenhouse in John Innes No.1. Take cuttings of herbs in early summer, half-hardy bedding plants such as geraniums, trailing petunias, marguerites and helichrysum in July and early August and chrysanthemums in late winter and early spring. Fuchsia cuttings will take at any time of the

▶ **When winter comes** the greenhouse becomes a safe haven. Tender container plants such as palms, agaves, bonsai, and Cape primroses can be moved inside until the danger of frost has passed.

▼ **Herbs root easily** in a warm place. Here cuttings of mint, purple sage and rosemary are given a dusting of hormone rooting powder before planting in trays.

year. To keep the cuttings alive during their first winter, a minimum temperature of 5-7ºC (40-45ºF) is necessary. Take care not to overwater.

OVERWINTERING PLANTS

Many half-hardy container plants, such as begonias, tender fuchsias, geraniums, marguerites and trailing petunias, need protection from frost during colder months. The best solution is to move them to a greenhouse kept frost-free with bubble wrap and heated to just above 0ºC (32ºF).

Other patio plants will overwinter at just above freezing, providing they are kept almost dry and not pruned until new growth begins to appear. Place them towards the centre of the greenhouse where the temperature is highest (not near the glass or the roof).

◄ **This row of tomatoes** is thriving in pots set in rings within a grow bag. The rings make it easier to direct water straight to the roots, since regular moisture is a key requirement of a good crop.

▲ **Hungarian Hot Wax peppers** produce mild, spicy rather than fiery fruits that change colour as they ripen. The plants are tied into a metal trellis, which straddles the grow bag.

hothouse crops for summer

Half-hardy vegetables can be raised successfully in containers outdoors, but growing them in a greenhouse throughout their lives will give you bigger crops over a longer period.

Half-hardy vegetables such as tomatoes, peppers, and aubergines can be raised in pots outdoors, but growing them in a greenhouse throughout their lives will give you bigger crops over a longer period.

Sow the seeds in small pots of seed compost in a heated propagator at a temperature of 15-20°C (60-68°F) in late February, and prick out the seedlings into small pots when they are large enough to handle.

Transfer the young plants to large pots filled with multi-purpose compost, or to grow bags, when about 10cm (4in) tall, in April, maintaining a temperature of around 12-15°C (55-60°F).

Provide canes, twine or wires for support as the plants grow. Tomatoes under glass are usually grown as cordons, with the side shoots removed as they appear to leave a single stem.

Feed with a liquid tomato fertiliser once flowers start to appear, and weekly throughout the cropping season thereafter.

▶ **Glossy purple aubergines** burgeon in a warm greenhouse. They are big plants, which need plenty of space around them and some support. They benefit from being misted regularly to keep down red spider mite.

◀ **Shiny red peppers** hang ready for picking. They are green until they reach their full size then turn colour over the next three weeks. Peppers are sprawling plants and need to be trained up canes for support.

TRY SOMETHING DIFFERENT

If you don't want to grow crops in your greenhouse, why not turn it into an alpine house, like the one in the picture below? A wide selection of alpines can be grown permanently in pots under glass. Those species which do not enjoy the cold and damp of the British winter are particularly suitable. Try *Androsaces*, encrusted saxifrages, lewisias, *Ranunculus asiaticus* and *Soldanella*.

• **No heat is needed:** the secret of growing alpines under glass is to give them as much light as possible and plenty of good ventilation. Leave doors, windows and vents open at all times, even in winter, and reduce watering to a minimum from October to February.

• **Put plants in shallow clay pots or pans** in a gritty, open, alpine compost. Top off with pea shingle or grit, and plunge the pots into grit or sharp sand to regulate the temperature, soil moisture and humidity.

It is usually necessary to shade the greenhouse with blinds or with white shading paint during the height of summer to prevent the foliage from being scorched by hot sunshine falling on the glass for long periods.

Water all the plants regularly, so that the compost is always moist but never waterlogged. If the watering is erratic it will cause problems with the developing fruits. Vegetables grown in the greenhouse usually produce their crops from July to October, depending on the variety.

PERMANENT ORNAMENTAL PLANTS

While you are tending to your vegetable crops, try to find a corner in the greenhouse where you can grow a selection of tender plants to give yourself an even more attractive working environment.

The most suitable are those plants that will overwinter without needing too high a temperature, such as abutilon, asparagus fern, bougainvillea, Christmas cactus, *Jasminum polyanthum*, oleander, passionflowers, plumbago, rhodochiton, sansevieria and spider plants. These will overwinter at 3-5ºC (37-40ºF), providing there is good light, watering is reduced to the minimum and the greenhouse is kept well insulated.

For extra pleasure early in the year, pot up some bowls of bulbs and leave them outside for winter, covered with old compost or sacking. Bring them into the greenhouse early in the new year and you will soon be surrounded by the welcome colours of spring flowers.

► **"The view over the river is so beautiful,"** says Moira, "always changing…" Here, scented white nicotianas tumble over the balcony fence and fragrant yellow lilies bask in the sun as deep purple clouds roll in from over the city.

a
place
to
unwind

High above
a sweep of the
River Thames
in the heart
of London,
designers Moira
and Nick Potter
have created
a container
garden in the
sky. Four floors up in a
converted Victorian warehouse, French
doors open onto a stunning balcony.
To the west lies the centre of London,
and looking east you can see the cranes
and skyscrapers of Docklands. But here
the only sounds come from wheeling
seagulls and the occasional tourist
steamer. "Giving up a real garden was
difficult at first," remembers Moira ▶

▲ **The south-facing
balcony** enjoys lots
of sun and is a
perfect spot for an
al fresco summer
lunch (right). It's
also warm enough
to use for much of
the autumn when
pots of burgundy,
orange and russet
chrysanthemums
glow in the evening
sunshine.

253

> " **I was so surprised – the lilies love windy weather and push their heads through the railings to catch more fresh air.** "

"but now, coming back in summer after work, we sit out here with a drink, the smell of flowers, the sound of the river and the boats."

The balcony has its own microclimate: "It is very exposed with odd bits of shelter," says Moira, "and can be windy and very sunny. Early on, I guessed it must be a bit like central Turkey – very hot in summer and cold in winter – although the river, and being in an inner city, keep it mostly above freezing."

A hunt for suitable plants turned up thrifts: "They're thriving, and flower from March right through to September. I've never had much time for thrifts before, but now I love their resilience and the way their button flowers float above the cushion of spiky green leaves."

A huge agapanthus is another favourite: "In spring, green leaf blades appear" says Moira. "Then 15 or so stalks with the flowers tightly bound in a green wrap which seems to take ages to burst. The blooms are lovely cobalt blue balls which then stay as seed heads catching cobwebs, frost and dew all winter…"

OF WIND AND WATER

But agapanthus does not like the wind. "We've put polycarbonate screening around half of the railings and tall screens at either end," says Nick. "It's what they use for riot shields – very strong, doesn't discolour or break, but it's expensive." He has since drilled the screens with a grid of large holes, as high winds

▶ **Drawbridge shelves,** hanging from sturdy chains anchored to the walls (above), hold the heaviest planters. Nick put up the shelves to lessen the risk of overloading the balcony. He and Moira usually opt for plastic pots to keep the weight down.

▼ **Colour is key,** but fragrance is an added bonus, provided by lilies and nicotianas. "The summer bedding petunias, which get fitted into gaps, also give off a surprising amount of scent", says Moira.

254

caused it to bow dramatically. Other plants, however, seem to relish river breezes. "I always put out pots of scented lilies and nicotianas when they're in flower," says Moira, "and I was so surprised – the lilies love windy weather and push their heads out through the railings to catch more fresh air. The nicotianas aren't bothered by summer winds either."

Moira and Nick got off to a good start when they first moved in, bringing with them some 80 plants in containers from their old garden. But it wasn't all plain sailing. Some plants couldn't stand the climate and Moira lost all her beloved hostas. "We also quickly realised that filling watering cans in the bathroom was not ideal," remembers Nick, "so we put in an outdoor tap and a watering system. But every time we turned it on the balconies below were deluged," he laughs "so we had to water when we were sure everyone was in bed! And then the little hoses got so tangled up whenever we moved the pots, we've pretty much given up on it."

There is room for both order and chaos in this container garden in the sky. A neat pair of square planters, placed so that they can be seen from inside, stands either side of the French doors. "I have two sets of pots" explains Moira. "The daffodils live in theirs permanently and go to the cellar in the summer. The other flowers are planted in sequence in the same pot."

Perhaps the greatest joy of this garden is its unpredictability. "Foxgloves from our old garden always self-seed in places I haven't planned, but they are such good fun," smiles Moira. "And blue morning glory seeds, sown midsummer, always take and scramble untidily through other plants. We just love it."

▲ **The view from inside** has a pleasing geometric symmetry. Large square planters sit on either side of the French doors, and a second pair at the front of the balcony frame and shelter an elegant filigree table and chairs.

▲ **Two conical box,** which act as formal bookends to the balcony for most of the year, come indoors over Christmas and are decorated with lights and ribbons.

◄ **Traditional border plants** and climbers do surprisingly well in their elevated container home (1). Among Moira's favourites are self seeded foxgloves (2), and a peony – a gift from Nick's grandmother (3).

novel ways to decorate containers

Fir cones, paints, ribbon and raffia can all be used to embellish containers. Here are some ideas for permanent transformations and quick fixes for special occasions.

Silvering the rim of a terracotta pot

The cheapest flowerpots can be given a touch of designer class using metallic paints. Sold by the tube in craft shops, they are simply applied ❶ with a finger tip. This flowerpot's shiny silver rim ❷ looks great with a creamy white hyacinth. Or you could paint the pots first. These pots ❸ were painted with olive-green emulsion and left to dry, before a metallic stripe was added around their middles. A glittering mulch of crystalline glass chippings (see pages 226-227) completed the transformation.

Using a verdigris kit to cover an urn

The attractive greenish coating that covers old, weathered copper is called verdigris. Its soft greeny grey colour makes a wonderful backdrop to foliage and flowers and is easy to achieve.

A typical verdigris kit, available from DIY stores, contains several small pots of paint – one for each layer – and a stippling brush. It can be used to transform wood, metal, plastic or terracotta containers.

A terracotta pot must be washed thoroughly and allowed to dry completely before beginning work. Then, paint it all over ❶ with the first colour in the kit. Once the paint has dried, apply the second, lighter, colour ❷ with the stippling brush.

The secret of stippling is to use an almost dry brush. Dip the brush into the paint and dab it on a piece of kitchen paper until it is almost dry. Then stipple the brush onto a scrap of paper.

What you want to achieve is an even, light-coloured impression. Once you are happy with the effect, begin stippling the pot. You should end up with an almost transparent layer of paint through which the base coat can be seen.

Repeat this process with each colour supplied in the kit, ending with the metallic paint.

◄ **Leftover emulsion paints** can be used to create this rainbow effect. First, paint the pot with three or four overlapping horizontal bands in different colours. When the paint is dry blend the stripes into one another by rubbing over the entire surface of the pot with a suede brush, which has fine, flexible metal bristles.

▲ **Tying ribbon or raffia** around a pot is the quickest way to decorate it, whether for a special occasion or to pick up on a colour scheme. Try gold braid for a party, tinsel at Christmas or lace for a wedding.

▲ **Cheer up a hanging basket** by poking a few fir cones through its mesh or wirework before you put in the coir or moss lining. Otherwise, the underside can look very bare.

To give pots a festive feel, see pages 218-219

Different ways with wooden barrels

Wooden half-barrels often look fine just as they are. However, you may like to paint yours to enhance a particular colour scheme (below left). The key to success is preparation ❶: use abrasive paper to rub down both wood and metal before you paint.

Then apply a coat of primer. When the primer is dry, paint the whole barrel, including the metal straps with your chosen colour, in this case bottle green.

When this has dried, you can paint the metal bands ❷ in a contrasting colour. Stop accidental drips running onto the wood by applying a strip of masking tape below the straps.

For a stripy fairground effect, you could paint alternate upright wooden slats in contrasting colours.

257

hide away those buckets and bags

Use natural materials such as bamboo, log edging or wood to disguise plastic pots or grow bags used for plants on a balcony, terrace or patio.

Camouflaging a plastic bucket

To disguise the plastic tub a new plant came in, and to avoid repotting, wrap it in a roll of bamboo, from a garden centre. Measure the height ❶ of the bucket and its circumference and use secateurs ❷ to cut a strip of bamboo tall enough to hide the rim and long enough to wrap all the way round. Hold it in place with a few twists of garden wire.

Hiding a grow bag

The garish covers of grow bags do little to enhance a garden or patio. And if you intend growing vegetables in a choice, south-facing position, the chances are that your grow bag will be in full view. However, you can solve the problem with this ingenious disguise. All you need ❶ is a length of log edging, two planks and five bricks. It takes just minutes to put together and can be dismantled for winter and used the following year.

Measure the length of the grow bag and buy two planks of preservative-treated 150x25mm (6x1in) softwood cut to that length. Measure around the edge of the bag and buy enough log edging (available by the roll from most garden centres) to go right round it.

Choose the growing site and sit the planks ❷ on the bricks – two bricks at each end and one in the middle. Unroll the log edging and place it in position – it is heavy, so enlist a helper if you can. Bang a few nails ❸ right through the logs and into the planks to keep the roll neatly in position. Put the grow bag on the planks ❹ – pummel it into shape for a snug fit – and cut the planting holes in it.

Making a Versailles planter

Wooden Versailles planters were traditionally used for orange trees and topiary. They had one removable side to allow gardeners access for root trimming, which stops trees in planters from growing too large.

Today, Versailles planters are made in plastic or wood in a range of sizes. Few have removable sides, but this one does. You can plant straight into the box or keep the tree or shrub in its original pot and stand this in the planter.

The planter is made with five planks of tongue-and-groove cladding deep and is about 460mm (18in) square. The 50x50mm (2x2in) corner posts extend about 50mm (2in) above the top slat and about 100mm (4in) below the base. The base is made from marine ply supported on 25x25mm (1x1in) battens. Four lengths of quadrant beading are used to neaten the corners.

FIRST STEPS

Make two sides by nailing sections of glued and interlocked cladding to the corner posts. Use a nail punch **1** to sink the nail heads so they lie just below the surface of the wood.

Glue and interlock the slats of the third section and nail this **2** to the two already-completed sides.

Measure the internal dimensions of the box and cut the base to size. Drill several drainage holes, each approximately 25mm (1in) in diameter, in the base using a spade bit. And cut 50mm (2in) right-angle notches out of the corners

to clear the upright posts (for more detail, see window box construction, pages 260-261). Glue and pin batten supports for the base to the inner faces of the box, flush with the bottom edges, and **3** slip the base into place.

For the removable fourth side, use an offcut from a corner post as a guide to mark vertical lines inside the section. Glue and pin battens along these lines, as well as the horizontal base support piece. Check the fit **4** – the vertical battens should fit snugly between the corner posts.

Then drill three or four holes straight through the section into the corner posts. Fix in place **5** using brass screws, which do not rust so will be easy to remove when you want access to the roots. Use brass screw cups, too, if you wish.

Neaten the corners of the planter using quadrant beading cut to length and fixed with glue – it's a good idea to hold the beading in place with masking tape while the glue sets. Finally, treat the finished planter inside and out with wood preservative and a paint, varnish or stain finish.

make a picket fence window box

This window box gives a pretty cottage garden feel to a window. The picket fence look is easy to achieve with a little patience.

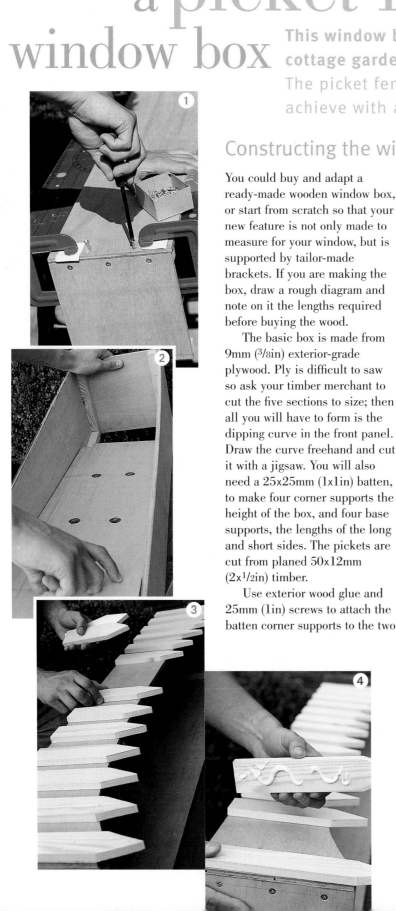

Constructing the window box

You could buy and adapt a ready-made wooden window box, or start from scratch so that your new feature is not only made to measure for your window, but is supported by tailor-made brackets. If you are making the box, draw a rough diagram and note on it the lengths required before buying the wood.

The basic box is made from 9mm (³/₈in) exterior-grade plywood. Ply is difficult to saw so ask your timber merchant to cut the five sections to size; then all you will have to form is the dipping curve in the front panel. Draw the curve freehand and cut it with a jigsaw. You will also need a 25x25mm (1x1in) batten, to make four corner supports the height of the box, and four base supports, the lengths of the long and short sides. The pickets are cut from planed 50x12mm (2x¹/₂in) timber.

Use exterior wood glue and 25mm (1in) screws to attach the batten corner supports to the two ends. Drill pilot holes and countersink them so that the screw heads lie flush. Then fix the back to the ends, screwing into the corner uprights ❶. You will need to use clamps or enlist help to support the structure. Fix battens along the bottom inside edges of both back and front sections to support the floor. Fix the front to the ends to make a four-sided structure.

Make drainage holes in the base using a 25mm (1in) spade bit. Wedge a piece of scrap wood underneath the hole and drill clean through the ply and into the scrap. This will stop the drill bit from splintering and tearing the ply as it emerges. Saw 25x25mm (1x1in) notches in each corner of the base to clear the corner supports. Then drop the base ❷ into the box.

Cut as many pickets as you need for the front of the box. Cut them in pairs, each pair slightly longer than the last and number them on the back. Position them ❸ evenly along the front and glue them ❹ in place.

Do not worry about being too perfect – the finished box will actually look better with a degree of irregularity. Three pickets will be enough for each end – the corner ones are useful for hiding the screw heads. Then treat the whole box with wood preservative before painting or varnishing it. A white lime-washed effect looks pretty.

Making the brackets

A planted window box is heavy – even more so when it has just been watered. You can either buy a pair of metal brackets or make wooden ones and paint them to match the box. Each of these brackets is made using three lengths of 50x25mm (2x1in) timber. The horizontal support needs to be the same length as the depth of the box from the wall, plus an extra 25-50mm (1-2in) to allow air behind it. The vertical support should be the same length or longer, for ease of fixing to the wall.

Create the right-angle bracket using 50mm (2in) screws and exterior wood glue. Then, roughly measure a diagonal ❶ that cuts across the right angle about 50mm (2in) from its ends. This is the length of the support. If you have a mitre saw or a mitre block, these will help you to cut the 45° angles at the ends of the diagonal support. Otherwise mark the mitres using a combination square and cut them with a tenon saw.

Hold the diagonal support in place ❷ using one of the mitred offcuts and a clamp. Then drill through from the back of the bracket. Fix the support with screws and glue. Repeat at the opposite end. Drill holes in the back piece for fixing to the wall. Then treat your brackets with preservative. If you are fixing the brackets to a masonry wall ❸ use wall plugs and 75mm (3in) screws. Use a spirit level to check that each upright is plumb.

using lead to create a stylish effect

This unusual window box, filled with kitchen herbs, has been covered with lead sheeting. The scalloped frill around the top was given a silvery mottled look by dabbing it with white malt vinegar.

Applying lead to a window box

You will need a plain window box (either buy one or make your own following the steps on pages 260-261), a length of 25x25mm (1x1in) softwood batten, a roll of lead flashing (sold at builders' merchants) and some galvanised clout nails. Measure the height of the box and the length of the front plus the two sides – you do not need to cover the back unless it will be visible. Use tin snips to cut a strip of lead just longer than this so you can bend any surplus behind to create neat corners. Flatten the lead onto the box ➊ using a small flat piece of wood and a hammer and nail it in place.

Cut three lengths of batten, one for each side and one to go along the front. The scalloped frill will be fixed to these so that it stands proud of the box. Fix the battens around the top of the box ➋: drill holes through the box from inside and drive screws through

the holes into the battens. Cut the scalloped trim (see tip box) ➌ and nail this to the top of the front batten.

Snip notches out at the corners ➍ and bend the scalloped edge down. Then bend the strip round the corners and fold it over the top edges of the side battens. Tap smoothly into place using a piece of wood and a hammer and fix in place with clout nails driven into the top of the battens.

To give the lead a weathered patina dab white malt vinegar onto the surface with a cloth until a whitish mottled effect appears. Paint the inside of the box if desired; the sage green used here ➎ would tone well with terracotta pots filled with herbs or flowers.

Securely fix two brackets to the wall (see pages 268-269) and sit the window box on them. Then drive screws up through the brackets into the base of the box to keep it firmly in place.

create your own stone trough

Stone troughs blend with any background and age beautifully. Their natural finish provides a perfect backdrop for even the subtlest planting. But solid stone troughs are expensive. Here are three ways to create your own.

Scoop some mortar up with your finger: if it remains stuck when you turn your hand upside down, it is ready.

Start applying the mortar to the trough using the trowel. You may find it easiest to pile the mixture along the base of the trough ③ and smooth it upwards. Mix more batches as needed. Do not worry about the finish: you will be applying a second coat later. Once you have completed the first coat, leave it to dry overnight.

The second layer of mortar contains compost. This will absorb moisture and attract algae, quickly giving the trough a weathered look. Crumble multi-purpose compost to a fine powder, and add a couple of handfuls to each small batch of the dry mix before stirring in the water. Slap the mix onto the trough. Then, wearing a pair of protective gloves ④, mould it with your hands to round off the edges – a slightly uneven surface will add to the authenticity. Rub off any loose mortar and leave the trough to dry overnight before planting.

Coating a plastic trough

The all-year-round container (pages 174–175) is a plastic trough coated in mortar mix. Mortar is available as a dry ready-mix from most DIY stores. But before mixing or applying it, you first need to paint the exterior sides of the plastic container (but not the base) with a thick coat of exterior grade PVA ①. This is a waterproof adhesive and bonding agent that will help the mortar

to stick. Leave the PVA to dry until tacky to the touch (an hour or so, but the length of time depends on drying conditions), and mix a small bucket of mortar. It is best to use several small batches of mortar rather than mixing it all at once as it hardens quite quickly.

Add water, a little at a time, stirring ② until the mix is smooth. A little PVA added to the mixture will strengthen it.

A lightweight trough

This trough is easy to move around and ideal for a roof garden or balcony where weight needs to be restricted. You will need a polystyrene box (the sort that fish or tender vegetables come in at the market is ideal). Cut away any angular corners **1** with a trimming knife, to soften the outline, and make a drainage hole in the base.

Coat the box, inside and out, with PVA and leave it to dry until tacky. Make a mortar mix with added compost, as described (below left). Wearing protective gloves, apply the mortar with your hands **2** and mould it over the edges until the trough is covered **3**. Once you are happy with the shape, leave it for an hour or so, then check to see if any of the mix has slipped. Slide it back into place while the mortar is still soft enough to mould. Leave to dry before planting up.

A moulded trough

Laminated board makes a good mould for a stone trough because its smooth sides slide easily from the solidified concrete. Decide on what size trough you require and screw together four pieces of wood to form a bottomless box. Make a second, smaller, version that will determine the thickness of the walls **1**, and add handles for easy lifting (simply nail two short lengths of batten to the inside).

Use dry ready-mix concrete to which you have added several handfuls of finely crumbled multipurpose compost. Mix these together **2** and slowly add water, stirring until you achieve a sloppy consistency.

Stand the outer mould on a plastic sheet and spread a layer of concrete to make the base of the trough. Push a piece of pipe into the middle to make a drainage hole. Sit the smaller mould squarely on the base, and then trowel the mixture down between the two.

Work evenly around the box **3**, gradually building height and tamping down with the trowel and a piece of wood to remove any air bubbles. Pay attention to filling the corners, as these are the weakest areas.

Pull out the inner mould as soon as the concrete feels just firm to the touch (leaving it any longer will make it hard to remove). Leave the trough to dry and harden overnight, then unscrew **4** and lift away the outer mould.

ways to brighten an empty space

Here are two simple ideas for decorating a wall, fence or trellis with plants. The beauty of both of these projects is that you can change the look as often as you like – it's just a question of changing the flowerpots.

Pot-swap plant shelf

This little pot shelf will brighten up any blank wall, and is light enough to hang from trellis screening or a wooden fence. You will need a piece of 20mm (³/₄in) thick planed softwood, 150mm (6in) wide and about 500mm (20in) long, a couple of shorter lengths for the brackets and two 150mm (6in) long battens, for the shelf supports, cut from 25x25mm (1x1in) softwood.

Mark three evenly spaced holes using a pencil, a ruler and a round template (a masking tape reel or a paint tin is ideal). To cut the holes, first drill right through the shelf inside one of the marked circles; then insert a padsaw or jigsaw blade ❶ to make the cut.

Ring the
changes
with spring
bulbs,
fresh herbs
and summer
flowers

Because the jigsaw cuts on the
upstroke, mark and cut the holes from
underneath. That way, any ragged
edges will end up on the underside of
the finished shelf.

The brackets can be any shape you
like. Here, a simple 'S' curve was cut to
make one bracket and was used as a
template to mark the second one. Drill
through the battens and use exterior-
grade wood glue and screws to fix them
to the brackets ❷ as shelf supports.
Countersink the screws so the heads lie
flush with the wood for a neater finish.

Fix the brackets to the shelf ❸ and
coat the finished article with clear
exterior wood preservative. You can
then paint or varnish it. This vibrant
blue is reminiscent of paintwork found
all over the Greek islands. Finally, drill
a hole through the top of each bracket,
fix the shelf in place with screws or
nails and add the pots.

A pot trellis

Brighten up a bare fence or wall with
this pot trellis. You can change the look
as often as you like: just unhook the
pots and pop in fresh plants. First,
measure the area you wish to cover and
buy a piece of trellis to suit – you
might like to paint it with an outdoor
wood stain. Then fix the trellis in place.

To make a pot loop, bend a length
of galvanised wire ❶ to fit snugly
beneath the pot rim. Twist one end of
the wire over itself and pinch tight ❷
with pliers leaving one long free end.
Bend this piece over ❸ to make a hook
that fits snugly over a horizontal piece
of the trellis. You can now create a
vertical herb garden or a wall of colour.

basic jobs in the container garden

Certain tasks are common to most container gardens. Nearly all pots need moving around from time to time, and pots or brackets need fixing to walls. In addition, you may wish to use the simple theft deterrent suggested below.

DETERRING THEFT

Pretty planters near a front door are easy targets for thieves. Complete security demands chains or steel rope, which are difficult to work with and unsightly. However, by making a pot hard to move, you may persuade a would-be pilferer to go for an easier target elsewhere.

• **Make an invisible deterrent** by fixing a pot in place. Drive a gate bolt, available from hardware stores, through one of the drainage holes in a pot before planting it up.

• **If the planter is to stand on a terrace** or other paved area, you first need to drill a hole large enough for the bolt to pass through the slabs or the concrete and hardcore. Next, hammer the bolt into the ground and pull it out to create the hole. Position the pot so that the drainage hole lies over this hole.

• **Gently push the bolt in** and drive it home (below) using a club hammer and a batten with a V-notch cut out of one end: this will reduce the likelihood of jarring the bolt or accidentally hitting the pot.

Moving pots made easy

Shifting a heavy pot can take its toll on your back. The job is made much easier with the help of a simple plant dolly. You can make one with a few timber offcuts, or buy a single wood decking tile (these are treated to make them weatherproof) and fix a castor at each corner. For a 380mm (15in) square dolly, you need seven 380mm lengths of 50x25mm (2x1in) planed softwood, wood screws, exterior-grade wood glue and four castors.

Create the square frame ❶ by joining four softwood lengths at the corners. Drill pilot holes at each end of the remaining three slats. Space these evenly between the end pieces and glue and screw in place ❷. Turn the platform over and fix a castor ❸ at each corner. Treat the bare wood with a weatherproof coating, and paint the dolly if you wish.

Putting up a bracket for a hanging basket

Hanging baskets are a popular decoration for the front door or porch. They are also a great way to break up a large dull expanse of wall. Choose a bracket that matches the basket in terms of style and, more importantly, size. A small basket hanging from a huge bracket looks mean; a large basket on a small bracket looks ridiculous and may pull it loose. If fixing the bracket to a masonry wall, mark the positions of the holes and drill them ❶ using a masonry drill bit. Tap in wall plugs and fix the bracket in place with 50mm (2in) screws ❷. Hang up the empty basket to make sure that you are happy with the placing. Then take it down, plant up and rehang.

Running water adds a magical touch to any garden. Containers can be used to incorporate water features in the most unlikely places – from a paved patio to a sunny roof terrace.

just add water for success

Installing a pebble fountain

Most garden centres now sell pebble or bubble fountain kits, consisting of a plastic bucket with a lid and a wide collar. You will also need a pond pump and a decorative disguise for the surface.

Start by digging a hole ❶ to take the bucket. The lip of the plastic collar should be flush with the surrounding earth and the feature must be level ❷ all the way round. When you are happy with the hole, line it with soft play-pit sand ❸ to prevent sharp stones from puncturing the plastic. Put the pond in place, position your pump in the base and run the electric cable away, hiding it among surrounding plants.

When wiring in the pump, follow the instructions that come with it, or call in an electrician. Outdoor electrics should always be connected via a residual current device (RCD) and installed with great care.

Fill the reservoir with water ❹ and test the pump. You may need to adjust the flow rate or positioning to achieve the effect you want. When you are happy, fit the lid ❺ and cover the top with your chosen decoration. Pebbles, gravel ❻ and large cobbles ❼ work well with a bubbling stream of water. You could build a display of tumbling flowerpots, or run a hose from the pump through a glazed terracotta ball with a hole drilled in the top. Or fit the pump with a spray attachment and hide it with pots of perennials that are happy being splashed, such as *Houttuynia*, ivies, *Lysimachia*, *Mimulus* and *Oenanthe*.

A FREE-STANDING POND

If you would like a fountain on your patio, you can fit a pump in any watertight pot. The pump must be completely submerged and will need space around it when you add your decorative topping. A good tip is to shield the pump with an upturned wire hanging basket and to arrange cobbles, plants, or both over the top.

An even easier way to bring moving water to your garden is to float a solar-powered fountain in a wide container, add a few water plants, and position the display in a sunny spot.

For more creative ways with water in the garden, see pages 76-77

PLANTS FOR A CONTAINER POND

All ponds need at least one oxygenating plant, and one floating plant for shade. Fill the rest of your container with marginal species. Stand pots on bricks so that the plants' roots will be the required depth below the water's surface.

• **Oxygenators:** hair grass (*Eleocharis acicularis*); hornwort (*Ceratophyllum demersum*); milfoil (*Myriophyllum spicatum*); water crowfoot (*Ranunculus aquatilis*).

• **Floating plants:** frogbit (*Hydrocharis morsus-ranae*); pygmy water lilies (*Nymphaea* 'Pygmaea Rubra'; *N.* 'Pygmaea alba'); water soldier (*Stratiotes aloides*).

• **Decorative marginals:** bog arum (*Calla palustris*); *Carex* spp; chameleon plant (*Houttuynia cordata*); corkscrew rush (*Juncus effusus* 'Spiralis'); *Iris* spp; marsh marigold (*Caltha palustris*); flowering rush (*Butomus umbellatus*); water mint (*Mentha aquatica*).

• **Avoid these invasive species** as they can escape and harm native British flora: Australian swamp stone-crop (*Crassula helmsii*); floating pennywort (*Hydrocotyle ranunculoides*); giant salvinia (*Salvinia molesta*); Indian balsam (*Impatiens glandulifera*); parrot's feather (*Myriophyllum aquaticum*); water chestnut (*Trapa natans*); water ferns (*Azolla caroliniana* and *A. filiculoides*); water hyacinth (*Eichornia crassipes*); water lettuce (*Pistia stratiotes*).

the pick of container plants

the pick of container plants

▶ **Pretty daisy-shaped flowers** from summer to mid autumn make argyranthemums (marguerites) a popular container plant.

To help you select the best plants for your containers, here are more than 200 chosen by experts and listed by colour and season. A cup symbol ♀ indicates plants that have won the Royal Horticultural Society's Award of Garden Merit (AGM).

white & cream flowers

spring

ANEMONE BLANDA 'WHITE SPLENDOUR'

Anemone blanda
'White Splendour'♀

Clump-forming perennial with irregularly lobed leaves and yellow-eyed, daisy-like flowers. This is a vigorous and free-flowering cultivar.
HEIGHT & SPREAD: 15x15cm (6x6in)

CULTIVATION: In autumn, soak tubers overnight and plant 5cm (2in) deep. Place in full sun. Keep damp, but stop watering once foliage dies back. Keep tubers dry in their pots or store in dry sand until you replant them in autumn. You can produce more plants by careful division of tubers.

Crocus chrysanthus
'Cream Beauty'♀

Early spring-flowering corm with rounded flowers that are buttery cream in colour. The

CROCUS CHRYSANTHUS 'CREAM BEAUTY'

grass-like leaves have a central silver stripe.
HEIGHT: 7.5cm (3in)
C. chrysanthus 'Ladykiller'♀ Slender flowers with fine purple feathering (vein-like markings) on the outer petals and a yellow eye.
C. chrysanthus 'Snow Bunting'♀ Rounded flowers, with grey-blue feathering on the outer petals.
CULTIVATION: Plant in autumn in John Innes No.1 with extra grit added. Place the corms at a depth of 7.5cm (3in). Site in sun or light shade. Keep the compost moist but avoid waterlogging. Increase by removing cormlets during dormancy. Mice and voles eat crocus corms, especially newly planted ones. Birds may damage the flowers.

Lamium maculatum
Dead nettle
'White Nancy'♀

Herbaceous perennial with a creeping habit. Heart-shaped silvery leaves have a green margin. The hooded flowers are borne in dense spikes.
HEIGHT & SPREAD: 15x40cm (6x16in)
CULTIVATION: Grow in shade in a humus-rich compost. Keep moist in spring and summer but drier in winter. Apply a balanced liquid feed monthly in the growing season.

LAMIUM MACULATUM 'WHITE NANCY'

MAGNOLIA STELLATA 'WATERLILY'

Magnolia stellata
Star magnolia
'Waterlily'♀

Large spreading deciduous shrub, bearing star-shaped flowers, which emerge from pointed silky buds. Flowers appear before the leaves.
HEIGHT & SPREAD: Limited, in a pot, to about 1.8x1.8m (6x6ft)
M. denudata♀ Yulan/lily tree Bears goblet-shaped, lemon-scented flowers.
CULTIVATION: Plant in early autumn in John Innes No.3 with added leaf-mould. Site in sun or partial shade, sheltered from cold winds and frosts, which will damage early flowers. Keep compost moist.

Apply a weak liquid feed every month in the growing season, and mulch with leaf-mould in autumn. Prune any frost-damaged branches in spring. Since magnolias are difficult to propagate, plants are best bought from a reputable nursery.

PIERIS JAPONICA 'GRAYSWOOD'

Pieris japonica
'Grayswood'♀

Compact, bushy evergreen shrub with glossy dark green leaves, coppery when young, and hanging clusters of creamy white flowers.

HEIGHT & SPREAD: 1.8x1.8m (6x6ft)
P. japonica 'Debutante'♀ Low-growing, to about 90cm (3ft) with flowers carried in dense, erect clusters.
CULTIVATION: Plant in autumn in acid compost, in dappled shade. Although hardy, frost will damage flower buds, so try to provide some shelter.

Keep compost moist at all times. Apply a liquid feed monthly in the growing season, and mulch in autumn with leaf-mould. Prune dead wood, and for shape, after the shrub has finished flowering.

TULIPA 'PURISSIMA'

Tulipa
Tulip
'Purissima'

Bulb producing large, cup-shaped, cream flowers and grey-green leaves.
HEIGHT: 20cm (8in)
T. 'Spring Green'♀ Large, cup-shaped ivory flowers with feathery green markings.
HEIGHT: 40cm (16in)
T. turkestanica♀ Species tulip bearing up to ten blooms, star-shaped with yellow eyes.
T. 'White Triumphator'♀ Lily-flowered tulip with pointed, reflexed petals.
CULTIVATION: Plant bulbs in autumn, 10cm (4in) deep in a loam-based compost. Site pot in a sunny sheltered spot, out of the wind. Deadhead, and keep moist in the growing season. Increase tulips by removing daughter bulbs and growing them on.

AGAPANTHUS AFRICANUS 'ALBUS'

Agapanthus africanus
African lily
'Albus'♀

Evergreen perennial with arching, strap-like leaves. Trumpet-shaped flowers are held in rounded flowerheads on long stalks.
HEIGHT & SPREAD: 90x50cm (36x20in)
A. 'Snowy Owl' Hardy, deciduous variety.
A. 'White Dwarf' Small, frost-tender, evergreen cultivar.
HEIGHT & SPREAD: 40x30cm (16x12in)
CULTIVATION: Grow in large pots of John Innes No.3, in a sunny sheltered site. Move tender varieties under glass in autumn. *A.* 'Snowy Owl' may be left outside if given a sheltered position and a dry mulch. Water freely in spring and summer but keep almost dry in winter. Give a balanced liquid feed from spring until the flower buds form. Increase by dividing clumps.

Ajuga reptans
Bugle
'Alba'

Low-growing, evergreen perennial spreading by creeping stems. Tubular

AJUGA REPTANS 'ALBA'

flowers are carried in whorls on erect spikes.
HEIGHT & SPREAD: 15x25cm (6x10in)
CULTIVATION: Grow in dappled shade in a humus-rich potting mix. Keep compost moist at all times, and feed monthly in growth with a balanced liquid feed. Create new plants by removing and repotting the plantlets that form at the end of the creeping stems.

ARGYRANTHEMUM FOENICULACEUM 'ROYAL HAZE'

Argyranthemum foeniculaceum
Marguerite
'Royal Haze'♀

Vigorous, evergreen sub-shrub with finely dissected, grey-green foliage. Produces a mass of daisy-like flowers over a long season.
HEIGHT & SPREAD: 70x70cm (28x28in)
A. gracile 'Chelsea Girl'♀ Has very finely cut, feathery foliage.
A. 'Snowflake' Has semi-double flowers.
CULTIVATION: Plant in spring in a good-quality potting mix and site in full sun. Water freely throughout summer but keep the compost almost dry in winter.

Feed fortnightly with a balanced liquid fertiliser. Encourage continued blooming by cutting off dead flowerheads.

Argyranthemums may be trained as standards and look particularly good in pairs on either side of a front door.

BRUGMANSIA SUAVEOLENS

Brugmansia suaveolens ♥
Syn. *Datura suaveolens*
Angel's trumpet
This tender shrub bears large, pendulous, trumpet-shaped flowers, which are highly scented, especially at night. Brugmansia is usually deciduous in Britain.

HEIGHT & SPREAD: 1.8x1.5m (6x5ft)

B. suaveolens 'Variegata' Slightly smaller plant with cream-margined leaves.

CULTIVATION: Grow in a large pot of John Innes No.3 in a greenhouse or conservatory at a minimum 7°C (45°F). In summer, move outside to a sunny spot. Frost-damaged plants usually rejuvenate. Water freely in summer but keep almost dry in winter. Once established, feed fortnightly with a diluted liquid fertiliser. Deadhead often. Prune hard in spring. *NB All parts of this plant are poisonous.*

COBAEA SCANDENS F. ALBA

Cobaea scandens f. alba ♥
Cup and saucer vine
Rapidly growing perennial vine, usually grown as an annual. Wide, cup-shaped flowers are white, ageing to cream. Cobaea climbs by means of tendrils.

HEIGHT & SPREAD: 2.4x1.5m (8x5ft)

CULTIVATION: Plant out young plants once the danger of frost has passed. Use a free-draining compost. Place pot in a sheltered sunny position. Provide support for the climbing stems, such as wires or trellis, on a wall.

The compost should be kept moist at all times, but avoid waterlogging. Feed throughout summer with a balanced liquid feed.

CONVOLVULUS CNEORUM

Convolvulus cneorum ♥
Silverbush, shrubby bindweed
The leaves of this dwarf evergreen shrub are covered in silky hairs, giving the plant a silvery appearance. Pink-tinged buds open into white funnel-shaped flowers.

HEIGHT & SPREAD: 50x50cm (20x20in)

CULTIVATION: Grow in pots of John Innes No.1 with added grit for extra drainage. Site in full sun. Water moderately while growing and sparingly in winter. Apply a weak liquid feed every month in the growing season.

May be pruned back hard in spring if outgrowing its space. Prone to fungal and bacterial diseases in warm, wet conditions.

DIMORPHOTHECA PLUVIALIS 'GLISTENING WHITE'

Dimorphotheca pluvialis
Star of the Veldt, Cape marigold
'Glistening White'
This compact, upright annual has deeply toothed, dark green leaves and bears a profusion of dark-eyed, daisy-like flowers.

HEIGHT & SPREAD: 30x23cm (12x9in)

D. sinuata 'Tetra Pole Star' Has large white flowers up to 7.5cm (3in) across.

CULTIVATION: Plant out after the last frosts in pots of John Innes No.2 and place containers in a sunny site. The flowers tend to close up in dull weather.

Although drought-tolerant, growth is better when the plant is watered moderately. Apply a weak liquid feed every two weeks once flowering starts. Deadhead regularly to prolong flowering.

FELICIA AMELLOIDES 'READ'S WHITE'

Felicia amelloides
'Read's White'

Evergreen sub-shrub, usually grown as an annual. Plants are compact and low-growing. Yellow-eyed, daisy-like flowers are carried on long stalks above the foliage from summer to early autumn.

HEIGHT & SPREAD: 30x40cm (12x16in)

F. amelloides 'White Variegated' Has cream stippled variegation on the foliage.

CULTIVATION: Plant out after danger of frost has passed into a good-quality potting mix and site the container in full sun.

Water freely and apply a balanced liquid feed every two weeks. Pinching out young plants will encourage bushiness. Cut off dead flower stalks to prolong flowering.

HEDYCHIUM SPICATUM

Hedychium spicatum
Ginger lily, garland flower
Tender, clump-forming perennial with large leaves and waxy spikes of exotic white flowers with orange bases and red stamens.

HEIGHT & SPREAD: 1.2mx60cm (4x2ft)

H. coronarium Fragrant, butterfly-shaped flowers.

CULTIVATION: Grow in pots of John Innes No.3 and site in a sunny, sheltered position. These hedychiums are tender and can be moved out of the greenhouse or conservatory only during the summer months. Water freely and apply a balanced liquid feed monthly while growing.

Move plants back under glass in autumn and keep the compost almost dry in winter. Remove spent flower spikes. Increase by dividing congested clumps in spring.

IBERIS AMARA

Iberis amara
Common candytuft

Vigorous, erect, branching annual bearing dense clusters of tiny, fragrant flowers.
HEIGHT & SPREAD: 30x15cm (12x6in)
I. amara 'Giant Hyacinth Flowered' Has particularly large flower spikes.
I. amara 'Pinnacle' Flowers are especially fragrant.
CULTIVATION: Plant out in spring in a free-draining compost and site in full sun. Water freely, taking care to avoid waterlogging, and apply a balanced liquid feed every two weeks. Prolong flowering by cutting back spent flower spikes.

LILIUM 'MONT BLANC'

Lilium
Lily
'Mont Blanc'

Bulb producing waxy, creamy white, upward-facing, star-shaped, fragrant flowers with conspicuous orange anthers.
HEIGHT: 60cm (2ft)
L. 'Casa Blanca'♀ Bears very large, heavily scented flowers.
L. 'Sterling Star' Upward-facing flowers, with tiny brown spots inside the petals.
CULTIVATION: Plant bulbs in autumn at a depth of three

times their own height. Use John Innes No.2, making sure there is a good layer of crocks in the bottom of the pot. Choose a sheltered position in full sun. Water freely while growing and give a high potash feed once a month. Store bulbs over winter in their pots, or lift them and store in boxes of damp sand in a cool dry place. Propagate by removing the outer scales of the bulbs and growing them in trays of compost. Lily beetle may be troublesome.

LOBULARIA MARITIMA 'SNOW CRYSTALS'

Lobularia maritima
Sweet alyssum
Syn. *Alyssum maritimum*
'Snow Crystals'

Low-growing, compact annual. Tiny, four-petalled flowers in dense, fragrant clusters are borne in profusion throughout summer.
HEIGHT & SPREAD: 10x20cm (4x8in)
L. maritima 'Carpet of Snow' Compact, mound-forming, profuse white variety.
L. maritima 'Creamery' Bears abundant cream-coloured flowers.
CULTIVATION: Grow plants in moderately fertile, free-draining compost in full sun. Water freely and feed every month with a liquid tomato feed. Clip over the first flush of blooms to encourage further flowering. Sow seed in pots outside in late spring or under glass in early spring.

MYRTUS COMMUNIS

Myrtus communis
Myrtle

Bushy evergreen shrub with glossy, dark green aromatic foliage, and fragrant flowers followed by small purple-black berries in autumn.
HEIGHT & SPREAD: 1.2mx60cm (4x2ft)
M. communis ssp. *tarentina* Shorter plant; pink flowers and white berries.
M. communis 'Variegata' Has leaves edged in cream.
CULTIVATION: Plant in autumn in large pots of John Innes No.3, and site in full sun. In very cold areas move the pot to a sheltered position over winter. Water freely while establishing – thereafter, myrtle is fairly drought-tolerant. Apply a balanced liquid feed monthly in the growing season.
Prune any branches damaged by frost, or to maintain the shape of the bush, in spring. Downy mildew may be a problem in damp conditions.

Nemophila maculata
Five spot

This compact, low-growing annual has bowl-shaped flowers. Each of the five

NEMOPHILA MACULATA

petals has purple veins and a deep violet blotch at the tip. The spreading prostrate plant has pale green, deeply lobed foliage.
HEIGHT & SPREAD: 15x20cm (6x8in)
N. maculata 'Freckles' Petals are heavily dotted with tiny black speckles.
CULTIVATION: Plant out after the last frosts in a good-quality potting compost, and site the container in sun or partial shade.
Nemophila does not tolerate drought and should be kept moist at all times. Feed monthly with a diluted tomato fertiliser.

NIEREMBERGIA CAERULEA 'MONT BLANC'

Nierembergia caerulea
Cup flower
'Mont Blanc'

Low, spreading tender perennial, usually grown as an annual, with tiny dark green leaves and an abundance of yellow-eyed, bowl-shaped flowers which appear from early summer until early autumn. It looks pretty around the rim of a pot.
HEIGHT & SPREAD: 20x20cm (8x8in)
CULTIVATION: Plant out in pots of John Innes No.1 after the last frosts. Site containers in a warm sunny position for best flowering.
Water moderately and apply a balanced liquid feed every month.

OSTEOSPERMUM 'SILVER SPARKLER'

Osteospermum
'Silver Sparkler'♀

Evergreen sub-shrub bearing an abundance of purple-eyed, daisy-like flowers. The leaves have cream margins.
HEIGHT & SPREAD: 45x30cm (18x12in)
O. 'Weetwood'♀ One of the hardiest cultivars, the white petals are flushed purple underneath, and the flowers have a yellow eye.
O. 'Whirlygig'♀ Spoon-shaped petals flushed blue on the reverse; grey-blue eye.
CULTIVATION: Grow in John Innes No.2 and site in full sun. Osteospermums are drought-tolerant but perform better if watered moderately in summer. Hardiness is increased by keeping them almost dry in winter.

Feed monthly in the growing season with a balanced liquid fertiliser. Deadhead to prolong flowering.

SUTERA 'SNOWFLAKE'

Sutera
Syn. *Bacopa*
'Snowflake'

Tiny heart-shaped leaves clothe the trailing, spreading stems. Masses of small five-petalled flowers are borne throughout summer. This makes an excellent trailing hanging basket plant.
HEIGHT & SPREAD: 40x30cm (16x12in)
CULTIVATION: Plant out after the danger of frost has passed in a moderately fertile, free-draining compost. Sutera thrives in a sunny site or in partial shade.

Water freely but avoid waterlogging. Apply a liquid tomato feed every two weeks.

Trim back after flowering and move plants to a heated greenhouse or conservatory over winter.

TAGETES ERECTA 'VANILLA'

Tagetes erecta
African marigold
'Vanilla'

Large, cream-coloured pompom flowers are held over deeply cut, dark green foliage. This cultivar is vigorous and free-flowering, and the palest of all marigolds.
HEIGHT & SPREAD: 35x20cm (14x8in)
CULTIVATION: Plant out in early summer after danger of frost has passed, in pots of John Innes No.2. Flowering is best in full sun.

Water freely in dry weather and apply a liquid tomato fertiliser every two weeks – overfeeding will encourage lush foliage at the expense of flowers. Deadhead regularly. These marigolds are prone to botrytis (grey mould) and loved by slugs.

autumn

ABELIA CHINENSIS

Abelia chinensis
Syn. *Abelia rupestris*

Small deciduous shrub with fragrant, funnel-shaped flowers, flushed pink on the outside. The flowers are carried in rounded clusters.
HEIGHT & SPREAD: 80x80cm (32x32in)
CULTIVATION: Plant in spring or autumn in pots of John Innes No.3, and site in full sun. *Abelia chinensis* benefits from the shelter of a south-facing wall.

Water freely in summer but avoid waterlogging. Apply a balanced liquid feed monthly in spring and summer.

Prune for shape directly after flowering.

CALLUNA VULGARIS 'WHITE LAWN'

Calluna vulgaris
Heather, Scots heather, ling
'White Lawn'

Dwarf, hardy evergreen shrub with a prostrate trailing habit that is ideal for troughs. 'White Lawn' is especially low-growing reaching just 5cm (2in) in height. It has white flowers amid clear green leaves.
HEIGHT & SPREAD: 5x30cm (2x12in)
C. vulgaris 'Kinlochruel'♀ Double-flowered cultivar. The foliage colour turns bronze in winter.
C. vulgaris 'Spring Cream'♀ Dark green foliage with cream-coloured tips in spring. Single white flowers.
HEIGHT & SPREAD: 25x30cm (10x12in)
CULTIVATION: Plant in autumn into ericaceous (acid) compost and site the pots in full sun. Do not allow the compost to dry out. Feed monthly in the growing season with a balanced liquid fertiliser.

Clip back flower spikes once they have gone past their best. Botrytis (grey mould) may be a problem in humid conditions.

CRINUM X POWELLII 'ALBUM'

Crinum x powellii
'Album'♀

Bulbous, deciduous perennial with long, arching strap-shaped leaves. Up to ten large, trumpet-shaped flowers are borne in umbels (rounded flowerheads) at the top of sturdy flower stalks.
HEIGHT & SPREAD: 90x60cm (3x2ft)
CULTIVATION: Plant in spring with the neck of the bulb just above soil level. Use John Innes No.2 with added sharp sand. Site in a sheltered,

sunny spot. Water freely while in growth, applying a diluted tomato fertiliser monthly. Remove spent flowers. Increase by carefully lifting and dividing congested clumps of bulbs in spring. Repot only when absolutely necessary.

winter

ERICA X DARLEYENSIS 'WHITE PERFECTION'

Erica x darleyensis
Heath, heather
'White Perfection' ♥

Compact, bushy evergreen shrub with small, bright green needle-like leaves and bell-shaped flowers in clusters at the tips of the shoots.
HEIGHT & SPREAD: 40x40cm (16x16in)
E. x *darleyensis* 'Springwood White' ♥ Very low-growing.
E. x *darleyensis* 'White Glow' Is compact at only 25cm (10in) tall.
HEIGHT & SPREAD: 15x40cm (6x16in)
CULTIVATION: Plant in autumn in humus-rich compost (the ericas listed here do not need special ericaceous compost). Site in full sun.

Water heathers freely and apply a weak liquid fertiliser every month. Clip dead flower spikes back to encourage a second flush. Botrytis (grey mould) may develop in warm, wet conditions.

GALANTHUS NIVALIS

Galanthus nivalis
Snowdrop

Bulb producing dainty, hanging flowers with three outer petals partially concealing three green-marked inner petals.
HEIGHT: 10cm (4in)
G. nivalis 'Flore Pleno' ♥ Vigorous, double-flowered.
G. nivalis 'Pusey Green Tip' Broad double flowers with green markings on both inner and outer petals.
CULTIVATION: In autumn plant bulbs 10cm (4in) deep in loam-based compost with extra leaf-mould. Site in sun or shade. Keep moist after planting. Increase by division after flowering.

SARCOCOCCA HOOKERIANA VAR. DIGYNA

Sarcococca hookeriana var. digyna
Christmas box

Compact evergreen shrub with glossy dark green, lance-shaped leaves. The small, highly scented flowers are borne in tassel-like clusters in the leaf axils. Flowers are followed by shiny, purple-black berries.
HEIGHT & SPREAD: 75x75cm (30x30in)
CULTIVATION: Plant in autumn in pots of John Innes No.3 and site in deep or partial shade. Sarcococca is drought-tolerant once established, but growth is better with moderate watering. Feed once a month from spring to autumn, using a balanced liquid fertiliser.

Prune as necessary to improve shape in spring. You can produce more plants by cutting off and transplanting rooted suckers in autumn.

VIBURNUM TINUS

Viburnum tinus

Bushy evergreen shrub with glossy dark green foliage. The flowers are carried in large flat heads and are pink or red when in bud.
HEIGHT & SPREAD: 1.8x1.8m (6x6ft)
V. tinus 'Lucidum' Very large flowerheads.
CULTIVATION: Plant in autumn in pots of John Innes No.3, and site in sun or partial shade. Keep the compost moist and feed the shrub every month during the growing season, using a balanced liquid fertiliser.

Trim shrub to shape after flowering. May be affected by aphids and sooty mould.

◄ **Viburnum offers year-round interest:** white flowers in winter, evergreen foliage, and sometimes autumn berries. The buds of *V. tinus* appear from mid autumn and open from midwinter. The berries are deep blue, later turning black.

◄ **Pretty in pink,** a seed pan filled with thrift (*Armeria maritima*) adds colour to a sunny balcony. Also known as sea pink, thrift does well in seaside gardens where it happily tolerates salt-laden breezes.

Primula
Primrose
'Groeneken's Glory'

Rosette forming, evergreen perennial producing deeply veined leaves and saucer-shaped bluish pink flowers with a yellow eye.
HEIGHT & SPREAD: 15x25cm (6x10in)
P. vulgaris 'Pink Shades' Vibrant pink blooms.
P. vulgaris 'Rose Shades' Flowers are pinkish red.
CULTIVATION: Plant primulas in early spring in a humus-rich compost and site in sun or light shade.

Water moderately and apply a balanced liquid feed once flowering begins.

Remove faded flowers to prolong flowering period. You can increase plants by dividing them after two years.

pink flowers

spring

Bellis perennis
Bedding daisy
'Dresden China' ♀

Double pompom flowers are carried on short stems above rosettes of green leaves.
HEIGHT & SPREAD: 15x10cm (6x4in)
B. perennis 'Galaxy Rose' Semi-double flowers with a yellow eye.
B. perennis 'Tasso Deep Rose' Flat-topped pompoms.

CULTIVATION: Plant in autumn in free-draining, humus-rich compost. Site the container in sun or partial shade. Water moderately and apply a balanced liquid feed once the buds have formed.

Deadhead regularly to prolong flowering.

Camellia x williamsii
'Donation' ♀

Broad, upright, evergreen shrub with glossy dark green foliage and masses of semi-double, rose-pink flowers with darker veins.
HEIGHT & SPREAD: 1.8x1.5m (6x5ft)
C. x williamsii 'Bowen Bryant' ♀ Erect open habit with bell-shaped flowers.
C. x williamsii 'Brigadoon' ♀ A small, dense upright shrub with large semi-double blooms.
CULTIVATION: Plant in autumn in large pots of ericaceous compost. To protect the flowers from frost and thaw damage, position the plant away from full early morning sun, ideally in dappled shade. Water freely in growth. If the rootball dries out in summer, the flower buds will abort the following spring.

Feed annually in late spring with a balanced liquid fertiliser. Top-dress in autumn with leaf-mould. Prune to shape after flowering. Scale insect may be troublesome.

Ranunculus asiaticus
'Accolade Pink'

Tuberous perennial producing large, fully double, peony-like flowers on slender, branched

stems above a ruff of foliage.
HEIGHT & SPREAD: 25x15cm
(10x6in)
R. asiaticus 'Bloomingdale Pink Shades' Very large and showy flowers.
CULTIVATION: Plant out in early spring into a good-quality potting mix. Site in full sun. These cultivars will tolerate moderate frost but should be moved to a sheltered position if a cold spell is severe or prolonged. Water moderately. Feeding is unnecessary. Remove spent flowers. For early spring flowers plant tubers in autumn.

TULIPA AUCHERIANA

Tulipa aucheriana
Tulip

Dwarf species tulip producing star-shaped flowers with a yellow eye.
HEIGHT: 10cm (4in)
T. 'China Pink'
Tall, stately, lily-like flowers with pointed reflexed petals.
HEIGHT: 50cm (20in)
T. 'Peach Blossom' Semi-double, deep rose flowers.
HEIGHT: 30cm (12in)
CULTIVATION: Tulips are completely hardy. Plant bulbs in autumn in a loam-based compost at a depth of 15cm (6in). Site in sun or light shade out of wind. Water when growing; no need to feed. Deadhead to encourage growth of new bulbs.
Lift the bulbs once the foliage fades and store in a dry place; remove daughter bulbs and grow them on.

ANTIRRHINUM MAJUS 'RIBBON LIGHT PINK'

Antirrhinum majus
Snapdragon
'Ribbon Light Pink'
Tubular, two-lipped flowers are carried in dense, upright spikes on bushy plants.
HEIGHT & SPREAD: 50x25cm (20x10in)
A. majus 'La Bella Rose' Open, rounded flowers of clear pink. Fragrant.
A. majus 'Chimes Pink' Yellow-throated flowers on bushy, dwarf plants.
HEIGHT & SPREAD: 20x20cm (8x8in)
CULTIVATION: Plant out after the last frosts in a good-quality, free-draining potting mix. Site in sun or partial shade. Water freely while growing and apply a liquid tomato feed every two weeks. Pinch out tips of young plants for bushy growth, and cut off spent flower spikes.

Argyranthemum
Marguerite
'Vancouver'
Vigorous evergreen sub-shrub with finely dissected, greyish green leaves. In a large tub on

ARGYRANTHEMUM 'VANCOUVER'

a sunny patio, marguerites will flower from early summer to late autumn. The pale pink, daisy-like flowers of 'Vancouver' have a central pompom.
HEIGHT & SPREAD: 60x30cm (24x12in)
A. 'Mary Cheek' Compact with pale pink pompom flowers.
A. 'Petite Pink' Compact in habit, silvery foliage and abundant pale pink flowers with a yellow eye.
HEIGHT & SPREAD: 30x30cm (12x12in)
CULTIVATION: Plant in a good-quality, free-draining potting mix after the risk of frost has passed, and site in full sun. Water freely in summer and keep almost dry in winter to improve hardiness.
Feed fortnightly with a balanced liquid fertiliser. Cut off dead flower stalks. Argyranthemums can be easily trained as standards.

ARMERIA JUNIPERIFOLIA 'BEVAN'S VARIETY'

Armeria juniperifolia
Thrift, sea pink
'Bevan's Variety'
Evergreen perennial forming dense cushions of narrow, linear leaves. The globular, dark pink flowerheads are held above the foliage on slender leafless stems.
HEIGHT & SPREAD: 5x15cm (2x6in)
A. 'Bee's Ruby' Taller variety with dark pink flowers.
A. maritima 'Vindictive'

A much larger variety with deep, rose-pink flowers.
CULTIVATION: Plant in spring to early summer in pots of John Innes No.2 with extra sand for good drainage. Site in full sun. Water moderately, avoiding overwetting the compost. Apply a balanced liquid feed monthly in the growing season. Cut off faded flower stalks. Increase by dividing established clumps in early spring.
Armeria grows wild on coasts and tolerates salt winds.

CATHARANTHUS ROSEUS

Catharanthus roseus
Madagascar periwinkle
Syn. *Vinca rosea*
Glossy-leaved perennial, usually grown as an annual. The flowers each have five satiny petals. *C. roseus* does not tolerate temperatures below 7°C (45°F).
HEIGHT & SPREAD: 30x30cm (12x12in)
C. roseus 'Blush Cooler' Pale pink with a deep pink eye.
C. roseus 'Pacifica Coral' Pale pink.
CULTIVATION: Plant out after the last frosts in a moist, humus-rich, free-draining potting mixture. Site the containers in full sun.
During the growing season water moderately and apply a balanced liquid feed monthly. Control growth and keep plants bushy by pinching out tips. Plants may be trimmed back and overwintered in a greenhouse or conservatory.

DIANTHUS CHINENSIS 'RASPBERRY PARFAIT'

Dianthus chinensis
Indian pink
'Raspberry Parfait'

Branching and compact perennial usually grown as an annual. The deep pink petals have a large crimson eye.

HEIGHT & SPREAD: 20x15cm (8x6in)

D. 'Ideal Fuchsia' Fuchsia pink flowers laced with paler patterning.

D. 'Princess Pink' Intense pink flowers.

CULTIVATION: Plant out after the last frosts in a good-quality potting mix. Position the container where it will receive continuous sun.

Water moderately, applying a balanced liquid feed every four weeks. Deadhead to prolong flowering.

DIASCIA 'TWINKLE'

Diascia
'Twinkle' ♀

Upright perennial usually grown as an annual. Compact plants with a profusion of shell-like, five-lobed flowers borne in dense spikes above heart-shaped leaves. The first flush appears in early summer and, if the plant is trimmed back, new shoots appear which flower later on.

HEIGHT & SPREAD: 30x20cm (12x8in)

D. 'Pink Queen' Loose spikes of rose pink, yellow-eyed flowers.

D. 'Ruby Field' ♀ Free-flowering over a long season.

CULTIVATION: Plant out after the last frosts in a good-quality potting mix and site in full sun. Do not allow the compost to dry out. Once established, feed every two weeks with a weak liquid fertiliser. Cut stems back after initial flowering. Diascia may be hardy in mild regions.

FUCHSIA 'PINK GALORE'

Fuchsia
'Pink Galore'

Free-flowering, trailing shrub producing double blooms with pink outer sepals and pale rose-pink inner petals.

HEIGHT & SPREAD: 20x30cm (8x12in)

F. 'Lady Thumb' ♀ Dwarf, upright shrub. Semi-double flowers have white inner petals with pink veins and pink outer sepals.

HEIGHT & SPREAD: 23x30cm (9x12in)

F. 'Rose of Denmark' Trailing in habit spreading up to 40cm (16in). Petals and sepals pink.

CULTIVATION: Plant out hardened-off plants after the last frosts. Plant in a good-quality potting mix, using a container large enough to ensure a reasonable root run.

Site in sun or light shade. Water frequently, especially in dry spells, and apply a balanced liquid fertiliser every three weeks. Deadhead to prolong flowering.

In autumn, move the plants into a cool shed or greenhouse. Water them just often enough to prevent the roots from drying out.

In spring, begin watering again to restart the plants into growth. Susceptible to red spider mite and aphids.

HYDRANGEA MACROPHYLLA 'PARZIFAL'

Hydrangea macrophylla
'Parzifal' ♀

Compact deciduous shrub with glossy serrated leaves, and large mophead flowerheads of dark pink.

HEIGHT & SPREAD: 1.2x1m (4x3ft)

H. macrophylla 'Ayesha' ♀ Lilac-like clusters of pale bluish pink flowers.

CULTIVATION: Plant in autumn in a large container of moisture-retentive, humus-rich compost. Pink-flowered hydrangeas do not need ericaceous compost; in fact, if you plant 'Parzifal' in acid soil, it will produce deep blue flowers. Site in sun or partial shade with some shelter from cold, drying winds.

Water generously while growing and apply a balanced liquid feed monthly.

Top-dress annually in autumn with garden compost or leaf-mould. Leave spent flowerheads on until spring, then prune back stems to a strong pair of buds.

LAVATERA 'PINK FRILLS'

Lavatera
Tree mallow
'Pink Frills'

Vigorous, semi-evergreen shrub with wide, funnel-shaped flowers.

HEIGHT & SPREAD: 90x60cm (3x2ft)

L. trimestris 'Pink Beauty' Slightly smaller, quick-growing hardy annual. Light pink flowers with darker veins; dark glossy leaves.

L. trimestris 'Salmon Beauty' Quick-growing hardy annual. Flowers are salmon-pink with darker veins.

CULTIVATION: Plant out in early summer in a light, free-draining compost in full sun. Avoid windy sites. Water freely and apply a balanced liquid feed every two weeks.

LILIUM PINK PERFECTION GROUP

Lilium
Lily
Pink Perfection Group ♀

Bulbous perennial producing clusters of five to eight heavily scented, pendulous blooms, in a range of pinks.

HEIGHT: 1.2m (4ft)

L. 'Journey's End' Pink petals with white margins. This lily is unscented.

L. 'Star Gazer' This lily bears heavily scented, star-shaped, upward-facing flowers.

HEIGHT: 90cm (3ft)

CULTIVATION: Plant bulbs in autumn at a depth of three times their own height. Use John Innes No.2, putting a good layer of crocks in the bottom of the pot. Select a sheltered position in full sun. Water freely while growing and give a high potash feed once a month.

Store lily bulbs over winter in their pots, or lift them and store in boxes of damp sand in a cool dry place.

You can increase bulbs by removing their outer scales in autumn and growing them in trays of compost. Lily beetle may be a problem.

LOBELIA ERINUS 'ROSAMUND'

Lobelia erinus
'Rosamund'

Bushy, mound-forming annual with tiny leaves on slender stems. Fan-shaped flowers are bright pink with a white eye.

HEIGHT & SPREAD: 15x10cm (6x4in)

L. erinus 'Rose Fountains' Vigorous trailing habit.

CULTIVATION: Plant out after the last frosts in a good-quality potting mix. Site the container or basket in sun or light shade. Do not allow the compost to dry out. Apply a liquid tomato feed every two to three weeks. Occasionally clip over the plants to encourage further flowering.

LOBULARIA MARITIMA 'PASTEL CARPET'

Lobularia maritima
Sweet alyssum
Syn. *Alyssum maritimum*
'Pastel Carpet'

Low-growing, compact, easy to grow annual. Tiny, four-petalled flowers are borne in profusion throughout summer in dense, fragrant clusters. The 'Pastel Carpet' seed mix produces white, pink and violet flowers.

HEIGHT & SPREAD: 10x20cm (4x8in)

L. maritima 'Rosie O'Day' Rose pink, very low-growing.

L. maritima 'Wonderland Pastel Pink' Pale pink.

CULTIVATION: Grow plants in a moderately fertile, free-draining compost in full sun. Water freely and feed every month with a high potash fertiliser, such as liquid tomato feed.

Clip after the first flush to encourage further flowering. You can sow seed directly into the container in late spring.

NICOTIANA X SANDERAE 'HAVANA APPLE BLOSSOM'

Nicotiana x sanderae
Tobacco plant
'Havana Apple Blossom'

One of the Havana Series, 'Havana Apple Blossom' is an upright, branching annual with loose clusters of tubular flowers, flared at the mouth. These hybrids are only slightly fragrant. The stems and oval leaves are sticky.

HEIGHT & SPREAD: 30x15cm (12x6in)

N. x *sanderae* 'Merlin Salmon Pink' Dwarf annual with soft pink flowers.

CULTIVATION: Plant out once the danger of frost has passed in a good-quality, moist but free-draining compost.

Site in sun or shade. Water liberally and apply a liquid tomato feed every two weeks. Deadhead regularly.

NB Nicotianas are poisonous.

◄ **Two-tone fuchsia blooms** are given a modern touch by tying strands of coloured raffia just under the rim of their pot. Fuchsias are ideal by a front door as they will flower right through from early summer to late autumn.

PENSTEMON 'HEWELL PINK BEDDER'

Penstemon
'Hewell Pink Bedder' ♀

Short-lived perennial with
oval, pointed leaves and tall
spikes of bright reddish pink
tubular flowers.
HEIGHT & SPREAD: 50x30cm
(20x12in)
P. 'Apple Blossom'♀ Pale
pink flowers with white
throats.
P. 'Hidcote Pink'♀ Pink
flowers with white and dark
pink streaks.
CULTIVATION: Plant in spring
into pots of John Innes No.2
and site in a sheltered, sunny
spot. Keep well watered and
feed every fortnight with a
balanced liquid fertiliser.
   Cutting off spent flower
spikes will encourage further
flowering.

ROSA 'QUEEN MOTHER'

Rosa
Patio rose
'Queen Mother'♀

Dwarf, cluster-flowered patio
rose bearing soft pink,
scented blooms that open flat.
HEIGHT & SPREAD: 35x35cm
(14x14in)

R. 'Judy Fischer' Miniature
rose, bearing slightly scented,
tiny dark pink flowers.
CULTIVATION: Plant in spring
in a fertile, humus-rich
compost and site in full sun.
Water freely and apply a
balanced liquid feed every
three weeks throughout spring
and summer. Add a layer of
well-rotted manure as a
mulch each spring.
   Prune annually in early
spring, cutting back main
stems to about 20cm (8in)
from the base. Remove
dead or damaged shoots.
Deadhead roses regularly
to prolong flowering.
   Roses are susceptible to
many pests and diseases,
especially aphids, black spot,
powdery mildew and rust.

VERBENA X HYBRIDA 'QUARTZ ROSE'

Verbena x hybrida
'Quartz Rose'

Vigorous, mound-forming
half-hardy dwarf perennial,
usually grown as an annual,
with large, domed heads of
bright pink flowers.
HEIGHT & SPREAD: 20x30cm
(8x12in)
V. x *hybrida* 'Sissinghurst'♀
Deep pink flowers borne on
trailing plants.
CULTIVATION: Plant out after
the last frosts in a good-
quality potting mix. Site the
containers in full sun.
   Water freely, especially
in dry spells. Apply a
balanced liquid feed every
month. Deadheading will
help to prolong flowering.

ZINNIA 'SHORT STUFF CORAL'

Zinnia
'Short Stuff Coral'

Low-growing, floriferous
annual with large, double,
soft pink flowers.
HEIGHT & SPREAD: 20x20cm
(8x8in)
Z. 'Dreamland Pink' Bright
pink blooms.
Z. 'Peter Pan Princess' Large
pale pink flowers on dwarf
plants, up to 10cm (4in) high.
CULTIVATION: Plant out after
the last frosts into a free-
draining compost. Site in full
sun. Water moderately and
apply a liquid tomato feed
every two weeks. Deadhead
to prolong flowering. Stagger
sowing for continuous
flowering into autumn.

autumn

CALLISTEPHUS CHINENSIS
'MILADY ROSE'

Callistephus chinensis
China aster
'Milady Rose'♀

Erect, bushy, fast-growing
annual with large, fully
double, chrysanthemum-like
flowers of rose pink.
HEIGHT & SPREAD: 25x25cm
(10x10in)
C. chinensis 'Asteroid Rose'

Abundant semi-double
flowers to 10cm (4in) across.
C. chinensis 'Compliment
Salmon Pink' Double flowers
on strong, upright stems.
HEIGHT & SPREAD: 65x20cm
(26x8in)
CULTIVATION: Plant out after
the last frosts in a good-
quality potting mix. Site in
full sun. Water moderately
and feed every two weeks
once established using a
balanced liquid fertiliser.
   Taller varieties may need
staking. Deadhead to prolong
flowering. Sow seed in early
spring. Repeated sowing in
early summer guarantees
autumn flowering plants.
Prone to callistephus wilt.

CRINUM X POWELLII

Crinum x powellii♀

Bulbous, deciduous perennial
with long, arching strap-
shaped leaves. Up to ten large
trumpet-shaped flowers are
borne in umbels (rounded
flowerheads), at the top of
sturdy flower stems.
HEIGHT & SPREAD: 90x60cm
(3x2ft)
CULTIVATION: Plant in spring
with the neck of the bulb just
above soil level. Use John
Innes No.2 with added sharp
sand. Site in a sheltered,
sunny position. Water freely
in growth but keep almost dry
in winter. Apply a diluted
tomato fertiliser every month
from spring to summer.
   Remove spent blooms.
Repot bulbs only when
absolutely necessary.

NERINE BOWDENII

Nerine bowdenii ♈

This bulbous perennial produces loose clusters of up to eight fragile, slender-petalled, rose-pink flowers.
HEIGHT: 45cm (18in)
N. bowdenii 'Pink Triumph' Has deep pink flowers.
CULTIVATION: Plant in spring in pots of John Innes No.2, at a depth of 10cm (4in). Site in a sheltered sunny spot. Keep warm and dry during summer dormancy, and begin watering freely as growth commences in late summer. Apply a balanced liquid feed as the flower buds open.

A dry winter mulch will protect against extreme winter cold. Propagate by dividing congested clumps during dormancy. Otherwise avoid disturbing the bulbs.

winter

CYCLAMEN COUM

Cyclamen coum ♈

Tuberous perennial with rounded dark green leaves marked with silver patterning. The distinctive flowers with swept-back petals are held on upright stalks above the rounded unlobed leaves.
HEIGHT & SPREAD: 7.5x10cm (3x4in)
C. persicum 'Miracle Rose' This large-flowered, scented cultivar is suitable for use under glass, or outdoors in only the mildest areas.
HEIGHT & SPREAD: 15x15cm (6x6in)
CULTIVATION: Use humus-rich, well-drained compost. Plant tubers of *C. coum* in late summer at a depth of about 5cm (2in). *C. persicum* cultivars are usually bought in flower and can be planted out immediately in mild, sheltered areas (such as window boxes in urban areas). While growing, water cyclamen moderately, taking care to avoid the crown, and apply a balanced liquid fertiliser when in flower. Reduce watering as the leaves wither after flowering.

Keep tubers of *C. coum* just moist through summer. *C. persicum* cultivars need a two to three month period of dry dormancy. Resume watering to restart growth in early autumn. Vine weevil may damage tubers.

▶ **Bushy heathers** provide year-round colour, in foliage and flower. Most need an acid compost although *Erica* x *darleyensis* is suitable for any soil making it useful for mixed plantings. It flowers from midwinter to mid spring.

Erica x darleyensis
Heath, heather
'Jenny Porter'♈

Compact, bushy evergreen shrub with small, bottle-green needle-like leaves and pale pink, bell-shaped flowers carried in clusters at the tips of the shoots.
HEIGHT & SPREAD: 40x40cm (16x16in)
E. x *darleyensis* 'Furzey'♈ Lilac-pink flowers and pink-tipped spring foliage.
E. x *darleyensis* 'Ghost Hills'♈ Bright green foliage tipped with cream in spring.
CULTIVATION: Plant in autumn in pots of humus-rich compost (the ericas mentioned here do not need ericaceous compost). Site in full sun. Water freely and apply a weak liquid feed every four weeks. Clip the flower spikes back once they are past their best. Botrytis (grey mould) may develop in warm, humid conditions.

ERICA X DARLEYENSIS 'JENNY PORTER'

GAULTHERIA MUCRONATA 'PINK PEARL'

Gaultheria mucronata
Syn. *Pernettya mucronata*
'Pink Pearl'♈

Woody, branching evergreen shrub with dense clusters of round, clear pink berries persisting through winter.
HEIGHT & SPREAD: 75x45cm (30x18in)
G. mucronata 'Mulberry Wine'♈ Mauve-pink berries.
G. mucronata 'Seashell'♈ Pale pink berries.
CULTIVATION: Plant in autumn into ericaceous compost. Site in full sun or partial shade. Water frequently, preferably with rainwater. Apply a liquid tomato feed monthly from spring to late summer. Prune to shape in winter. For berries the next year, a male plant must be grown nearby.

◄ Dwarf red tulips fill a terracotta pot. The variety 'Plaisir' is recommended for its pretty striped foliage as well as its soft red flowers.

semi-double flowers with golden stamens.

CULTIVATION: Plant this acid-loving camellia in autumn in a large pot of ericaceous compost. To protect flowers from frost/thaw damage, position the plant where it will not be exposed to full early morning sun. Camellias grow best in dappled shade. Water freely while growing: if the rootball becomes dry in summer the flower buds will abort the following spring.

Feed annually in late spring with a balanced liquid fertiliser. Top-dress in autumn with leaf-mould. Prune to shape after flowering. Scale insect may be troublesome.

ERYSIMUM CHEIRI 'RUBY GEM'

red flowers

spring

BELLIS PERENNIS 'TASSO DEEP ROSE'

Bellis perennis
'Tasso Deep Rose'

Fully double pompom flowers are held on short stems above mats of bright green leaf rosettes. These daisies are hardy perennials but are often grown as biennials because flower size and quality decline with each flowering.
HEIGHT & SPREAD: 15x10cm (6x4in)
B. perennis 'Galaxy Red' Semi-double flowers with a yellow eye.
CULTIVATION: Plant in autumn in free-draining, humus-rich compost. Site in full sun or partial shade. Water plants moderately and apply a balanced liquid feed once the buds form. Deadhead to prolong flowering. Increase plants by dividing every two years, after flowering.

CAMELLIA JAPONICA 'COQUETTII'

Camellia japonica
'Coquettii' ♀

Slow-growing, compact, erect evergreen shrub with glossy dark foliage. Bears profuse, double, deep red flowers.
HEIGHT & SPREAD: 2.4x1.2m (8x4ft)
C. japonica 'Miss Charleston' ♀ Neat, upright shrub with large, deep red

Erysimum cheiri
Syn. *Cheiranthus cheiri*
Wallflower
'Ruby Gem'

Biennial sub-shrub with lance-shaped leaves and clusters of sweetly scented, four-petalled flowers.
HEIGHT & SPREAD: 30x25cm (12x10in)
E. cheiri 'Scarlet Bedder' Slightly shorter variety.
CULTIVATION: Plant bedding wallflowers in early autumn in a free-draining, neutral or slightly alkaline compost and site in a sheltered sunny position. Water moderately. Feeding is unnecessary.

Pinch out the growing tips to encourage bushiness, and trim after flowering to encourage further blooms.

RANUNCULUS ASIATICUS
'ACCOLADE RED SHADES'

Ranunculus asiaticus
'Accolade Red Shades'

Striking tuberous perennial
producing large, fully double,
peony-like flowers in a range
of red shades.
HEIGHT & SPREAD: 25x15cm
(10x6in)
R. asiaticus 'Bloomingdale
Red Shades' Very large
showy flowers in a range from
coppery to blood red.
CULTIVATION: Plant out in
early spring in a good-quality,
moist, potting mix. Site the
containers in a sunny
position. These cultivars will
tolerate moderate frost, but
should be moved to a
sheltered position if a cold
spell is severe or prolonged.
Water moderately. Feeding
is unnecessary. Deadhead any
spent flowers to encourage
further flowering.

TULIPA 'OXFORD'

Tulipa
'Oxford'

Large scarlet flowers flushed
with blood red, and brilliant
red inside, are held at the top
of tall stems.
HEIGHT: 50cm (20in)
T. 'Plaisir' Much shorter
variety. Carmine with pale
sulphur at the base. Striking

maroon stripes on the leaves.
HEIGHT: 15cm (6in)
CULTIVATION: Plant bulbs from
early to late autumn, 15cm
(6in) deep in a free-draining
loam-based compost. Apply
potash-rich fertiliser in late
winter and water well while
growing. Site the container in
a sunny, sheltered spot, out of
the wind. Deadhead and keep
moist while growing.
Increase by removing
daughter bulbs and growing
them on. Prone to tulip fire,
a fungal disease.

summer

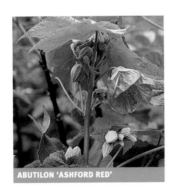

ABUTILON 'ASHFORD RED'

Abutilon
Flowering maple
'Ashford Red'

Fast-growing, twiggy shrub
with heart-shaped, serrated
leaves and exotic hanging
bell-shaped flowers.
HEIGHT & SPREAD: 90x60cm
(3x2ft)
A. 'Cannington Carol'
Dwarf plant whose leaves
are mottled with yellow.
HEIGHT & SPREAD: 45x45cm
(18x18in)
CULTIVATION: Grow in pots of
John Innes No.3 with added
leaf-mould. Select a sunny,
sheltered site. While growing,
water freely and feed monthly.
Overwinter plants under
glass, and in spring prune
back by about two-thirds of
the previous year's growth.

ALONSOA WARSCEWICZII

Alonsoa
warscewiczii
Mask flower

Fast-growing, branching
annual with glossy oval leaves
and abundant small scarlet
flowers borne on upright,
dark red stems.
HEIGHT & SPREAD: 40x25cm
(16x10in)
CULTIVATION: Plant out after
the last frosts in a free-
draining compost. Site in full
sun in a sheltered position
or grow in a conservatory.
Water moderately and
apply a balanced liquid feed
every month during the
growing season.
Pinch out the tips of young
plants to promote branching.
Susceptible to aphids and to
powdery mildew in dry spells.

AMARANTHUS CAUDATUS

Amaranthus caudatus
Love-lies-bleeding

Bushy half-hardy annual with
pale green leaves and long,
drooping tassel-like clusters
of tiny blood-red flowers.
HEIGHT & SPREAD: 60x40cm
(24x16in)

A. cruentus 'Foxtail'
(syn *A. paniculatus*) Has
upright flower spikes and
bronze-tinted foliage.
CULTIVATION: Plant out after
the last frosts in a humus-rich
compost. Site in full sun and
support taller plants with
stakes, especially those in
windy areas.
Water freely in summer and
apply a balanced liquid feed
every month. Pinch out tips
of young *A. cruentus* plants to
encourage bushiness.

ANTIRRHINUM MAJUS
'CORONETTE CRIMSON'

Antirrhinum majus
Snapdragon
'Coronette Crimson'

Fragrant, tubular, two-lipped
flowers are carried in dense,
upright spikes on bushy,
branching plants. Usually
grown as an annual.
HEIGHT & SPREAD: 50x25cm
(20x10in)
A. majus 'La Bella Red'
Spikes of open, rounded,
fragrant flowers.
A. majus 'Chimes Red'
Rich red flowers are borne
on dwarf, bushy plants.
HEIGHT & SPREAD: 15x15cm
(6x6in)
CULTIVATION: Plant out in
spring after the last frosts
in a good-quality potting mix.
Site in sun or partial shade.
Water freely in growth and
apply a liquid tomato feed
every two weeks. Remove
spent flower spikes to
encourage repeat flowering.
Plants may suffer from rust.

ARCTOTIS X HYBRIDA 'FLAME'

Arctotis x hybrida
African daisy
'Flame'

Orange-red, daisy-like flowers are carried on long stems above silvery green lobed leaves.

HEIGHT & SPREAD: 45x30cm (18x12in)

CULTIVATION: Grow in pots of John Innes No.2 and site in full sun because the flowers close up in dull weather. Arctotis is drought-tolerant but performs better with moderate watering. Feed once a month with a balanced liquid fertiliser. Deadhead to prolong flowering. Susceptible to grey mould and slugs in damp weather.

CAPSICUM ANNUUM 'REDSKIN'

Capsicum annuum
Chilli pepper
'Redskin'

Compact annual producing numerous small, bell-pepper fruits to 5cm (2in) long. They turn from green or white to bright red as they mature.

HEIGHT & SPREAD: 15x10cm (6x4in)

C. annuum 'Treasures Red' Produces small, conical, upward-pointing fruits.

HEIGHT & SPREAD: 30x30cm (12x12in)

CULTIVATION: Plant in humus-rich compost and site in a sunny, sheltered position once the risk of frost has passed. Support will be needed. Water freely while growing and give a liquid tomato fertiliser every two weeks until the fruits begin to colour. Pinch out tips of young plants to encourage bushiness. Susceptible to red spider mite and aphids.

DAHLIA 'BEDNALL BEAUTY'

Dahlia
'Bednall Beauty'

Fast-growing, dwarf, bushy, tuberous perennial with bronze foliage, bearing double scarlet flowers.

HEIGHT & SPREAD: 30x20cm (12x8in)

D. 'Ellen Houston'♀ Striking plant with purple foliage and very dark double flowers.

D. 'Figaro Red Shades' Yellow eyed semi-double flowers.

HEIGHT & SPREAD: 50x30cm (20x12in)

CULTIVATION: Plant out after the last frosts in a free-draining, humus-rich compost. Site in full sun. Water freely while growing and apply a balanced liquid feed every two weeks. Deadhead to encourage more shoots and flowers.

In late autumn, lift tubers, trim off dead stems and store them upside down in boxes of dry sand in a frost-free greenhouse or shed. Increase by division of tubers in early spring. Dahlias are prone to powdery mildew.

GAILLARDIA 'DAZZLER'

Gaillardia
Blanket flower
'Dazzler'♀

Short-lived, bushy annual with daisy-like flowers. The tips of the petals are yellow.

HEIGHT & SPREAD: 60x20cm (24x8in)

G. 'Dwarf Goblin' Similar flowers on shorter plants.

HEIGHT & SPREAD: 25x15cm (10x6in)

CULTIVATION: Plant in spring in a free-draining compost and position in full sun. Taller flowers may need staking for support. Water moderately and apply a liquid tomato feed monthly in the growing season. Deadhead to prolong flowering. Divide in autumn to increase.

LOTUS BERTHELOTII

Lotus berthelotii♀
Parrot's beak

Trailing evergreen sub-shrub with needle-like, silvery green leaves and a mass of curved, beak-like flowers.

HEIGHT & SPREAD: 20x45cm (8x18in)

CULTIVATION: Grow in pots of John Innes No.2 with extra grit. Ideally plant in a basket so that stems can trail down.

Position in full sun in a sheltered position. Flowering may disappoint in poor summers. Water moderately while growing, giving a balanced liquid feed monthly. Overwinter in a warm greenhouse or conservatory, keeping compost almost dry.

LYCOPERSICON LYCOPERSICUM 'TUMBLER'

Lycopersicon lycopersicum
Tomato
'Tumbler'

Specifically bred for containers, this trailing annual bears dozens of tasty cherry tomatoes from midsummer to autumn.

HEIGHT & SPREAD: 60x45cm (24x18in)

L. lycopersicum 'Red Alert' Bushy, upright annual producing cherry tomatoes.

HEIGHT & SPREAD: 50x40cm (20x16in)

CULTIVATION: Plant out after the last frosts in a moisture-retentive, humus-rich compost. Site in full sun in a sheltered position. Water freely while growing (dry spells cause the fruits to split) and apply a liquid tomato feed once a week.

Neither variety mentioned here requires pinching or staking. Remove ripe or spoiling fruits regularly. Tomatoes are prone to various moulds, rots and viruses.

MIMULUS 'WHITECROFT SCARLET'

Mimulus
Monkey flower
'Whitecroft Scarlet'♀

Open, trumpet-shaped flowers
are borne in profusion on this
low-growing, bushy annual or
short-lived perennial.
HEIGHT & SPREAD: 10x15cm
(4x6in)
M. 'Mystic Scarlet' Compact
and free-flowering.
HEIGHT & SPREAD: 15x15cm
(6x6in)
CULTIVATION: Plant out in
late spring in a humus-rich,
moisture-retentive compost.
Site in light shade. Do not
allow the compost to dry out.
Apply a balanced liquid
fertiliser every four weeks.

NICOTIANA X SANDERAE
'SARATOGA RED'

Nicotiana x sanderae
Tobacco plant
'Saratoga Red'

Upright, branching annual
with loose clusters of slightly
fragrant, tubular flowers.
Leaves and stems are sticky.
HEIGHT & SPREAD: 30x15cm
(12x6in)
N. x *sanderae* 'Havana Red'
Bright crimson flowers.
CULTIVATION: Plant out after
the last frosts in a moist but
free-draining potting mix, in
sun or partial shade. Water
liberally and apply a liquid
tomato feed every two weeks.
Deadhead regularly.

PELARGONIUM 'CAROLINE SCHMIDT'

Pelargonium
Geranium
'Caroline Schmidt'♀

This erect and bushy zonal
pelargonium has silvery
white margins to the leaves
and large, rounded clusters
of double scarlet flowers.

HEIGHT & SPREAD: 45x30cm
(18x12in)
P. 'Ann Hoysted'♀ Upright,
bushy, regal pelargonium
bearing large clusters of
crimson flowers whose upper
petals are flushed black-red.
HEIGHT & SPREAD: 45x30cm
(18x12in)
P. 'Rote Mini-cascade'
This trailing, ivy-leaved
pelargonium bears open
clusters of small, deep red
starry flowers above glossy
deep green leaves.
HEIGHT & SPREAD: 10x45cm
(4x18in)

CULTIVATION: Plant out after
the last frosts in a good-
quality compost. Site in full
sun. Ivy-leaved pelargoniums
make good subjects for
hanging baskets.

Water freely while growing
but sparingly in winter. In
summer, fertilise with a
balanced liquid feed every
three weeks. Deadhead
regularly and break off any
yellowing leaves.

Lift plants before the first
hard frosts and store almost
dry over winter in a frost-free
shed or greenhouse.

◀ **Easy to grow,**
and with brilliant
flowers and
handsome foliage,
pelargoniums
give a cheerful
note to any
summer patio.

289

ROSA 'RED ACE'

Rosa
Patio rose
'Red Ace'

Bushy and upright dwarf evergreen shrub with clusters of fragrant, velvety flowers.

HEIGHT & SPREAD: 40x35cm (16x14in)

R. 'Boy's Brigade' Red flowers with white eyes. This has a long flowering season.
R. 'Little Buckaroo' Crimson flowers with white eyes and golden stamens.

CULTIVATION: Plant in spring into a fertile, humus-rich compost and site in full sun. Water freely and apply a balanced liquid feed every three weeks throughout spring and summer. Add a layer of well-rotted manure as a mulch each spring.

Prune annually in early spring, cutting back main stems to 20-25cm (8-10in) from the ground. Remove dead or damaged shoots. Deadheading roses regularly will prolong flowering.

Many roses are susceptible to a variety of pests and diseases, particularly black spot, powdery mildew and rose rust, so they require regular spraying.

SALVIA SPLENDENS 'FURY'

Salvia splendens
'Fury'

Bushy annual with dense spikes of long tubular scarlet flowers emerging from conspicuous red bracts and toothed-edged leaves.

HEIGHT & SPREAD: 25x20cm (10x8in)

S. splendens 'Salsa Scarlet Bicolor' The tips of the petals are white and the bracts are streaked with white.
S. splendens 'Scarlet King' Intense scarlet flowers and very dark green foliage.

CULTIVATION: Plant out after the last frosts in a good-quality, moist, but free-draining compost. Site in full sun or light shade. Water liberally while growing and apply a liquid tomato feed every two weeks. Remove all faded flower spikes.

TROPAEOLUM MAJUS 'HERMINE GRASHOFF'

Tropaeolum majus
Nasturtium
'Hermine Grashoff' ♀

Fast-growing annual with rounded leaves and double, scarlet flowers.

HEIGHT & SPREAD: 1.2x1.2m (4x4ft)

T. majus 'Empress of India' Dwarf and bushy, semi-double flowers, purplish foliage.

HEIGHT & SPREAD: 30x45cm (12x18in)

T. majus 'Scarlet Gleam' Velvety, semi-double flowers and a trailing habit.

CULTIVATION: Grow in John Innes No.1 (a richer compost will encourage leaf growth at the expense of flowers). Site in sun or partial shade. Water well until established; after this nasturtiums are fairly drought-tolerant. Support scramblers or allow them to trail. Sow seed in pots in spring. Prone to blackfly.

◄ **Bright red cyclamen blooms** contrast with deep green foliage. These low-growing plants, here grouped around the base of a container-grown tree, thrive in winter sun but will tolerate partial shade.

VERBENA 'LAWRENCE JOHNSON'

Verbena
'Lawrence Johnson'♀

Bushy and mound-forming perennial, usually grown as an annual, bearing brilliant scarlet flowers held in large, domed clusters.

HEIGHT & SPREAD: 25x30cm (10x12in)

V. x *hybrida* 'Quartz Scarlet' White-eyed red flowers are borne on mound-forming, vigorous plants.

CULTIVATION: Plant out after the last frosts in a good-quality potting mix. Taller varieties will need staking for support. Site in full sun.

Water the plants well, especially during dry spells. Apply a balanced liquid fertiliser every month. Deadhead spent flowerheads regularly to encourage further displays of flowers.

autumn

CALLISTEPHUS CHINENSIS 'POMMAX DEEP RED'

Callistephus chinensis
China aster
'Pommax Deep Red'

This erect, bushy, fast-growing dwarf annual bears large, double, chrysanthemum-like flowers with yellow centres.

HEIGHT & SPREAD: 25x25cm (10x10in)

C. chinensis 'Milady Scarlet'♀ Shorter-stemmed fully double flowers to 10cm (4in) across, on a dwarf plant.

C. chinensis 'Matsumo Red' Tall semi-double flowers with a yellow eye.

HEIGHT & SPREAD: 75x40cm (30x16in)

CULTIVATION: Plant out in spring in a good-quality potting mix. Site the container in full sun. Taller varieties may need staking.

Water moderately and fertilise every two weeks once established, using a balanced liquid feed. Deadhead to prolong flowering.

Prone to callistephus wilt (a soil-borne disease) and to attack by aphids.

CANNA 'LUCIFER'

Canna
Canna lily
'Lucifer'

Tropical-looking rhizomatous perennial producing tall spikes of iris-like flowers. The red petals have yellow margins. The large, oval, slightly bluish green leaves spiral up the stem. Canna lilies make an excellent tall feature in a large container.

HEIGHT: Up to 60cm (2ft)

C. 'Endeavour' Bluish green foliage and iris-like flowers.

HEIGHT: Up to 1.5m (5ft)

C. 'King Humbert' Another tall lily with purple leaves and bright red flowers.

HEIGHT: Up to 1.5m (5ft)

CULTIVATION: Plant rhizomes in large pots of humus-rich, free-draining compost in late winter or early spring. Grow in frost-free conditions until early summer. Pots can then be moved outside to a sheltered sunny spot.

Water liberally and apply a tomato fertiliser every four weeks. Deadhead to prolong the flowering period.

After the first frost blackens the foliage, lift the rhizomes, trim off any dead growth and store in slightly moist compost in a frost-free place over winter.

winter

CYCLAMEN PERSICUM 'MIRACLE SCARLET'

Cyclamen persicum
'Miracle Scarlet'

Tuberous perennial with heart-shaped, silver-patterned leaves. The distinctive scented flowers with swept-back petals are held on upright stalks above the patterned foliage.

HEIGHT & SPREAD: 10x10cm (4x4in)

C. persicum 'Laser Scarlet' Bright, intense red flowers.

CULTIVATION: Plant out in winter in a humus rich, free-draining compost. Site in full sun in a very sheltered position, such as a window box. In all but the mildest areas, *C. persicum* cultivars should be grown in a porch or conservatory.

While growing, water moderately, avoiding the crown. Apply a balanced liquid feed while in flower. Reduce watering as the leaves wither after flowering, and keep dry for two to three months in summer. Resume watering in early autumn. Vine weevils may damage the corms.

SKIMMIA JAPONICA 'NYMANS'

Skimmia japonica
'Nymans'♀

Evergreen female shrub with red-tinged stalks bearing profuse, bright red berries throughout winter. These are preceded by clusters of small off-white flowers.

HEIGHT & SPREAD: 75x75cm (30x30in)

S. japonica 'Veitchii' (syn. 'Foremanii') Vigorous upright female plant with large clusters of scarlet berries.

HEIGHT & SPREAD: Up to 1.5x1.5m (5x5ft)

CULTIVATION: Plant in autumn into pots of John Innes No.3 with added organic matter such as leaf-mould. Site in partial to deep shade. Keep the compost moist and apply a balanced liquid feed monthly from spring to late summer. For these female skimmias to continue producing flowers and berries, a male plant, such as *S. japonica* 'Fragrans'♀, must be grown nearby.

orange flowers

spring

EPIMEDIUM X WARLEYENSE

Epimedium x warleyense

Evergreen perennial with cross-shaped flowers and heart-shaped leaves that flush red in spring and autumn.
HEIGHT & SPREAD: 40x40cm (16x16in)
E. x *versicolor* 'Cupreum' Has coppery orange flowers.
CULTIVATION: Plant in autumn in humus-rich, free-draining compost, in light shade. Water freely while growing and apply a liquid feed monthly. Mulch with leaf-mould in autumn. Remove the old foliage in spring to allow the new growth to show through.

ERYSIMUM CHEIRI 'ORANGE BEDDER'

Erysimum cheiri
Syn. *Cheiranthus cheiri*
Wallflower
'Orange Bedder'

A biennial sub-shrub with lance-shaped leaves and clusters of sweetly scented,

four-petalled flowers.
HEIGHT & SPREAD: 25x25cm (10x10in)
E. hieraciifolium♀ (syn. *E.* x *allionii*) Tall species with brilliant orange flowers with hairs on the backs of the petals.
HEIGHT & SPREAD: 50x30cm (20x12in)
CULTIVATION: Plant in early autumn into a free-draining, neutral to alkaline compost and site in full sun. Water moderately. Feeding is unnecessary. Pinch out the growing tips after planting to encourage bushiness. Prone to club root and root rot.

RANUNCULUS ASIATICUS 'ACCOLADE TANGERINE'

Ranunculus asiaticus
'Accolade Tangerine'

Tuberous perennial producing large, peony or poppy-like flowers on compact plants.
HEIGHT & SPREAD: 25x15cm (10x6in)
R. asiaticus 'Bloomingdale Orange Bi-colour' This bears orange flowers with petals shading to white at the base.
CULTIVATION: Plant out in early spring into a good-quality potting mix. Site in full sun. These cultivars will tolerate light frost but should be moved to a sheltered position if cold weather is severe or prolonged. Water moderately. Feeding is unnecessary. Remove spent flowers.

TULIPA 'PRINSES IRENE'

Tulipa
Tulip
'Prinses Irene'♀

Bulb producing large, cup-shaped flowers with purple feathering on the outer petals.
HEIGHT: 30cm (12in)
T. 'Orange Banquet' ♀ Deep orange cup-shaped flowers with a pale yellow base.
T. 'Orange Favourite' The flowers have finely and irregularly cut petals.
HEIGHT: 50cm (20in)
CULTIVATION: In autumn, plant bulbs 10cm (4in) deep in a loam-based compost. Place the bulbs close together. Site in sun or shade in a sheltered position out of the wind. In growth, water moderately. Remove spent flowers.

summer

CALENDULA OFFICINALIS 'FIESTA GITANA'

Calendula officinalis
Pot marigold
'Fiesta Gitana'♀

Dense, branching, dwarf plant with scented leaves and semi-double, daisy-like flowers.
HEIGHT & SPREAD: 25x20cm (10x8in)

C. officinalis 'Orange King' Taller with double flowers.
HEIGHT & SPREAD: 45x30cm (18x12in)
CULTIVATION: Plant in spring in John Innes No.1, to promote flowers rather than foliage, and site in sun or shade. Water moderately but do not feed. Deadhead to prolong flowering.

CUPHEA CYANAEA

Cuphea cyanea

This evergreen sub-shrub has glossy oval leaves and bears green-tipped, orangey red, tubular flowers.
HEIGHT & SPREAD: 60x60cm (2x2ft)
C. ignea♀ Cigar plant The scarlet tubular flowers have white tips, like ash on cigars.
CULTIVATION: Plant in a good-quality potting mix and place in a sunny sheltered position. Water freely while growing, applying a balanced liquid feed every three weeks. Pinch out growing tips to encourage bushiness. Overwinter in a warm conservatory.

Dahlia
'Figaro Orange Shades'

Bushy and fast-growing dwarf tuberous perennial producing a mass of semi-double orange

DAHLIA 'FIGARO ORANGE SHADES'

flowers with a yellow eye.
HEIGHT & SPREAD: 30x20cm
(12x8in)
D. 'Inflammation' Produces
abundant smaller blooms.
CULTIVATION: Plant out after
the last frosts in a free-
draining, fertile, humus-rich
compost. Site in full sun.
Water freely while growing
and apply a liquid feed every
two weeks.

Deadhead to prolong
flowering. In late autumn,
once frost has blackened the
foliage, lift the tubers, trim
off dead stems, and store
upside down in boxes of
dry sand in a frost-free
greenhouse or conservatory.

Increase by seed or
division of tubers in early
spring. These plants are
prone to powdery mildew.

DIASCIA 'BLACKTHORN APRICOT'

Diascia
'Blackthorn Apricot' ♀

Upright perennial grown as an
annual. Compact plant with
heart-shaped leaves and loose
spikes of pale apricot flowers.
HEIGHT & SPREAD: 20x40cm
(8x16in)
D. 'Joyce's Choice' ♀ Soft
apricot-coloured blooms.
CULTIVATION: Plant out after
the last frosts in a good-
quality potting mix. Site in
full sun. Keep the compost
moist at all times. Feed
every fortnight with a weak,
balanced liquid fertiliser.
Cut back after flowering to
encourage a second flush.

ECCREMOCARPUS SCABER

Eccremocarpus
scaber ♀
Chilean glory vine

Fast-growing perennial
climber with clusters of long
tubular flowers and dark
green leaves. Climbs by
means of tendrils.
HEIGHT & SPREAD: 3x1m
(10x3ft)
CULTIVATION: Plant out in
late spring in a light, free-
draining potting mix. Select
a sheltered site in full sun.
Provide a trellis or wigwam
support for the climbing
stems. Water freely while
growing, applying a balanced
liquid feed every month. Keep
almost dry in winter, adding
a deep, dry mulch to improve
hardiness. If frost kills the top
growth, the plant usually
resprouts in spring.

GAZANIA 'COOKEI'

Gazania
'Cookei' ♀

Low-growing bushy
perennial with grey foliage
and daisy-like orange flowers
with a slate-blue ring around
a yellow centre.
HEIGHT & SPREAD: 25x25cm
(10x10in)
G. 'Daybreak Bright Orange'
Has a brown ring around the
yellow eye and silvery leaves.
G. 'Kiss Bronze' Particularly

useful as it blooms well even
in dull weather, which causes
many gazania flowers to close.
CULTIVATION: Plant in a sunny
spot in early summer in
free-draining compost. Water
moderately until established;
after this gazanias are fairly
drought-tolerant. Feeding is
unnecessary. Overwinter in
a frost-free greenhouse.

HELIANTHUS ANNUUS 'TEDDY BEAR'

Helianthus annuus
Sunflower
'Teddy Bear'

Fast-growing annual with
large, fully double, orange-
yellow pompom flowers.
HEIGHT: 60cm (2ft)
H. annuus 'Sunspot' Single
flowers, to 20cm (8in) across,
with a yellow-green eye.
CULTIVATION: Grow in free-
draining compost in a sunny,
sheltered position. Water
freely while growing and feed
fortnightly. The short varieties
mentioned here do not require
staking unless the site is
exposed. Sow seed in the pot.

Hemerocallis fulva
Day lily
'Flore Pleno'

Evergreen perennial with
strap-shaped leaves and
double lily-like flowers.

HEMEROCALLIS FULVA 'FLORE PLENO'

HEIGHT & SPREAD: 90x90cm
(3x3ft)
H. 'Bertie Ferris' Herbaceous
perennial with apricot flowers.
HEIGHT: 45cm (18in)
H. 'Outrageous' Coppery
orange flowers with dark
brown eyes.
CULTIVATION: Plant in spring
in large pots of John Innes
No.3 with added organic
matter such as leaf-mould.
Site in full sun, but note that
they tolerate windy sites, too.
Water freely while growing,
and apply a balanced liquid
fertiliser every fortnight from
spring until the buds form.
Divide clumps every two
years or so, in spring.

IMPATIENS WALLERIANA
'ACCENT APRICOT'

Impatiens walleriana
Busy Lizzie
'Accent Apricot'

Low-growing, bushy perennial
usually grown as an annual.
Free-flowering with soft
orange blooms and fleshy,
wavy-edged, oval leaves.
HEIGHT & SPREAD: 20x20cm
(8x8in)
I. walleriana 'Tempo
Orange' Bright orange flowers.
I. walleriana 'Mega Orange
Star' Salmon-orange flowers
with radial white stripes.
CULTIVATION: Plant out in
spring after the last frosts.
Busy Lizzies do well in sun
or light shade. Water freely
while growing, applying a
balanced liquid fertiliser
every three weeks. Pinch out
tips to promote bushiness.

LILIUM 'ENCHANTMENT'

Lilium
Lily
'Enchantment' ☙

Bulb producing up to 12 upward-facing, bright orange, star-shaped flowers, each 10cm (4in) in diameter, which have black-spotted throats.
HEIGHT: 90cm (3ft)
L. bulbiferum var. *croceum* ☙ Large, bowl-shaped blooms.
L. 'Orange Pixie' Up to five upward-facing, starry flowers on short, sturdy stems.
HEIGHT: 50cm (20in)
CULTIVATION: Plant bulbs in autumn at a depth of three times their own height. Use John Innes No.2 and put a good layer of crocks in the bottom of the pot. Site in a sheltered position in partial shade. Water freely while growing and give a high potash feed once a month.

Overwinter bulbs in their pots, or store in boxes of damp sand in a cool, dry place. Remove outer scales of bulbs and grow them on.

MIMULUS 'HIGHLAND ORANGE'

Mimulus
Monkey flower
'Highland Orange'

Trumpet-shaped flowers, loved by bees, are borne in profusion on this bushy, often short-lived perennial.

HEIGHT & SPREAD: 25x25cm (10x10in)
M. 'Magic Orange' Bright orange flowers.
M. 'Magic Peach' Soft, peachy orange flowers.
CULTIVATION: Plant in a humus-rich, moisture-retentive compost in light shade. Apply a balanced liquid fertiliser every month.

NEMESIA STRUMOSA 'ORANGE PRINCE'

Nemesia strumosa
'Orange Prince'

Bushy, erect annual bearing an abundance of two-lipped, vivid orange flowers.
HEIGHT & SPREAD: 25x15cm (10x6in)
CULTIVATION: Plant out in spring after the last frosts into a moisture-retentive compost. Position the containers in a sheltered, sunny site.

Water frequently in dry weather and apply a liquid tomato feed every two weeks. Cut back hard after the first flush of blooms to encourage further flowering.

Sanvitalia procumbens
Creeping zinnia

Mat-forming annual with bright yellow-orange, daisy-like flowers with a black eye.

SANVITALIA PROCUMBENS

HEIGHT & SPREAD: 15x30cm (6x12in)
S. procumbens 'Irish Eyes' Golden-orange petals surround a greenish eye.
CULTIVATION: Plant in late spring in free-draining, preferably light compost. Position at the edge of the container so that the stems can trail down. Site in full sun. Water moderately. Feed monthly with a balanced liquid fertiliser.

TAGETES PATULA 'AURORA ORANGE'

Tagetes patula
French marigold
'Aurora Orange'

Fast-growing upright annual with aromatic, divided leaves and large double flowers.
HEIGHT & SPREAD: 20x15cm (8x6in)
T. patula 'Alamo Flame' Double flowers, the outer petals are coppery red.
T. patula 'Orange Boy' Compact and free-flowering.
T. erecta 'Inca Orange' African marigold with fully double, pompom flowers on erect plants.
HEIGHT & SPREAD: 35x20cm (14x8in)
CULTIVATION: Plant out after the last frosts in John Innes No.2 and site in full sun. Water moderately, and more frequently during dry spells, and apply a balanced liquid feed every two weeks.

Deadhead occasionally to prolong flowering. French marigolds are prone to attack from slugs and snails.

THUNBERGIA ALATA

Thunbergia alata
Black-eyed Susan

Fast-growing, annual climber with twining stems and black centred, pale orange flowers.
HEIGHT & SPREAD: 1.5mx25cm (5ftx10in)
CULTIVATION: Plant out after the last frosts into a free-draining compost. Site in full sun. Water freely and apply a balanced liquid feed every two weeks. Provide support for the twining stems, such as trellis or wires against a wall.

ZINNIA 'SHORT STUFF ORANGE'

Zinnia
'Short Stuff Orange'

Low-growing, free-flowering annual which bears double, bright orange flowers up to 5cm (2in) across.
HEIGHT & SPREAD: 20x20cm (8x8in)
Z. haageana (syn. *Z. mexicana*) 'Orange Star' Has single, daisy-like blooms.
Z. 'Peter Pan Orange' Very compact dwarf plant with large double flowers.
CULTIVATION: Plant out after the last frosts into a good-quality potting mix in full sun. Water freely while growing; feed every fortnight. Deadheading regularly will help to prolong flowering.

◄ **Pyracantha 'Golden Charmer' berries** radiate a warm orange glow and, with a basket of windfalls and a pumpkin, create a wonderful scene of mellow autumn fruitfulness.

PYRACANTHA 'GOLDEN CHARMER'

Pyracantha
Firethorn
'Golden Charmer'

This hardy evergreen shrub bears long-lasting berries in brilliant golden-orange. Upright at first, the branches arch over as the plant ages.
HEIGHT & SPREAD: 1.5x1.2m (5x4ft)
P. 'Navaho' Small reddish orange berries.
HEIGHT & SPREAD: 1x1.2m (3x4ft)
P. 'Orange Glow'♀ Upright shrub; deep orange berries.
HEIGHT & SPREAD: 1.8x1.8m (6x6ft)
CULTIVATION: Plant in humus-rich compost and site in sun or shade. Water moderately and feed monthly. Support with trellis or wires if grown against a wall.

HEIGHT & SPREAD: 1.2x1.2m (4x4ft)
CULTIVATION: Plant tubers 15cm (6in) deep in spring. Use a humus-rich compost. Site in sun or partial shade. Ideally the container should be in shade and the stems in the sun. Water freely while growing and apply a balanced liquid feed monthly. Provide support, such as trellis, for the twining stems, or allow the plant to ramble through another shrub.

In very cold districts move the pot inside after frost has killed off the top growth. It can be increased by dividing tubers in early spring.

winter

VIOLA X WITTROCKIANA 'UNIVERSAL ORANGE'

Viola x wittrockiana
Winter pansy
'Universal Orange'♀

Low-growing perennial, grown as an annual, with large, round, clear orange flowers produced during mild spells all through winter.
HEIGHT & SPREAD: 16x20cm (6x8in)
V. x *wittrockiana* 'Turbo Orange Blotch' Brown blotch in centre of each flower.
CULTIVATION: Plant in autumn and site in sun or shade. Water in dry spells. Deadhead regularly to prolong flowering. Loved by slugs and snails.

autumn

tall spikes. The broad, oval leaves are brownish purple.
HEIGHT & SPREAD: 1.5mx50cm (5ftx20in)
C. 'Striata' Pale green leaves with bright yellow veins.
CULTIVATION: Plant rhizomes in large pots of humus-rich compost in early spring. Grow on in frost-free conditions until early summer. Pots can then be moved outside to a sheltered sunny spot. Water liberally and apply a tomato fertiliser every four weeks. Remove spent flowers.

After the first frost blackens the foliage, lift the rhizomes and store in slightly damp compost in a frost-free shed or greenhouse over winter. Increase by division of rhizomes in early spring.

CANNA X GENERALIS 'WYOMING'

Canna
Canna lily
'Wyoming'

This exotic, tropical-looking, rhizomatous perennial is half-hardy in Britain. It bears striking gladiolus-like flowers with frilly tangerine petals on

TROPAEOLUM TUBEROSUM

Tropaeolum tuberosum

Perennial, deciduous climber with five-lobed, grey-green leaves and trumpet-shaped, orange-red flowers.

AURINIA SAXATILIS

Aurinia saxatilis ♀
Syn. *Alyssum saxatile*
Gold dust

Compact evergreen sub-shrub forming a low hummock of grey-green foliage. In late spring bears dense clusters of small, bright yellow flowers.
HEIGHT & SPREAD: 20x20cm (8x8in)
A. saxatilis 'Citrina' ♀ Pale lemon-yellow flowers.
A. saxatilis 'Flore Pleno' Double flowers.
CULTIVATION: Site in full sun. Water moderately and feed monthly. Clip back after flowering to maintain shape.

CROCUS CHRYSANTHUS 'ELEGANCE'

Crocus chrysanthus
'Elegance'

Cormous perennial which flowers in early spring, producing bright golden-yellow flowers with brown feathering on the outer petals.
HEIGHT: 7.5cm (3in)

C. chrysanthus 'Gipsy Girl' Pale yellow with pronounced purple feathering.
C. 'Dutch Yellow' ♀ Large-flowered cultivar.
CULTIVATION: Plant in autumn in John Innes No.1 with extra grit. Place the corms at a depth of 7.5cm (3in), in sun or shade. Keep the compost moist but avoid waterlogging. Mice and voles eat newly planted crocus corms.

HYACINTHUS ORIENTALIS 'CITY OF HAARLEM'

Hyacinthus orientalis
Hyacinth

'City of Haarlem' ♀

Bulb producing erect spikes of up to 40 bell-shaped, very fragrant flowers.
HEIGHT: 20cm (8in)
H. orientalis 'Yellow Hammer' Creamy yellow.
CULTIVATION: Plant in autumn, 10cm (4in) deep in John Innes No.2, in sun or partial shade.

Narcissus
Daffodil

'Tête-à-tête' ♀

Dwarf bulb producing up to three dainty flowers a stem.
HEIGHT: 15cm (6in)

NARCISSUS 'TÊTE-À-TÊTE'

N. 'Bantam' ♀ Yellow petals and orangey red central cup.
N. 'February Gold' ♀ Golden flowers to 7.5cm (3in) across.
HEIGHT: 30cm (12in)
N. 'Jumblie' ♀ Dwarf daffodil. Deep gold trumpet with pale yellow reflexed petals.
CULTIVATION: Plant bulbs in autumn at a depth of one-and-a-half times their own height in free-draining compost. Site in sun or dappled shade.

Water moderately. Feeding is unnecessary. After flowering the bulbs may be planted in the open ground. Prone to fungal infections in wet compost. Narcissus fly may damage bulbs.

RHODODENDRON 'PRINCESS ANNE'

Rhododendron
'Princess Anne' ♀

Compact and rounded dwarf evergreen shrub bearing clusters of funnel-shaped, pale yellow flowers. The pale green leaves are bronze when young.
HEIGHT & SPREAD: 75x75cm (30x30in)
R. 'Patty Bee' ♀ Very free-flowering. The leaves turn bronze in winter.
CULTIVATION: Plant in autumn in ericaceous compost and add slow-release fertiliser. Site in sun or light shade. Water liberally, especially in dry weather, preferably with rainwater. Trim as necessary after flowering to maintain a compact shape. Mulch in autumn with leaf-mould.

ABUTILON 'CANARY BIRD'

Abutilon
Flowering maple
'Canary Bird' ♀

Fast-growing, twiggy shrub bearing bell-shaped flowers and glossy, evergreen leaves.
HEIGHT & SPREAD: 1.2mx60cm (4x2ft)
CULTIVATION: Grow in John Innes No.3 with organic matter added. Water freely and feed while growing. Lightly prune to shape in spring and pinch out tips to promote bushiness. Over-winter in a warm greenhouse.

Allium moly
Golden garlic
'Jeannine' ♀

Bulb producing up to 40 starry flowers in exuberant large loose clusters.
HEIGHT: 30cm (12in)
A. flavum ♀ Pendent clusters of small flowers with prominent stamens.
CULTIVATION: Plant bulbs in autumn at a depth of twice their height. Use John Innes No.2 with added organic matter. Water while growing, avoiding excessive winter wet. Apply a balanced liquid feed once the buds form.

ALLIUM MOLY 'JEANNINE'

ARGYRANTHEMUM 'JAMAICA PRIMROSE'

Argyranthemum
Marguerite
'Jamaica Primrose' ♀

Vigorous evergreen sub-shrub with finely dissected, grey-green leaves, and pale yellow daisy-like flowers deepening to a darker yellow eye.

HEIGHT & SPREAD: 75x75cm (30x30in)

A. 'Cornish Gold' ♀ Has mid-green foliage.

CULTIVATION: Site in full sun. Water freely in summer but keep almost dry in winter. Feed fortnightly. Cut off dead flower stalks.

PROCUMBENS

Asarina procumbens
Creeping snapdragon

Evergreen perennial with trailing stems and pale yellow 'snapdragon' flowers.

HEIGHT & SPREAD: 10x60cm (4x24in)

A. procumbens 'Nuria' Dwarf, good for small pots.

CULTIVATION: Site in partial shade. Water freely in spring and summer. Keep compost just moist in winter.

ASTERISCUS MARITIMUS

Asteriscus maritimus

Low-growing perennial with rosettes of grey-green leaves and large, bright yellow, daisy-like flowers.

HEIGHT & SPREAD: 15x20cm (6x8in)

CULTIVATION: Plant in spring in free-draining compost and site container in full sun. Water moderately in summer but protect from excessive winter wet. Apply a balanced liquid fertiliser monthly in the growing season. Deadhead to prolong flowering. A useful plant for seaside gardens.

BIDENS FERULIFOLIA

Bidens ferulifolia

Slender-stemmed spreading perennial, usually grown as an annual. Bears abundant star-shaped flowers among finely divided, ferny foliage. Particularly suitable for hanging baskets.

HEIGHT & SPREAD: 30x45cm (12x18in)

CULTIVATION: Plant out after the last frosts in a good-quality potting mix. Site in full sun. Bidens is fairly drought-tolerant but likes some water. Give a liquid tomato feed every three weeks. Pinch out growing tips to encourage bushiness.

CALCEOLARIA INTEGRIFOLIA 'SUNSHINE'

Calceolaria integrifolia
Slipper flower
'Sunshine' ♀

Compact perennial sub-shrub, usually grown as an annual, producing a mass of rounded yellow flowers.

HEIGHT & SPREAD: 25x25cm (10x10in)

C. integrifolia 'Gold Bunch' Large, golden-yellow flowers.

CULTIVATION: Plant out after the last frosts in a good-quality potting mix. Site in sun or partial shade. Keep the compost moist at all times, and apply a liquid tomato feed every three weeks.

CELOSIA ARGENTEA 'CENTURY YELLOW'

Celosia argentea
'Century Yellow'

Upright annual bearing conical, feathery plumes of bright golden-yellow flowers.

HEIGHT & SPREAD: 50x20cm (20x8in)

C. argentea 'Kimono Yellow' Dwarf variety, 20cm (8in) tall.

CULTIVATION: Plant out after the last frosts into a moist but free-draining compost. Select a sunny, sheltered site.

COREOPSIS VERTICILLATA 'ZAGREB'

Coreopsis verticillata
'Zagreb'

Bushy perennial with finely divided, fern-like leaves and abundant, starry blooms.

HEIGHT & SPREAD: 40x30cm (16x12in)

C. grandiflora 'Domino' Upright plant. Daisy-like flowers with ragged petals.

HEIGHT & SPREAD: 25x20cm (10x8in)

CULTIVATION: Plant out in late spring in full sun. Water moderately. Deadhead to prolong flowering.

Gazania
'Kiss Yellow'

Compact and bushy perennial with abundant daisy-like flowers with a brown circle around the eye.

HEIGHT & SPREAD: 25x25cm (10x10in)

G. 'Daybreak Yellow' Bright yellow flowers with dark eyes.

G. 'Talent Yellow' ♀ This plant has silvery grey foliage and pure yellow flowers.

CULTIVATION: Plant out in early summer in free-draining compost. Site in full sun as flowers close in dull weather. Gazanias are drought-tolerant but do better if watered. Protect from winter cold.

GAZANIA 'KISS YELLOW'

Helianthus annuus
Sunflower
'Moonwalker'

Fast-growing, upright and branching annual, producing several large flowers with light yellow petals and dark brown centres.
HEIGHT & SPREAD: 1.2mx50cm (4ftx20in)
H. annuus 'Pacino' Dwarf annual bearing several small-centred, bright yellow flowers.
HEIGHT & SPREAD: 60x20cm (24x8in)
H. annuus 'Sunbeam' Dwarf, with golden-yellow flowers with a greenish centre.
CULTIVATION: Grow in free-draining fertile compost in full sun. Water generously and feed every three weeks. The dwarf varieties mentioned here do not require staking.

Helichrysum italicum ♀
Curry plant

Hardy evergreen sub-shrub with narrow, silvery grey, aromatic leaves. Produces tight, flattened clusters of

mustard-yellow flowers.
HEIGHT & SPREAD: 60x60cm (2x2ft)
H. 'Schwefellicht' Herbaceous perennial with grey, woolly foliage and bearing clusters of fluffy flowers.
CULTIVATION: Plant in spring in John Innes No.2 with extra grit and site in full sun. Water moderately throughout summer, keeping the compost just moist in winter. Remove flowerheads once they have faded, and prune any frost-damaged shoots in spring.

Hemerocallis
Day lily
'Eenie Weenie'

Compact and free-flowering perennial with arching, linear leaves and exotic lily-like flowers, each lasting just one day, held on upright stems.
HEIGHT & SPREAD: 25x40cm (10x16in)
H. 'Little Gypsy Vagabond' Evergreen; pale yellow flowers with purple eyes.
H. 'Yellow Lollipop' Very narrow leaves and large bright yellow flowers.
CULTIVATION: Plant in spring in pots of John Innes No.3 with added organic matter such as leaf-mould. Site in full sun. Water freely while growing and apply a balanced liquid feed every two weeks from spring until the buds form. Divide clumps every two years in spring to maintain vigour. Slugs may attack young foliage in spring.

Lilium
Lily
'Connecticut King'

Strong-growing bulb producing up to 15 upward-facing, star-like flowers.
HEIGHT: 90cm (3ft)
L. 'Grand Cru' Upward-facing flowers with an orange 'brush mark' at base of each petal.
CULTIVATION: Plant bulbs in autumn at a depth of twice their height. Use John Innes No.2, putting a good layer of crocks in the base of the pot. Site in a sunny sheltered position, keeping roots shaded. Water freely and give a high potash feed monthly. Store bulbs in their pots over winter, or store in boxes of damp sand in a cool place.

Lysimachia nummularia
Creeping Jenny

Vigorous, creeping evergreen perennial. Trailing stems bear saucer-shaped flowers and small, heart-shaped leaves.
HEIGHT & SPREAD: 5x45cm (2x18in)
L. nummularia 'Aurea' ♀ Has golden-yellow foliage.
CULTIVATION: Plant in spring and allow stems to trail. Site in sun or partial shade. Keep the compost moist.

Rudbeckia hirta
'Sonora'

Stout, branching perennial usually grown as an annual. The daisy-like flowers are golden-yellow with a maroon eye and a broad maroon band encircling it.
HEIGHT & SPREAD: 40x30cm (16x12in)
R. hirta 'Goldilocks' Semi-double with a black eye.
R. fulgida 'Goldsturm' Daisy-like golden flowers with brown centres.
HEIGHT & SPREAD: 60x30cm (2x1ft)
CULTIVATION: Plant in spring in a moisture-retentive compost. Site in a sunny position and water freely, especially in hot weather. Deadhead to prolong flowering.

Santolina chamaecyparissus ♀
Cotton lavender

Dense, rounded evergreen sub-shrub with tiny white woolly leaves and pompom flowers on slender stems.
HEIGHT & SPREAD: 50x50cm (20x20in)
CULTIVATION: Plant in spring in a free-draining compost. Site in full sun. Water moderately and feed monthly.

SEDUM SPATHULIFOLIUM 'CAPE BLANCO'

Sedum spathulifolium
'Cape Blanco' ♀

Mat-forming perennial with fleshy stems and a white bloom on the central rosettes of silvery leaves. Clusters of star-shaped flowers are held just above the foliage.
HEIGHT & SPREAD: 10x20cm (4x8in)
S. kamtschaticum var. *ellacombeanum* ♀ Compact with large pale yellow flowers.
CULTIVATION: Plant in spring in free-draining compost in full sun. Sedums are drought-tolerant but do better with moderate watering. No need to feed. Cut off faded flower stems. Protect plants from excessive winter wet: prone to rot in wet conditions.

TAGETES PATULA 'AURORA YELLOW'

Tagetes patula
French marigold
'Aurora Yellow'

Fast-growing, bushy, upright annual with aromatic divided leaves and double flowers.
HEIGHT & SPREAD: 20x15cm (8x6in)
T. patula 'Naughty Marietta' Single, deep yellow flowers, with a maroon blotch at the base of each petal.
T. erecta 'Antigua Primrose'

African marigold with fully double pompom flowers on erect plants.
HEIGHT & SPREAD: 20x15cm (8x6in)
CULTIVATION: Plant out after the last frosts in John Innes No.2 and site in full sun. Water moderately and apply a balanced liquid feed every two weeks. Deadhead to prolong flowering.

ZINNIA 'SHORT STUFF GOLD'

Zinnia
'Short Stuff Gold'

Low-growing, floriferous annual with double flowers.
HEIGHT & SPREAD: 20x20cm (8x8in)
CULTIVATION: Plant out after the last frosts into well-drained compost. Site in full sun. Water moderately and apply a liquid tomato feed every two weeks. Deadhead to prolong flowering.

autumn

Kniphofia
Red hot poker, torch lily
'Ice Queen'

Herbaceous perennial with numerous, tubular flowers, packed densely together at

KNIPHOFIA 'ICE QUEEN'

the top of sturdy flower stalks. The flowers are pale creamy yellow tinged with green, ageing to creamy white.
HEIGHT & SPREAD: 1.2mx60cm (4x2ft)
K. 'Bee's Lemon' Lemon-yellow flowers emerge from greenish buds.
HEIGHT & SPREAD: 90x60cm (3x2ft)
K. 'Little Maid' ♀ Has ivory blooms tipped with soft yellow and shorter than most.
HEIGHT: 55cm (22in)
CULTIVATION: Plant in autumn in a free-draining compost. Site in sun or light shade. Water moderately and feed monthly in the growing season. Remove dead flower spikes and foliage in winter. Thrips may mottle the foliage in hot, dry summers.

STERNBERGIA LUTEA

Sternbergia lutea

Bulbous perennial producing rich yellow, crocus-like flowers on short sturdy stems, and long, bright green, strap-like leaves.
HEIGHT: 15cm (6in)
CULTIVATION: Plant bulbs 10cm (4in) deep in late summer, using John Innes No.2 with extra grit. Site in full sun. Water sparingly while growing – overwatering can rot the bulbs – and allow the pots to dry out completely as the bulbs become dormant. These plants need a warm summer dormancy in order to flower. Resume watering in late summer.

winter

ERANTHIS HYEMALIS

Eranthis hyemalis ♀
Winter aconite

Tuberous perennial with yellow cup-shaped flowers above a ruff of divided leaves.
HEIGHT & SPREAD: 15x15cm (6x6in)
CULTIVATION: In autumn, soak tubers overnight before planting 5cm (2in) deep in humus-rich compost. Or plant eranthis in leaf in spring. Site in sun or partial shade. Allow tubers a period of dry dormancy in summer.

Jasminum nudiflorum ♀
Winter jasmine

Small bright yellow flowers are carried on the slender, leafless stems of this scrambling deciduous shrub.
HEIGHT & SPREAD: 1.5x1.5m (5x5ft)
CULTIVATION: Plant in autumn in large pots of John Innes No.3. Site in sun or partial shade. Water freely in summer and less in winter. Feed monthly in the growing season. Provide some support for the scrambling stems. Prune out about a third of the shoots in spring.

JASMINUM NUDIFLORUM

299

◄ **A tub filled with crocuses** and grape hyacinths looks particularly stunning under its blanket of spring snow.

HEIGHT & SPREAD: 2.4x2.4m (8x8ft)

C. alpina 'Frances Rivis' ♀ This clematis bears mid-blue flowers with twisted petals.

CULTIVATION: Plant in early spring in large pots of John Innes No.3 with added organic matter such as leaf-mould. Ideally, select a site where the container, but not the plant, is in shade.

Water moderately while growing, applying a balanced liquid feed monthly in the growing season. Provide some support, such as a trellis, pergola, or another shrub, for the tendrils to cling to. Prune lightly after flowering until the plant outgrows its space or becomes straggly. Then it can be cut back hard.

CROCUS TOMMASINIANUS 'RUBY GIANT'

blue & purple flowers

spring

ANEMONE BLANDA 'INGRAMII'

Anemone blanda

'Ingramii' ♀

Clump-forming tuberous perennial with irregularly lobed leaves and deep blue, daisy-like, flowers.

HEIGHT & SPREAD: 15x15cm (6x6in)

A. blanda 'Violet Star' Violet-coloured flowers.
A. blanda 'Blue Mist' Pale blue flowers.

CULTIVATION: In autumn, plant the tubers 5cm (2in) deep in free-draining compost. The tubers should first be soaked overnight. Site the container in full sun. Water moderately while growing, but cease watering once the foliage dies back. Either keep the tubers dry in their pots, or lift and store them in a box of dry sand during summer. Replant and recommence watering in autumn. Increase by careful division of tubers.

CLEMATIS ALPINA 'PAMELA JACKMAN'

Clematis alpina

'Pamela Jackman'

Robust and free-flowering deciduous climber bearing pendent, four-petalled deep blue flowers with cream anthers. The flowers are followed by fluffy seed heads.

Crocus tommasinianus ♀

'Ruby Giant'

This early spring flowering corm produces large, rounded, rich purple flowers with orange stamens.

HEIGHT: 10cm (4in)

C. vernus 'Purpureus Grandiflorus' Intense violet flowers; very free-flowering.

CULTIVATION: Plant in autumn in John Innes No.2 with extra grit. Place corms very close together at a depth of 7.5cm (3in). Site in sun or shade. Keep the compost moist but avoid waterlogging. Mice and voles eat newly planted crocus corms.

HYACINTHUS ORIENTALIS 'DELFT BLUE'

Hyacinthus orientalis
Hyacinth

'Delft Blue'♀

Bulb producing erect spikes of up to 40 bell-shaped, very fragrant flowers.

HEIGHT: 20cm (8in)

H. orientalis 'Blue Jacket'♀ Very dark blue flowers with purple veins.

H. orientalis 'Ostara'♀ Violet-blue flowers.

CULTIVATION: Plant in autumn 10cm (4in) deep in John Innes No.2. Position in sun or partial shade and water moderately while growing, but avoid excessive winter wet. Hyacinth bulbs are best discarded after one season and bought fresh each autumn as the second year's flowering is usually poor. Prone to various rots and moulds.

MUSCARI ARMENIACUM

Muscari armeniacum ♀
Grape hyacinth

Bulb producing dense, erect spikes of tiny, bright blue flowers. The linear leaves appear before the flowers the preceding autumn.

HEIGHT: 20cm (8in)

M. armeniacum 'Blue Spike' The tiny bell-like flowers are double.

M. azureum ♀ Has pale blue flowers.

CULTIVATION: Plant the bulbs 5-7.5cm (2-3in) deep in John Innes No.2 in summer. Site in sun or partial shade. Water moderately while growing. Feeding is unnecessary.

Bulbs are best planted out in the open ground once the leaves start to wither, as a second year's flowering in pots is usually poor.

MYOSOTIS SYLVATICA 'BLUE BALL'

Myosotis sylvatica
Forget-me-not

'Blue Ball'♀

Compact and rounded biennial with hairy leaves and small, saucer-shaped flowers held in dense clusters.

HEIGHT & SPREAD: 15x15cm (6x6in)

M. sylvatica 'Blue Basket' Taller forget-me-not with a more erect habit.

HEIGHT & SPREAD: 25x25cm (10x10in)

M. sylvatica 'Ultramarine'♀ Deep indigo-blue flowers.

CULTIVATION: Plant in autumn in humus-rich compost. Site in light shade.

Water moderately. Feeding is unnecessary. Sow seed in their containers in early summer or allow to self seed. Susceptible to aphids and to powdery mildew in a dry spring.

summer

AGAPANTHUS CAMPANULATUS 'ISIS'

Agapanthus campanulatus
African lily

'Isis'

Clump-forming perennial with arching, strap-like leaves. Trumpet-shaped flowers are held in loose, rounded clusters on long stalks.

HEIGHT & SPREAD: 75x45cm (30x18in)

A. campanulatus ssp. *patens* ♀ Pale blue flowers on shorter plants.

A. caulescens ♀ Mid-blue flowers on tall plants.

HEIGHT & SPREAD: 1.2mx60cm (4x2ft)

CULTIVATION: Grow in large pots of John Innes No.3 in full sun, sheltered from wind. Water freely from spring to autumn, but keep almost dry in winter. Apply a balanced liquid feed from spring until the flower buds form. Divide congested clumps to increase.

Ageratum houstonianum
Floss flower

'Champion Blue'

Compact annual bearing large clusters of powder-puff flowers over a long season.

AGERATUM HOUSTONIANUM 'CHAMPION BLUE'

HEIGHT & SPREAD: 15x15cm (6x6in)

A. houstonianum 'Atlantic Plus' Very dark blue flowers.

A. houstonianum 'Blue Danube' This plant is very compact and vigorous.

CULTIVATION: Plant out after the last frosts in a good-quality potting mix and site in full sun. Water generously in the growing season and apply a liquid tomato feed every three weeks.

Regular deadheading will prolong flowering.

ALLIUM SCHOENOPRASUM

Allium schoenoprasum
Chives

Bulb producing edible, onion-scented leaves and spherical heads of papery, pale purple flowers.

HEIGHT: up to 30cm (12in)

A. cyaneum ♀ Pendent, violet flowers in loose, rounded clusters.

A. sikkimense Rounded clusters of blue flowers.

HEIGHT: 10-25cm (4-10in)

CULTIVATION: Plant bulbs in autumn at a depth of twice their height. Use John Innes No.2 with added organic matter such as leaf-mould. Water moderately while growing, but avoid excessive winter wet. Apply a balanced liquid fertiliser once the buds form.

After flowering, bulbs are best lifted and planted out in the open ground. Increase by dividing congested clumps.

BRACHYSCOME IBERIDIFOLIA

Brachyscome iberidifolia
Swan river daisy

Bushy, spreading annual with finely dissected foliage. The abundant, fragrant daisy-like flowers are usually violet or blue with a yellow eye.
HEIGHT & SPREAD: 30x45cm (12x18in)
B. iberidifolia 'Blue Star' The unusual petals are curled to form 'quills'.
B. iberidifolia 'Brachy Blue' Dwarf variety, blue flowers.
HEIGHT & SPREAD: 15x15cm (6x6in)
CULTIVATION: Plant out after the last frosts in a good-quality potting mix. Site the container in sun or partial shade. Water moderately and apply a liquid tomato feed every three weeks. Deadhead to prolong flowering.

CAMPANULA ISOPHYLLA

Campanula isophylla ♀
Italian bellflower

Trailing perennial which is usually grown as an annual. It bears masses of pale

mauve-blue, star-shaped flowers on short stalks, and has heart-shaped leaves on trailing stems.
HEIGHT & SPREAD: 20x30cm (8x12in)
C. isophylla 'Stella Blue' Violet-blue flowers.
CULTIVATION: Plant out after the last frosts in a good-quality potting mix. It should be sited in full sun or in partial shade.

Water freely while the plant is growing, applying a balanced liquid feed monthly. Deadheading regularly will help to prolong flowering.

FELICIA AMELLOIDES 'SANTA ANITA'

Felicia amelloides
Blue Marguerite
'Santa Anita' ♀

Bushy evergreen sub-shrub which is usually grown as an annual. The daisy-like, yellow-eyed, light blue flowers are carried on slender stalks above the bright green, oval leaves.
HEIGHT & SPREAD: 30x40cm (12x16in)
F. amelloides 'Santa Anita Variegated' ♀ Has cream-splashed leaves.
CULTIVATION: Plant out after the last frosts in a good-quality potting mix and site the containers in full sun. These marguerites should be watered generously and given a balanced liquid feed every two weeks. Pinch out young plants to encourage bushiness. Cut off dead flower stalks to prolong flowering.

HELIOTROPIUM ARBORESCENS 'MARINE'

Heliotropium arborescens
Heliotrope, cherry pie
'Marine' ♀

Compact evergreen sub-shrub with dark green leaves and bearing dense clusters of richly fragrant purple flowers.
HEIGHT & SPREAD: 45x45cm (18x18in)
H. arborescens 'Chatsworth' ♀ Vigorous with very fragrant flowers.
H. arborescens 'Dwarf Marine' Compact with a height and spread of just 30cm (12in).
CULTIVATION: Plant out after the last frosts in a good-quality potting mix. Site in full sun. Water moderately, applying a balanced liquid feed monthly. Remove faded flowerheads. May be overwintered in a frost-free greenhouse or conservatory.

HYDRANGEA MACROPHYLLA 'GENERAL VICOMTESSE DE VIBRAYE'

Hydrangea macrophylla
'General Vicomtesse de Vibraye' ♀

This deciduous shrub has large, glossy, serrated leaves and dense, rounded, mop head flowers of clear mid blue, provided that they are grown in acid compost.

HEIGHT & SPREAD: 1.2x1m (4x3ft)
H. macrophylla 'Mariesii Perfecta' ♀ Syn. 'Blue Wave' Has rich blue 'lacecap' flowerheads in acid compost.
CULTIVATION: Plant in autumn in large pots of ericaceous compost. The flowers will be pink if a neutral or limey compost is used.

Site in partial shade with some shelter from cold, drying winds. Water generously while growing, using rainwater if possible (because tap water is alkaline), and feed every month. You could also add a blueing compound to guarantee blue flowers. Top-dress annually in autumn with garden compost or leaf-mould. In spring, prune back the stems to a strong pair of buds.

IPOMOEA TRICOLOUR 'HEAVENLY BLUE'

Ipomoea tricolour
Morning glory
'Heavenly Blue'

Fast-growing, twining annual with heart-shaped leaves and funnel-shaped flowers with a white throat.
HEIGHT & SPREAD: 2.4x1m (8x3ft)
I. purpurea Has mauve to purple flowers.
CULTIVATION: Plant out after the last frosts in a good-quality potting mix and site in full sun. Provide support for the climbing stems, such as a wigwam of canes or a trellis against a wall. Water freely and apply a balanced liquid feed monthly.

LAVANDULA ANGUSTIFOLIA 'HIDCOTE'

Lavandula angustifolia
Lavender
'Hidcote' ♀

Compact, bushy shrub with aromatic, grey-green leaves and small, purple flowers held in short, dense spikes.
HEIGHT & SPREAD: 60x60cm (2x2ft)
L. stoechas ssp.
pedunculata ♀ (French lavender) The fragrant flowers are topped with conspicuous purple-pink bracts.
CULTIVATION: Plant in spring in John Innes No.2 and site in full sun. Once established, lavender is reasonably drought-tolerant but for best results and good growth the plants should be watered moderately.

Apply a balanced liquid feed monthly. Clip off faded flower spikes in autumn. Prune lightly in spring to maintain bushiness.

LOBELIA ERINUS 'RIVIERA BLUE SPLASH'

Lobelia erinus
'Riviera Blue Splash'

Compact, bushy annual forming low mounds. The fan-shaped flowers are a pale lilac-blue.
HEIGHT & SPREAD: 10x10cm (4x4in)

L. erinus 'Blue Fountains' Vigorous trailing type with a profusion of pale blue flowers.
L. erinus 'Kathleen Mallard' Double flowered form that must be raised from cuttings.
L. erinus 'Regatta Sky Blue' Trailing habit and abundant pale blue flowers.
CULTIVATION: Plant out after the last frosts in a good-quality potting mix. Site the plants in sun or light shade. Keep moist at all times – the compost should never dry out.

Apply a liquid tomato feed every two to three weeks. Occasionally clip the plants over, and remove any faded flowerheads in order to encourage further flowering.

PETUNIA 'PURPLE WAVE'

Petunia
'Purple Wave'

Vigorous, bushy and spreading Multiflora type with abundant, weather-resistant, magenta flowers.
HEIGHT & SPREAD: 40x50cm (16x20in)

P. 'Daddy Blue' Grandiflora type with large, silver-blue flowers, variegated with dark blue veins.
P. 'Frenzy Blue' This Multiflora type petunia bears purple flowers.
CULTIVATION: Plant out into containers after the risk of frost has passed, selecting a sheltered site in full sun.

Use a good-quality potting mix. Water the plants freely and apply a liquid tomato feed every two weeks.

Deadhead all petunias regularly. Large-flowered (Grandiflora) types should have some shelter as their flowers may get damaged by wind and rain.

◀ **The purple, daisy-like heads** and frilly foliage of *Brachyscome* 'Tinkerbell' sit prettily in a tiny ornate wrought-iron bird cage. Well suited to hanging baskets, this plant also benefits from the support the cage provides.

SALVIA SPLENDENS 'SALSA PURPLE'

Salvia splendens
'Salsa Purple'

Bushy annual with dense spikes of long, tubular flowers emerging from conspicuous dark purple bracts.
HEIGHT & SPREAD: 25x20cm (10x8in)
S. farinacea 'Rhea' (Mealy sage) Tall, slender spikes of dark purple flowers. Densely branched stems are covered by a white 'mealy' dust.
HEIGHT & SPREAD: 35x20cm (14x8in)
CULTIVATION: Plant out after the last frosts in a good-quality, moist but free-draining compost. Site in full sun to light shade. Water liberally while growing and apply a liquid tomato feed fortnightly. Remove faded flowerheads regularly.

Scaevola aemula
Fan flower
'Blue Wonder'

Evergreen perennial, usually grown as an annual, with lax stems and distinctive lilac-blue fan-shaped flowers.
HEIGHT & SPREAD: 30x50cm (12x20in)
CULTIVATION: Plant out after the last frosts in a good-quality potting mix and site in sun or partial shade.
Water plants moderately while growing and apply a liquid tomato feed every two to three weeks. Pinch out the tips of young plants to encourage bushiness.

SCAEVOLA AEMULA 'BLUE WONDER'

SOLENOPSIS AXILLARIS 'BLUE STARS'

Solenopsis axillaris
Syn. *Isotoma axillaris*, *Laurentia axillaris*
'Blue Stars'

Woody sub-shrub, almost spherical in habit, bearing a profusion of starry, pale violet-blue flowers.
HEIGHT & SPREAD: 30x30cm (12x12in)
CULTIVATION: Plant out in a free-draining compost after the last frosts. Site in full sun. Water moderately and feed monthly in the growing season. Deadheading will help to prolong flowering. Overwinter in a frost-free greenhouse or conservatory.

TRACHELIUM CAERULEUM 'PASSION IN VIOLET'

Trachelium caeruleum ♆
'Passion in Violet'

Upright, branching perennial which is usually grown as an annual. The tiny violet flowers are borne in large domed clusters.
HEIGHT & SPREAD: 60x30cm (2x1ft)
CULTIVATION: Plant out after the last frosts in a good-quality potting mix and site the containers in full sun. Water the plants moderately while growing, applying a weak tomato fertiliser every two weeks. Deadheading will help to prolong flowering.

VERBENA X HYBRIDA 'IMAGINATION'

Verbena x hybrida
'Imagination'

This spreading and mound-forming dwarf perennial is usually grown as an annual. It bears dense, domed clusters of deep, violet-blue flowers.
HEIGHT & SPREAD: 20x30cm (8x12in)
V. x *hybrida* 'Quartz Blue' White-eyed violet flowers.
V. x *hybrida* 'Tapien Purple' Has a cascading habit.
CULTIVATION: Plant out after the last frosts in full sun. Water freely, especially in dry spells and feed every month.

◄ **Winter-flowering pansies** bring a welcome splash of colour and do particularly well in containers, producing a succession of blooms through winter and into spring. Many do equally well in sun or partial shade.

autumn

BILLARDIERA LONGIFLORA

Billardiera longiflora
Climbing blueberry

Evergreen, wiry-stemmed, twining climber. Shiny, purple, oval fruits are preceded by tubular yellow green flowers in summer.
HEIGHT & SPREAD: 1.5x1.5m (5x5ft)
CULTIVATION: Grow in pots of ericaceous compost in a sheltered, lightly shaded position. Provide support for the twining stems by using a trellis against a wall, for example.

Water freely while the plants are growing, applying a balanced liquid fertiliser monthly. Top-dress annually in spring with ericaceous compost. Trim lightly in spring as needed.

HEBE 'AUTUMN GLORY'

Hebe
'Autumn Glory'

Evergreen shrub forming a mound of rounded leaves and bearing abundant short spikes of purple flowers.
HEIGHT & SPREAD: 60x60cm (2x2ft)
H. 'Mrs Winder' Produces long spikes of violet-blue flowers. Young leaves turn dark purple in winter.
HEIGHT & SPREAD: 90x90cm (3x3ft)
CULTIVATION: Plant in spring or autumn in pots of John Innes No.3. Site in full sun. Water freely in the growing season and apply a balanced liquid feed monthly. Prune shrubs lightly to shape in spring if necessary. These plants are prone to powdery mildew.

LIRIOPE MUSCARI

Liriope muscari

Evergreen perennial with tufts of dark green, grass-like leaves. Small purple, bell-shaped flowers are borne in dense upright spikes.
HEIGHT & SPREAD: 30x45cm (12x18in)
L. exiliflora Has narrower leaves and taller, lavender-blue flowers.
L. muscari 'Gold Banded' Compact plant with leaves edged in yellow.
CULTIVATION: Plant in spring in free-draining, humus-rich compost. Site in full or partial shade. Water liriopes moderately until established; they are drought-tolerant thereafter. Apply a balanced liquid feed monthly. Remove faded flower spikes and old leaves regularly as new foliage emerges.

PLUMBAGO AURICULATA

Plumbago auriculata
Leadwort

A climbing evergreen shrub bearing rounded clusters of sky-blue flowers.
HEIGHT & SPREAD: 1.5x1.5m (5x5ft)
CULTIVATION: Grow in pots of John Innes No.3. Provide support, such as a trellis, for the whippy stems. Tying in will be necessary. Site containers in a lightly shaded, sheltered spot. Water the plants moderately and apply a balanced liquid feed monthly in the growing season.

Shorten back flowering shoots after they have finished blooming. May be hard pruned in spring if it is outgrowing its space. Overwinter in a frost-free greenhouse or conservatory.

winter

Primula vulgaris
Primrose
'Quantum Blue'

Very early flowering evergreen perennial producing violet-blue, saucer-shaped flowers with a yellow eye.

PRIMULA VULGARIS 'QUANTUM BLUE'

HEIGHT & SPREAD: 20x20cm (8x8in)
P. vulgaris 'Danova Purple' Large, pale purple flowers.
CULTIVATION: Plant in early winter in humus-rich compost and site containers in a position where they will gain maximum winter sun. Water moderately and apply a balanced liquid fertiliser once the buds are formed.

Remove spent flowers to prolong the flowering period. Increase by dividing vigorous clumps in early spring.

VIOLA X WITTROCKIANA 'UNIVERSAL PURPLE'

Viola x wittrockiana
Winter pansy
'Universal Purple'

Low-growing perennial, usually treated as an annual. It produces large, velvety, dark purple flowers. This pansy will continue to flower throughout winter in mild spells.
HEIGHT & SPREAD: 16x20cm (6x8in)
V. x wittrockiana 'Sorbet Blue Heaven' Violet-blue flowers.
V. x wittrockiana 'Ultima True Blue' Violet-blue blooms with a yellow eye.
CULTIVATION: Plant in autumn in a good-quality, free-draining compost and site in sun or light shade. Water freely during dry spells.

Remove any dead flowerheads regularly to prolong blooming. May be damaged by slugs and snails.

◄ **Hostas provide interest** from spring to the first frosts. They are especially useful for bringing living colour to a shady spot on the patio or in the garden. A mulch of marble chippings looks good and helps to retain moisture.

foliage

spring & summer

ACER PALMATUM 'GARNET'

Acer palmatum
Japanese maple
'Garnet'♀

Mound-forming deciduous tree with deeply and finely cut palmate leaves. These are dark purple-red in colour.
HEIGHT & SPREAD: 2x2m (6x6ft)

A. palmatum var. *dissectum*♀ This tree's green leaves turn red and then yellow in autumn.
A. palmatum 'Red Pygmy'♀ Upright with linear leaves that are dark red in spring, green in summer and yellow in autumn.
CULTIVATION: Plant in spring or autumn in large pots of John Innes No.3. Site in partial shade with protection from cold winds and late frosts, which may damage foliage. Water freely while growing, applying a balanced liquid feed monthly from spring to midsummer. Prune out any weak or damaged branches in winter. Prone to aphids and mites, and leaf scorch in exposed positions.

ATRIPLEX HORTENSIS

Atriplex hortensis var. rubra
Purple orache

Fast-growing, erect annual with reddish stems and purple-green foliage.
HEIGHT & SPREAD: 90x30cm (3x1ft)
CULTIVATION: Plant out after the last frosts in a good-quality potting mix. Site the containers in full sun in a sheltered position.
   Water freely and apply a balanced liquid feed every month. Seeds can be sown directly into their container in late spring.

CHLOROPHYTUM COMOSUM 'VITTATUM'

Chlorophytum comosum
Spider plant
'Vittatum'♀

Popular evergreen perennial with arcing, linear leaves, striped white along the centre. May produce a series of plantlets on arching stems.
HEIGHT & SPREAD: 30x30cm (12x12in)
C. comosum 'Variegatum'♀ Leaves have white margins.
CULTIVATION: Plant out in early summer. Site in sun or light shade. Water freely and feed monthly in the growing season. Overwinter indoors on a sunny windowsill.

HELICHRYSUM PETIOLARE 'VARIEGATUM'

Helichrysum petiolare
'Variegatum'♀

Trailing perennial, usually grown as an annual, with oval, felted, silvery green leaves, each with a dark green central blotch marking.
HEIGHT & SPREAD: 30x60cm (1x2ft)
H. petiolare 'Limelight'♀ Yellowy green leaves.
CULTIVATION: Plant out after the last frosts in a good-quality potting mix at the edge of a container or basket, so that the trailing stems can hang down. Site in full sun but be careful not to allow the compost to dry out.
   Apply a balanced liquid feed every two or three weeks. Pinch out the tips of young plants to promote bushiness.

HOSTA 'HALCYON'

Hosta
Plantain lily
'Halcyon'♀

Clump-forming perennial with glaucous, grey-blue, heart-shaped leaves.

HEIGHT & SPREAD: 40x50cm (16x20in)

H. 'Golden Prayers' Deep yellow leaves are cupped and puckered. Prefers shade.

H. 'Golden Tiara'♀ Leaves are mid green with irregular bright yellow margins.

CULTIVATION: Plant in spring or autumn in large pots of John Innes No.2 with added organic matter. Site in light shade. Yellow-leafed cultivars generally colour best with some exposure to sun. Shelter from cold, drying winds.

Water freely while growing, never allowing the compost to dry out, and feed in mid spring and midsummer. Mulch annually in spring with leaf-mould. Hostas are particularly prone to attack from slugs and snails.

IRESINE HERBSTII 'AUREORETICULATA'

Iresine herbstii
'Aureoreticulata'

Short-lived, erect branching perennial with succulent red stems. The oval, pointed leaves are marked with yellow along the veins.

HEIGHT & SPREAD: 40x30cm (16x12in)

I. herbstii 'Brilliantissima' Has rich crimson leaves with pink veins.

CULTIVATION: Plant in early summer in pots of John Innes No.2 in full sun for best leaf colour. Water freely and apply a balanced liquid fertiliser monthly. Pinch out tips of young plants for bushiness. Overwinter indoors.

MENTHA GRACILIS 'VARIEGATA'

Mentha gracilis
Ginger mint
'Variegata'

Spreading perennial with reddish upright stems clothed in ginger-scented, oval, yellow-marked leaves.

HEIGHT & SPREAD: 30x30cm (12x12in)

M. suaveolens 'Variegata' (Pineapple mint) Vigorously spreading with wrinkled greyish green leaves, irregularly marked in cream.

CULTIVATION: Plant in spring in a moisture-retentive compost. Site in full sun, but be careful not to allow the compost to dry out. Apply a balanced liquid feed in spring and summer. All plants are easily increased by division.

OCIMUM BASILICUM VAR. PURPURASCENS

Ocimum basilicum var. purpurascens
Sweet basil

Bushy aromatic annual with reddish purple leaves that can be used in cooking.

HEIGHT & SPREAD: 30x30cm (12x12in)

CULTIVATION: Plant out after the last frosts in a good-quality potting mix. Site the containers in a sunny, sheltered position.

Water freely, especially in dry spells. Pinch out flowerheads as they appear to encourage more leaf production. You can sow basil seed straight into the pot in early summer. Basil is prone to slug damage.

PERILLA FRUTESCENS VAR. CRISPA

Perilla frutescens var. crispa♀

Vigorous annual with broadly oval, dark purple, frilly margined leaves.

HEIGHT & SPREAD: 90x30cm (3x1ft)

CULTIVATION: Plant out in spring in fertile, moist but free-draining compost in sun or partial shade. Water freely, applying a balanced liquid feed monthly. Pinching out the tips of young plants will encourage bushiness.

PLECTRANTHUS MADAGASCARIENSIS 'VARIEGATED MINTLEAF'

Plectranthus madagascariensis
Swedish ivy
'Variegated Mintleaf'

Creeping tender perennial with firm fleshy oval leaves, smelling of mint when crushed. The leaves are mid green with scalloped edges and white margins.

HEIGHT & SPREAD: 20x40cm (8x16in)

P. forsteri Oval, dark green, scallop-edged leaves; prostrate, trailing stems.

CULTIVATION: Plant out hardened-off plants after the danger of frost has passed, using a good-quality potting mixture. Site the container in sun or light shade.

Pinch out the growing tips of young plants to encourage bushiness. Swedish ivy may be overwintered indoors.

RICINUS COMMUNIS 'IMPALA'

Ricinus communis
Castor-oil plant
'Impala'

This fast-growing, erect evergreen shrub, usually grown as a half-hardy annual or as a conservatory plant, has striking foliage. The large, palmate, reddish purple leaves are 25cm (10in) across.

HEIGHT & SPREAD: 1.2x1m (4x3ft)

R. communis 'Zanzibarensis' The reddish purple leaves have white veins.

CULTIVATION: Plant out after the last frosts in John Innes No.2 with added organic matter, such as leaf-mould. Site pots in full sun.

Water plants freely and apply a balanced liquid feed every three weeks. Ricinus tends to self-seed. *NB The seeds of ricinus are very poisonous.*

◄ **Dwarf fan palms** add an exotic note to a sunny terrace, but need to be brought indoors in winter. Occasionally, they will produce bunches of greenish yellow flowers.

AUCUBA JAPONICA 'CROTONIFOLIA'

Aucuba japonica
Spotted laurel
'Crotonifolia' ♀

Easily grown evergreen shrub with glossy leaves heavily splashed with yellow. Red berries may be produced in autumn on female plants.
HEIGHT & SPREAD: 1.2x1.2m (4x4ft)
A. japonica f. *longifolia* ♀ This female plant has long, narrow, pale green leaves.
CULTIVATION: Plant in spring or autumn into John Innes No.3. Aucuba is tolerant of sun or shade. Water moderately and apply a balanced liquid fertiliser monthly in the growing season. Trim to size and shape in spring.

SENECIO CINERARIA 'SILVER DUST'

Senecio cineraria
Syn. *Cineraria maritima*
'Silver Dust' ♀

Evergreen sub-shrub usually grown as an annual with deeply divided, almost white, felted leaves.
HEIGHT & SPREAD: 30x30cm (12x12in)
S. cineraria 'Cirrus' Silvery grey lobed oval leaves.

CULTIVATION: Plant out hardened-off plants in spring, in a good-quality potting mix. Site in full sun.

Water moderately and feed monthly with a balanced liquid feed. Snip out flower buds as they form.

Solenostemon
Syn. *Coleus* 'Royal Scot'
Flame nettle
'Royal Scot' ♀

Upright bushy evergeen perennial with square stems bearing long, deep red,

SOLENOSTEMON 'ROYAL SCOT'

triangular leaves marked with yellow-green margins.
HEIGHT & SPREAD: 50x50cm (20x20in)
S. scutellarioides 'Wizard Series' Compact and bushy cultivars with foliage variously marked with shades of red, yellow, pink, purple and cream.
HEIGHT & SPREAD: 20x30cm (8x12in)
CULTIVATION: Plant out hardened off plants after the last frosts into a good-quality potting mix. Site in sun (with some shelter from midday sun) or light shade.

Water freely and apply a high nitrogen fertiliser every month. Pinch out growing tips to promote bushiness, and pinch out flower buds as soon as they appear.

BUXUS SEMPERVIRENS 'MARGINATA'

Buxus sempervirens
Box
'Marginata'

This slow-growing, dwarf evergreen shrub forms a low mound of small dark green leaves with yellow margins.
HEIGHT & SPREAD: 1x1m (3x3ft)

B. sempervirens
'Suffruticosa'♀ Dense shrub with bright green leaves, good for formal clipping.
CULTIVATION: Plant in spring or autumn in John Innes No.3. Site in partial shade. Water freely, especially while becoming established. Feed monthly in the growing season. Trim in summer.

CHAMAECYPARIS LAWSONIANA 'AUREA DENSA'

Chamaecyparis lawsoniana
'Aurea Densa'♀

Dwarf evergreen conifer with a rounded, conical habit. The foliage is made of tiny greeny gold scale-like leaves.
HEIGHT & SPREAD: 1.2mx90cm (4x3ft)
C. lawsonia 'Gimbornii'♀ Neat, dense blue-green globe.
C. lawsonia 'Pygmaea Argentea'♀ Silver-tipped, bluish foliage; likes shade.
CULTIVATION: Plant in John Innes No.3 in full sun. Water well. Trim lightly in summer.

Chamaerops humilis♀
Dwarf fan palm

Small palm producing a crown of palmate leaves held on prickly stems.

CHAMAEROPS HUMILIS

HEIGHT & SPREAD: 90x90cm (3x3ft)
CULTIVATION: Grow in pots of John Innes No.3, putting plants outdoors only after the last frosts. Site in a sunny, sheltered position. Water freely and apply a balanced liquid feed monthly in the growing season. Reduce watering and move to a greenhouse or conservatory over winter and cut away dying leaves.

You can produce more plants by growing suckers in small pots. Red spider mite, scale and mealy bugs may be a problem for palms grown under glass.

CORDYLINE AUSTRALIS 'TORBAY DAZZLER'

Cordyline australis
Cabbage tree
'Torbay Dazzler'

Erect, palm-like evergreen, with linear, arching leaves which have cream and grey-green stripes running through. It gradually develops a trunk.
HEIGHT & SPREAD: 1.8x1.8m (6x6ft)
C. australis 'Purple Tower' Has dark purple leaves.
CULTIVATION: Plant in spring in pots of John Innes No.3 and site in full sun. Water freely while establishing, after which it is drought-tolerant. Feed in mid spring and midsummer. Gently pull away dead leaves from the base of the trunk. In cold areas during winter, give plants the shelter of a house wall.

ERICA CARNEA 'FOXHOLLOW'

Erica carnea
Alpine heath
'Foxhollow'♀

Low-growing, spreading evergreen shrub with tiny, linear leaves. The foliage is yellow with bronze tips which deepens to reddish orange in very cold weather. Bears purplish pink flowers from winter to mid spring.
HEIGHT & SPREAD: 15x40cm (6x16in)
E. carnea 'Golden Starlet'♀ Has lime-green foliage turning a glowing yellow in summer; white flowers.
E. carnea 'Vivellii'♀ Bronze foliage; magenta flowers.
CULTIVATION: Plant in autumn in ericaceous compost. Site the containers in full sun. Water freely and apply a weak liquid fertiliser once a month in the growing season.

Clip the flower spikes back once they have gone over. Grey mould (botrytis) may develop in warm, wet conditions.

EUONYMUS FORTUNEI 'SILVER QUEEN'

Euonymus fortunei
'Silver Queen'♀

Upright, evergreen shrub with glossy oval leaves, that have broad creamy white margins tinted rose in winter.

HEIGHT & SPREAD: 90x90cm (3x3ft)
E. fortunei 'Emerald 'n' Gold'♀ Spreading habit; bright green, yellow-edged leaves.
E. fortunei 'Emerald Cushion' Compact and mound forming; lustrous dark foliage.
HEIGHT & SPREAD: 30x30cm (12x12in)
CULTIVATION: Plant in John Innes No.2. Site in sun for best leaf variegation. Shelter from cold winds. Water moderately and feed monthly in the growing season. Lightly prune in late spring. Cut out shoots of variegated plants that have reverted to green.

FATSIA JAPONICA

Fatsia japonica♀
Syn. *Aralia japonica*

Slow-growing, rounded evergreen shrub with large, glossy, dark green palmate leaves. In autumn it bears round clusters of creamy white flowers.
HEIGHT & SPREAD: 1.5x1.5m (5x5ft)
F. japonica 'Variegata'♀ Leaves margined with cream at the tips of the lobes.
CULTIVATION: Plant in spring in large pots of John Innes No.3. Site in sun or partial shade and shelter from cold, drying winds.

Keep the compost moist throughout summer, but drier in winter. Apply a balanced liquid feed in spring and summer. Fatsia does not need pruning, but can be trimmed to shape in spring.

GLECHOMA HEDERACEA 'VARIEGATA'

Glechoma hederacea
Ground ivy
'Variegata'

Vigorous evergreen perennial
with trailing stems. The
leaves are kidney-shaped,
with scalloped margins,
irregularly marked with white
blotches. It is especially
suited to hanging baskets.
HEIGHT & SPREAD: 15x90cm
(6x36in)
CULTIVATION: Plant in spring
in a good-quality potting mix.
Site in sun or partial shade.
Position plants so that stems
can trail down. Water freely
while growing and give a
balanced liquid feed monthly.

HEDERA HELIX 'GLACIER'

Hedera helix
Ivy
'Glacier'

Easily grown and adaptable
evergreen that can be
encouraged to either climb
or hang down. The five-lobed
leaves are mottled green and
silvery green and have narrow
white margins.
HEIGHT & SPREAD: 1x1m (3x3ft)
H. helix 'Cavendishii' ♥
Large, three-lobed leaves,
mottled with grey. The leaf
margins are cream.
H. helix 'Golden Easter'
Light green leaves with an

irregular yellow margin.
CULTIVATION: Plant in spring
or autumn in pots of John
Innes No.3. Site containers or
baskets in sun or light shade:
although ivies tolerate deep
shade, their leaf variegation
will be less pronounced if
deprived of sun.
  Water freely in dry spells.
Apply a balanced liquid feed
monthly in the growing
season. Clip plants to shape,
if necessary, in spring.

JUNIPERUS HORIZONTALIS
'EMERALD SPREADER'

Juniperus horizontalis
Juniper
'Emerald Spreader'

Slow-growing dwarf conifer,
low and spreading in habit.
The small, needle-like leaves
are bright green.
HEIGHT & SPREAD: 30x80cm
(12x32in)
J. communis 'Compressa' ♥
Dwarf, slow-growing variety,
conical in habit with grey-
green foliage.
HEIGHT & SPREAD: 80x45cm
(32x18in)
J. squamata 'Blue Star' ♥
Compact rounded bush with
silvery blue foliage.
HEIGHT & SPREAD: 40x80cm
(16x32in)
CULTIVATION: Plant in autumn
in John Innes No.3, selecting
a site in full sun. Water well
while establishing; after this,
junipers are fairly drought-
tolerant. Pruning is rarely
necessary unless the plant
is outgrowing its space.

LAURUS NOBILIS

Laurus nobilis ♥
Bay laurel, bay tree, sweet bay

Striking evergreen shrub or
tree with dark green, glossy,
aromatic foliage used in
cooking. Bay tolerates
clipping and is commonly
shaped into formal round-
headed (lollipop) or pyramid-
shaped standards.
HEIGHT & SPREAD: 1.2mx80cm
(4ftx32in)
L. nobilis 'Aurea' ♥ Golden-
yellow foliage at its best in
late winter and early spring.
CULTIVATION: Plant in spring
or autumn in John Innes
No.3. Site in full sun to
partial shade. Shelter from
cold, drying winds. Clip to
size or shape in summer. Bay
is prone to scale insect, leaf
spot and sooty mould.

NANDINA DOMESTICA

Nandina domestica ♥
Sacred bamboo

Evergreen or semi-evergreen
shrub forming a clump of
erect, leafy stems, looking
similar to bamboo. The leaves

are reddish purple when
young, becoming green in
summer and turning red
in winter. In midsummer,
sprays of creamy white, starry
flowers appear. After a hot
summer, the flowers are often
followed by a show of bright
red berries.
HEIGHT & SPREAD: 90x75cm
(36x30in)
CULTIVATION: Plant in spring
in John Innes No.3. Site in
full sun in a sheltered spot.
Water moderately and apply a
balanced liquid feed in spring
and summer. Prune out old or
weak shoots in spring.

OPHIOPOGON PLANISCAPUS
'NIGRESCENS'

Ophiopogon planiscapus
Lily turf, mondo grass
'Nigrescens' ♥

Clump-forming, evergreen
grass with dark, purplish
black leaves, dark purple
flowers and black fruits.
HEIGHT & SPREAD: 25x30cm
(10x12in)
O. jaburan 'Vittatus' Taller
growing with green leaves
margined and striped cream.
HEIGHT & SPREAD: 60x30cm
(2x1ft)
CULTIVATION: Plant in spring
in John Innes No.2 with
added organic matter, such
as leaf-mould. Site pots in
sun or partial shade. Water
moderately while growing, but
sparingly in winter. Apply a
balanced liquid feed in spring
and summer. Mulch with leaf-
mould in autumn.

PHORMIUM 'SUNDOWNER'

Phormium
New Zealand flax
'Sundowner'♀

Clump-forming evergreen perennial making a tuft of rigid, upright, pointed linear leaves. These are green-bronze with pink margins.
HEIGHT & SPREAD: 1.2x1m (4x3ft)
P. 'Dazzler' Arching bronze leaves with red, orange and pink stripes.
P. tenax 'Variegatum'♀ Dark green leaves with yellow stripes and margins.
CULTIVATION: Plant in John Innes No.3 in a sunny, sheltered spot. Water freely in summer but sparingly in winter. Apply a liquid feed in spring and summer.

PITTOSPORUM TENUIFOLIUM 'PURPUREUM'

Pittosporum tenuifolium
'Purpureum'

Evergreen shrub or small tree with lustrous, wavy-edged, dark purple leaves.
HEIGHT & SPREAD: 1.5x1m (5x3ft)
P. tenuifolium 'Abbotsbury Gold' Green leaves with dark margins and yellow midribs.
P. tenuifolium 'Silver Queen'♀ Grey-green leaves with white margins.

CULTIVATION: Plant in spring in John Innes No.3. Site in full sun for best leaf colour. Shelter from cold, drying winds. Water well while establishing; after this, plants are drought-tolerant. Keep almost dry in winter. Apply a balanced liquid feed in spring and summer. Scale insects may be troublesome.

PLEIOBLASTUS AURICOMUS

Pleioblastus auricomus♀
Syn. *Arundinaria auricoma*
Bamboo

A bamboo producing upright, branching, purplish canes clothed in lance-shaped leaves. The leaves are bright yellow with dark and pale green stripes running through.
HEIGHT & SPREAD: 1.2mx60cm (4x2ft)
P. gramineus Arching canes and grass-like, drooping, mid-green leaves.
P. pygmaeus Dwarf bamboo with bright green leaves held horizontally.
HEIGHT & SPREAD: 20x30cm (10x12in)
CULTIVATION: Plant in spring or autumn in large pots of John Innes No.3 with added leaf-mould. Shelter from strong winds and site variegated varieties in full sun; other varieties prefer light shade. Water liberally, especially while establishing. Apply a balanced liquid feed monthly in the growing season. Canes that have flowered will die off, so prune these out.

SEMPERVIVUM 'RUBIN'

Sempervivum
Houseleek
'Rubin'

Clump-forming, evergreen perennial, with rosettes of fleshy foliage. These leaves are flushed bronze-red. At flowering, the rosette elongates into a fat leafy spike bearing many starry pink flowers.
HEIGHT & SPREAD: 7.5x7.5cm (3x3in)
S. arachnoideum♀ (cobweb houseleek) The leaf tips are crisscrossed with fine, white, cobweb-like hairs.
S. tectorum♀ Green leaf rosettes flushed red.
CULTIVATION: Plant in spring in a light, free-draining compost and site in full sun.
   Though sempervivums are drought-tolerant, water moderately. Feeding is not necessary. *S. arachnoideum* should be protected from excessive winter wet. Easily increased by planting offsets.

Thymus
Thyme
'Doone Valley'

This mat-forming evergreen sub-shrub has small aromatic dark green leaves splashed with yellow. Purple-pink

THYMUS 'DOONE VALLEY'

flowers are borne in dense heads in summer.
HEIGHT & SPREAD: 13x35cm (5x14in)
T. serphyllum 'Annie Hall' (Creeping thyme, wild thyme) Mat-forming aromatic plant with shell-pink flowers.
T. vulgaris 'Silver Posie' Upright and shrubby with white margined green leaves.
HEIGHT & SPREAD: 20x20cm (8x8in)
CULTIVATION: Plant in spring in a free-draining compost and site in full sun. Water moderately while growing. No need to feed. Clip over after flowering to keep compact.

YUCCA FILAMENTOSA 'BRIGHT EDGE'

Yucca filamentosa
'Bright Edge'♀

Stemless evergreen shrub forming a rosette of stiffly erect, linear, dark green leaves with broad yellow margins. Bears tall plumes of creamy white flowers.
HEIGHT & SPREAD: 60x75cm (24x30in)
Y. whipplei Dense tufts of slender grey-green leaves.
CULTIVATION: Plant in spring in John Innes No.2. Site in a sunny position sheltered from the wind. Although yuccas are drought-tolerant, they should be watered moderately in summer and sparingly in winter. Feeding is not necessary. After flowering the leaf rosettes die off, although varieties of *Y. filamentosa* produce offsets. Protect from severe frosts in colder areas.

index

Italic page numbers refer to entries in the Pick of Container Plants directory. References to particular varieties of plant genera are grouped together at the end of each entry. For plants grouped by colour and season, see pages *274-311*.

PLANTING

bulbs 150, 231
flower balls 233
flower pouches 231
hanging baskets 232
herb pots 230
mixed containers 228-9
strawberry pots 230
trees and shrubs 229
window boxes 230

acknowledgments

The following abbreviations are used throughout the photography credits:
t top; **c** centre; **b** bottom; **l** left; **r** right.
© RD indicates images that are copyright of The Reader's Digest Association Limited. PL indicates pictures from the Reader's Digest Plant Library, which may previously have appeared in *Reader's Digest New Encyclopedia of Garden Plants & Flowers*. DP Debbie Patterson JS Jason Smalley JW Joanna Walker FY Francesca Yorke CS Colegraves Seeds Ltd.

Front cover © RD/Linda Burgess **Spine** © RD/DP **Back cover** © RD/DP **Endpapers** © RD/DP **2-3** © RD/DP **4-5** © RD/JW **6-7** © RD/DP **8-9** © RD/DP **10 t** Garden Picture Library/Ann Kelley **10-11** John Glover **11 tr** Jerry Harpur/Yaccout Restaurant Marrakech, Morocco **12 bl** John Glover **12-13** © RD/DP **13** Andrew Lawson/Hestercombe, Somerset **14-15 l, r** © RD/DP **c** © RD/DP **16 l** Andrew Lawson **b** Jacqui Hurst **17** © RD/Nick Clark **18-19** © RD/DP **20** © RD/DP **21** © RD/DP **22** © RD/DP except for **Glass fibre: tl** © RD/FY **bl** photography ©Andrea Jones/Exposures Photo Library **23** © RD/DP **24-27** © RD/DP **28 tl** © RD/DP **r** Garden Picture Library/Janet Sorrell **29 tl** John Glover **c, r** © RD/DP **bl** © RD/JW **30 c** © RD/FY **bc, br** © RD/DP **31** Debbie Patterson **32 tr, br** © RD/DP **cr, bl** John Glover **32-33** © RD/DP **33 t** Andrew Lawson **34 tl, tr, br** © RD/DP **tc** © RD/JW **35** © RD/JW **36 tl** Garden Picture Library/Mark Bolton **r, bl** © RD/DP **37 tl** John Glover **tr, br** © RD/FY **bl** © RD/DP **38 c** Debbie Patterson **bl** © RD/FY **38-39** © RD/DP **39 tr** © RD/FY **br** John Glover **40-41** © RD/FY **42** © RD/DP **43 l** © RD/FY **r** © RD/DP **44** © RD/DP **45** © RD/FY **46 l** © RD/Linda Burgess **r** © RD/DP **47 l** © RD/FY **c** © RD/DP **r** John Glover **48-49** Jacqui Hurst **50-53** © RD/FY **54-55** © RD/DP **55 tr** © RD/DP **cr** © RD/Linda Burgess **br** © RD/FY **56 tl** © RD/DP **56-57** © RD/FY **58** © RD/DP **58-59** © RD/DP **59 t** © RD/FY **60-61** © RD/DP **62** Jerry Harpur/Design Penny Crawshaw **62-63** Andrew Lawson **63 tr** © RD/DP **64** © RD/JW **65** © RD/JS **66** © RD/JW **66-67** © RD/DP **68** © RD/DP **69** © RD/FY **70-73** © RD/FY **74-75** © RD/DP **76 tl** © RD/DP **b** © RD/JS **77** © RD/DP **78-79** © RD/DP **80** © RD/FY **81** © RD/DP **82** © RD/DP **83** © RD/DP **84-85** © RD/FY **85 tl, tr** © RD/FY **br** © RD/DP **86-89** © RD/FY **90 l** © RD/FY **90-91** © RD/DP **92 t** © RD/DP **b** © RD/FY **93** © RD/FY **94** © RD/FY **95 tl, bl** © RD/FY **tr, br** © RD/DP **96-97** © RD/FY **98** © RD/FY **98-99** © RD/DP **99 tl** © RD/PL **tr** © RD/DP **100-101** © RD/DP **102** © RD/DP **103 t** © RD/JW **bl** John Glover **br** © RD/Nick Clark **104 tl** © RD/FY **bl** © RD/DP **104-105** © RD/DP **106 l** © RD/FY **r** © RD/DP **107 t, cl, bl** © RD/DP **br** Clive Nichols/Designer: Elisabeth Woodhouse **108** © RD/DP **109** © RD/DP except for **tl** Clive Nichols/Designer: Anthony Noel **111 bl** Clive Nichols/Schenies Manor, Bucks **bc** Garden Picture Library/John Glover **br** © RD/DP **112 tl** Garden Picture Library/Steven Wooster **112-113** © RD/DP **113** © RD/DP **114-115** © RD/DP **116-117** © RD/DP except for **116 b** IPC International Syndication/© New Eden/Photographer Andrea Jones **118-121** © RD/FY except for **121 br** © RD/DP **122-123** © RD/PL **124-125** Andrew Lawson **bl** © RD/JS **du** © RD/FY **124-125** Andrew Lawson Garden Picture Library/Marianne Majerus **126-129** © RD/DP **130 tl, bc** © RD/JS **br** © RD/DP **131** © RD/DP **132** © RD/DP **133 tl** IPC International Syndication/June Buch **tr** © RD/DP **br** © RD/JS **134-135** © RD/DP except for **135 br** © RD/JW **136 t, b** Jerry Harpur **137 t** Garden Picture Library/Linda Burgess **138** © RD/DP **139 tl** Francesca Yorke **tr** John Glover/Designer: Michael Miller **bl, bc, br** © RD/PL **140 l** Garden Picture Library/Friedrich Strauss **140-141** © RD/Nick Clark **141 t** © RD/Nick Clark **br** Garden Picture Library/Marie O'Hara **142-145** © RD/DP except for **142 bl** © RD/Artist, Cherry Burton **tl** © RD/Alison Candlin **146-147** © RD/JS **148-149** © RD/DP except for November © RD/FY **150-151** © RD/DP **152 tl** © RD/Linda Burgess **c, r** © RD/DP **153** © RD/DP **154-155** © RD/DP except for **bc, bl,**

br © RD/PL **156-157** © RD/DP **158** © RD/DP **159 tr** © RD/DP **bl, bc, br** © RD/PL **160-161** © RD/FY except for **160 bl** © RD/DP **162 tl, br** © RD/DP **tc, tr, bl** © RD/FY **163** © RD/FY except for **br** © RD/DP **164-165** © RD/DP **166-167** © RD/FY **168 l** © RD/DP **168-169** © RD/FY **170-171** © RD/FY **172 l** John Glover **c** © RD/DP **b** Garden Picture Library/Christopher Fairweather **173** © RD/DP **174-175** © RD/FY **b** © RD/DP **176 tl, cl, bl** © RD/FY **r** © RD/DP **177 l, tr** © RD/FY **c** © RD/Nick Clark **178** © RD/DP **179 l** Interior Archive Limited/Simon McBride **r** © RD/DP **180-181** © RD/DP **182-183** © RD/Linda Burgess **184-185** © RD/DP except for **184 tl** Jerry Harpur/Lisette Pleasance **186-189** © RD/DP except for **186 tl** © RD/JW **190-191** © RD/FY **192** © RD/DP **193** © RD/DP **194 tl, tc, tr** © RD/PL **194-195** © RD/DP **195** © RD/DP **196 tl, tr, tc** © RD/FY **b** © RD/DP **196-197** © RD/FY **197 tr** John Glover **198-199** © RD/DP **200-201** © RD/DP **202 tl** Garden Picture Library/Steven Wooster **202-203** © RD/DP **204-205** © RD/DP **206-207** © RD/DP **208-211** © RD/JS **212-213** © RD/DP **214-215** © RD/DP **216-217** © RD/DP **218-219** © RD/DP **220** © RD/DP **221 t, b** © RD/DP **c** © RD/JW **222-223** © RD/JS **224** © RD/DP **225** © RD/DP except for **cr** © RD/FY **226 bl** © RD/DP **Natural mulches:** © RD/DP **Standard trees:** © RD/DP **227 Stones & gravel:** © RD/FY except for **tl, bl** © RD/DP **Coloured mulch:** © Alex McDonald except for **tr, c, bcl** © RD/DP **228-229** © RD/DP **230-231** © RD/DP **232-233** © RD/DP except for **233 br** John Glover **234 bl, br** © RD/DP **tr** © RD/FY **235** © RD/DP **236 tl, cl** © RD/DP **b** © RD/FY **237 l** © RD/DP **r** © RD/FY **238** © RD/DP **239 t, c** © RD/FY **cr, br** © RD/DP **240** © RD/DP **241 l** © RD/FY **c, r** © RD/DP **242-243** © RD/DP **244 l** © RD/FY **244-245** © RD/FY **245 tr** © RD/FY **c** Garden Picture Library/Vaughan Fleming **b** Photo Horticultural Photo Library **246** © RD/FY **247 t** Holt Studios Ltd/Nigel Cattlin **cl** Harry Smith Collection **c** Photo Horticultural Photo Library **bl** Garden Picture Library/Christi Carter **br** Garden Picture Library/Friedrich Strauss **248 tl, tr** © RD/DP **bl** Harry Smith Collection **br** Emap Gardening Picture Library **249 t** Harry Smith Collection **b** Garden Picture Library/Mel Watson **250 l, r** Emap Gardening Picture Library **250-251** Andrew Lawson **251 t** Harry Smith Collection **252-255** © RD/Nick Clark **256 tl, c, bl** © RD/DP **tc, b** © RD/Linda Burgess **257** © RD/DP except for **tr** © RD/JW **258-259** © RD/DP **260-261** © RD/DP **262-263** © RD/DP **264** © RD/DP **265** © RD/JS **266-267** © RD/DP **268-269** © RD/DP **270-271** © RD/DP **272-273** © RD/DP **274-275** © RD/PL except for **274 tr** © RD/FY **276-277** © RD/PL except for **276 tr** Harry Smith Collection **277 b** Garden Picture Library/Howard Rice **278-279** © RD/PL except for **278 bl** Garden Picture Library/Friedrich Strauss **279 b** © RD/DP **280-281** © RD/PL except for **280 tl** © RD/Nick Clark **br** CS **281 t** CS **282-283** © RD/PL except for **282 bl** CS **283 tr** CS **bl** © RD/DP **284 tl, cr** © RD/PL **tr, cl, bl** CS **285 tl, cr, bl, b** © RD/PL **tr** © RD/DP **286** © RD/PL **bl** CS **br** © RD/PL **287** © RD/PL except for **tl** CS **288** © RD/PL except for **cr** Harry Smith Collection **bl** CS **289** © RD/PL except for **bl** CS **br** © RD/DP **290 tl, br** © RD/PL **tr** CS **bl** © RD/DP **291** © RD/PL except for **c** CS **292** © RD/DP except for **c, bl, br** CS **bc** Garden Picture Library/Marie O'Hara **293** © RD/PL except for **cr** CS **294 tl, tr, bl** © RD/PL **cl, c, cr, br** CS **295** © RD/PL except for **tl** © RD/DP **cr** CS **296** © RD/PL except for **c** Harry Smith Collection **297** © RD/PL except for **br** CS **298** © RD/PL **299** © RD/PL except for **cl, c** CS **300 tl** Linda Burgess **tr, bl** © RD/PL **br** John Glover **301** © RD/PL except for **cl, br** CS **302** © RD/DP **tr, cr, bl** CS **303** © RD/PL except for **bl** CS **br** © RD/FY **304 tl, tc, tr** CS **cl** Harry Smith Collection **bl** © RD/DP **br** © RD/PL **305** © RD/PL except for **cr, br** CS **306** © RD/PL **307** © RD/PL **308** © RD/PL except for **cl** CS **309** © RD/PL **310** © RD/PL **311** © RD/PL **312-313** © RD/DP **314-315** © RD/DP except for **315 c** © RD/JS **316 l** © RD/DP **c, r** © RD/FY **317 l** © RD/DP **r** © RD/FY **318 tl** © RD/DP **tc, tr** © RD/FY **319** © RD/DP

The Reader's Digest Association Ltd would like to thank the following individuals for their contribution to this book

For allowing us to feature their gardens: Ian Brownhill and Michael Hirschl; Susan Campbell; Nick Clark and Moira Clinch; Elsa Day; Oliver and Sallyanne Greenwood; Catherine Horwood; Sheila Jackson; London Buddhist Centre; Penny Snell; Richard and Liz Tite.

For allowing us to use their gardens for photography: Mr and Mrs J. Adams; Steve Adams; Barry Arbon and Sally Williams; Marc and Janet Berlin; Mr and Mrs Ray Breame; John Hawkridge, Cobble Cottage Gardens; Mike Lawrence; Biddy Marshall; Adele and Sydney Morris; Lance Percival; Sarah Raven's Cutting Garden; Trudi Procter; Jenny Raworth; Mr and Mrs Simon Wainwright.

For their help with planning and producing the book: John Amand; Ray Breame; Cherry Burton Garden Design; Roger Houghton; Julian Hunt; Mike Lawrence; John Lister; Stuart Lowen; Biddy Marshall, National Garden Scheme, Yorkshire; Jonathan Mount; Richard Rosenfeld; Penny Snell, National Garden Scheme, London; Huw Stevenson, Oaklands Landscape Design and Garden; Jean Weatherell; Julia Young, St Andrews Pottery and Shop

For providing plants for photography: Architectural Plants, Horsham; Fulham Palace Garden Centre, run by the charity Fairbridge, which supports socially and economically alienated young people in deprived inner city areas; Living Colour, Winnall Down Farm, Winchester, Hants SO21 1HF; KinderGarden Plants Ltd, Wragg Marsh, Spalding, Lincs PE12 6HH Tel 01406 371200, www.kindergarden.co.uk Unwins Seeds Ltd, Histon, Cambridge, CB4 9LE

For providing props and containers: Birchgrove Garden Centre, Spalding; Lakeland Plastics; Roger Oates Design; Whichford Pottery, classic handmade flowerpots, Whichford, near Shipston on Stour, Warwickshire CV36 5PG Tel: 01608 684416, Fax: 01608 684833, www.whichfordpottery.com

Container Gardening for All Seasons was edited and designed by The Reader's Digest Association Limited, London.

First edition Copyright © 2001
The Reader's Digest Association Limited,
11 Westferry Circus, Canary Wharf, London E14 4HE

Reprinted 2003

We are committed to both the quality of our products and the service we provide to our customers. We value your comments, so please feel free to contact us on **08705 113366**, or via our web site at **www.readersdigest.co.uk**
If you have any comments about the content of our books, you can email us at: **gbeditorial@readersdigest.co.uk**

The typefaces used in this book are Bodoni, European Pi3, FFJustlefthand, Gill sans, Meta, New Baskerville and Trixie

READER'S DIGEST ASSOCIATION BOOK PRODUCTION
Book Production Manager: Fiona McIntosh
Pre-Press Manager: Howard Reynolds
Pre-Press Technical Analyst: Martin Hendrick

Origination: Colour Systems Limited, London
Printed by Partenaires, France

ISBN 0 276 42486 7
BOOK CODE 400-011-03
CONCEPT CODE UK1231/IC